MAKING SENSE OF
MATHEMATICS
FOR TEACHING

Grades 3–5

JULI K. DIXON

EDWARD C. NOLAN

THOMASENIA LOTT ADAMS

JENNIFER M. TOBIAS

GUY BARMOHA

Solution Tree | Press
a division of
Solution Tree

555 North Morton Street
Bloomington, IN 47404
800.733.6786 (toll free) / 812.336.7700
FAX: 812.336.7790

email: info@solution-tree.com
solution-tree.com

Visit **go.solution-tree.com/mathematics** to download the free reproducibles in this book.

Printed in the United States of America

ISBN: 978-1-942496-42-7

Library of Congress Control Number: 2016931408

Solution Tree
Jeffrey C. Jones, CEO
Edmund M. Ackerman, President

Solution Tree Press
President: Douglas M. Rife
Senior Acquisitions Editor: Amy Rubenstein
Managing Production Editor: Caroline Weiss
Senior Production Editor: Rachel Rosolina
Proofreader: Elisabeth Abrams
Text and Cover Designer: Abigail Bowen
Compositor: Laura Kagemann

Acknowledgments

My deepest love and gratitude to my daughters, Alex and Jessica, who continue to allow me to understand mathematics more deeply through their eyes, and to my husband, Marc, who supports me to spend countless hours doing so. Thanks to Rachel Rosolina for her expertise and flexibility in supporting us to make the best book possible. Finally, thanks to Jeff Jones, Douglas Rife, and Stefan Kohler from Solution Tree for believing and investing in our vision to make sense of mathematics for teaching.

—Juli Dixon

Many thanks to my family, Michele and Calvin, for the wonderful support they continue to provide me in all of my endeavors. I also wish to thank our wonderful team of authors—Juli, Thomasenia, Jennifer, and Guy—from whom I have learned so much in the writing of this book.

—Ed Nolan

I am most grateful for the presence of my husband, Larry, and our sons, Blake, Philip, and Kurt, in my life. Many others support me and my work, and they include my mother, T. R. Lott, my six siblings, my pastors, and many dear friends. I am also thankful for the Dixon Nolan Adams Mathematics associates for working as a collaborative team to refine the delivery of the contents of this book.

—Thomasenia Adams

I would like to thank my family and future husband, Lee, for all of their support and guidance. I would like to also thank my coauthors as well as all of the other Dixon Nolan Adams Mathematics associates for the collaborative work that we have done. You have taught me more than I could have imagined.

—Jennifer Tobias

I would like to thank my family and friends for all the support they have given me in this and all my efforts. A special thank you to my wife, Jennifer, who has inspired me to always take the next step forward and never stand in one place; her patience with me in this process has been amazing. Finally, thanks to the entire Dixon Nolan Adams Mathematics team—the collaborative work on this book and all other projects has made me a better mathematics educator.

—Guy Barmoha

Solution Tree Press would like to thank the following reviewers:

Jennifer Basner
Fifth-Grade Teacher
Berlin Community School
Berlin, New Jersey

Kristopher J. Childs
Assistant Professor, STEM Education
Texas Tech University
Lubbock, Texas

Rebecca Elder
Fourth-Grade Teacher
McMillan Elementary
Murray, Utah

Becky Elliott
Assistant Principal
Academy of the Holy Names
Tampa, Florida

Amanda Miliner
Fourth-Grade Teacher
Miller Elementary School
Warner Robins, Georgia

Amanda L. Miller
Assistant Professor of Middle
School Mathematics Education
Illinois State University
Normal, Illinois

Amanda Northrup
Fifth-Grade Teacher
The Exploris School
Raleigh, North Carolina

Sarah Reed
Third-Grade Teacher
Field Elementary School
Louisville, Kentucky

Donald Sarazen
Fifth-Grade Teacher
White Knoll Elementary School
West Columbia, South Carolina

Visit **go.solution-tree.com/mathematics** to
download the free reproducibles in this book.

Table of Contents

CHAPTER 5
Geometry 117

CHAPTER 6
Measurement. 145

EPILOGUE

About the Authors

Juli K. Dixon, PhD, is a professor of mathematics education at the University of Central Florida (UCF) in Orlando. She coordinates the award-winning Lockheed Martin/UCF Academy for Mathematics and Science for the K–8 master of education program as well as the mathematics track of the doctoral program in education. Prior to joining the faculty at UCF, Dr. Dixon was a secondary mathematics educator at the University of Nevada, Las Vegas and a public school mathematics teacher in urban school settings at the elementary, middle, and secondary levels.

She is a prolific writer who has authored and coauthored books, textbooks, chapters, and articles. A sought-after speaker, Dr. Dixon has delivered keynotes and other presentations throughout the United States. She has served as chair of the National Council of Teachers of Mathematics Student Explorations in Mathematics Editorial Panel and as a board member for the Association of Mathematics Teacher Educators. At the state level, she has served on the board of directors for the Nevada Mathematics Council and is a past president of the Florida Association of Mathematics Teacher Educators.

Dr. Dixon received a bachelor's degree in mathematics and education from State University of New York at Potsdam, a master's degree in mathematics education from Syracuse University, and a doctorate in curriculum and instruction with an emphasis in mathematics education from the University of Florida. Dr. Dixon is a leader in Dixon Nolan Adams Mathematics.

To learn more about Dr. Dixon's work supporting children with special needs, visit www.astrokeofluck.net or follow @thestrokeofluck on Twitter.

Edward C. Nolan is preK–12 director of mathematics for Montgomery County Public Schools in Maryland. He has nineteen years of classroom experience in both middle and high schools and was department chair for fifteen years, all in Montgomery County. An active member of the National Council of Teachers of Mathematics (NCTM), he is president-elect of the Maryland Council of Supervisors of Mathematics. Nolan is also a consultant for Solution Tree as one of the leaders of Dixon Nolan Adams Mathematics, providing support for teachers and administrators on rigorous standards for mathematics.

Nolan has been published in the *Banneker Banner*, a publication of the Maryland Council of Teachers of Mathematics, and *Mathematics Teaching in the Middle School*, an NCTM publication, and he has conducted professional development at the state, regional, and national level, including webinars for NCTM and TODOS: Mathematics for ALL. His research interests lie in helping students and teachers develop algebraic thinking and reasoning. In 2005, Nolan won the Presidential Award for Excellence in Mathematics and Science Teaching.

He is a graduate of the University of Maryland. He earned a master's degree in educational administration from Western Maryland College.

To learn more about Nolan's work, follow @ed_nolan on Twitter.

Thomasenia Lott Adams, PhD, is an associate dean and professor of mathematics education in the College of Education at the University of Florida. She has mentored many future teachers of mathematics and mathematics teacher educators, and has served as a mathematics coach for grades K–12. She is the author of an elementary mathematics text series, academic books, and numerous peer-reviewed journal articles. Dr. Adams is a presenter at U.S. conferences and for professional development in school settings, which often includes teaching mathematics. She is also a trained National School Reform Faculty Certified Critical Friends Group coach.

Dr. Adams previously served as editor for the Mathematical Roots Department in *Mathematics Teaching in the Middle School* and coeditor for the Investigations Department of *Teaching Children Mathematics*. She is a past board member for the Association of Mathematics Teacher Educators and the School Science and Mathematics Association. She is also a past president of the Florida Association of Mathematics Teacher Educators and a recipient of the Mary L. Collins Teacher Educator of the Year Award from the Florida Association of Teacher Educators.

Dr. Adams has engaged in many high-impact mathematics education projects, including Algebra Nation, an online platform for supporting the teaching and learning of algebra. She was also the team leader for mathematics and science job-embedded professional development for middle and high school mathematics and science teachers. Dr. Adams is a leader in Dixon Nolan Adams Mathematics.

Dr. Adams received a bachelor of science in mathematics from South Carolina State College and a master of education and doctorate of philosophy in instruction and curriculum with an emphasis in mathematics education from the University of Florida.

To learn more about Dr. Adams's work, follow @TLAMath on Twitter.

Jennifer M. Tobias, PhD, is an associate professor of mathematics education at Illinois State University. Her specialization is in elementary mathematics with a research emphasis on the preparation of prospective elementary teachers and their development of understanding elementary mathematics, specifically in the area of rational numbers. Prior to coming to Illinois State, she taught mathematics at the middle and high school level for three years. She also conducts professional development workshops for teachers.

Dr. Tobias received an Outstanding University Teaching Award from Illinois State University for the 2012–2013 academic year. She has also served on committees for the Association of Mathematics Teacher Educators and the National Science Foundation. She also reviews articles for many national and international journals.

Dr. Tobias has had numerous publications in state, national, and international journals and books focusing on her research and on teaching practices. She has also presented at several state, national, and international conferences on her teaching and research with prospective and practicing elementary teachers.

Dr. Tobias received a bachelor of science in elementary education, master's of education in elementary education, and master's of science in applied mathematics from the University of Illinois. She received her doctorate in education with an emphasis on mathematics education from the University of Central Florida.

To learn more about Dr. Tobias's work follow @tobimath3 on Twitter.

Guy Barmoha is the director of the Mathematics, Science, and Gifted Department at Broward County Public Schools, Florida, the sixth largest school district in the nation. Barmoha has also worked as the Elementary Mathematics Curriculum Supervisor for Broward County Public Schools. In both roles, Barmoha has designed and delivered engaging mathematics and science professional learning for in-service teachers and administrators in grades K–12.

Barmoha taught middle school mathematics for twelve years as well as two years of mathematics distance-learning classes. He received the prestigious Edyth May Sliffe Award for Excellence in Teaching in 1997. In 2001, he was a finalist for the Broward County, Florida, Teacher of the Year Award. In 2004, the local council of mathematics teachers awarded Barmoha the distinction of Broward County's Middle School Mathematics Teacher of the Year.

While managing his responsibilities with Broward Schools, Barmoha worked as a part-time instructor for the Institute for Mathematics and Computer Science (IMACS) from 1995 to 2013. He taught courses in mathematics enrichment, logic puzzles, computer enrichment, and electronics. Barmoha was a lead instructor and trainer for the IMACS mathematics enrichment curriculum, which is tailored to mathematically talented students in grades K–12. He was awarded the honor of being IMACS teacher of the year twice during his time there.

Barmoha has written curriculum for Broward County Public Schools, Florida Atlantic University, and IMACS. He continues to train preservice and in-service teachers in mathematics content knowledge and pedagogy. He holds a bachelor of science in mathematics education from Florida State University and a master of science in teaching mathematics from Florida Atlantic University.

To learn more about Barmoha's work, follow @gbarmoha on Twitter.

To book Juli K. Dixon, Edward C. Nolan, Thomasenia Lott Adams, Jennifer M. Tobias, or Guy Barmoha for professional development, contact pd@solution-tree.com.

Introduction

The only way to learn mathematics is to do mathematics.

—Paul Halmos

When teaching, much of the day is spent supporting students to engage in learning new content. In mathematics, that often means planning for instruction, delivering the planned lessons, and engaging in the formative assessment process. There are opportunities to attend conferences and other professional development events, but those are typically focused on teaching strategies or on administrative tasks like learning the new gradebook program. Opportunities to take on the role of *learner* of the subject you teach are often neglected. As you read *Making Sense of Mathematics for Teaching Grades 3–5*, you will have the chance to become the learner once again. You will *learn* about the mathematics you teach by *doing* the mathematics you teach.

There is a strong call to build teachers' content knowledge for teaching mathematics. A lack of a "deep understanding of the content that [teachers] are expected to teach may inhibit their ability to teach meaningful, effective, and connected lesson sequences, regardless of the materials that they have available" (National Council of Teachers of Mathematics [NCTM], 2014, p. 71). This lack of deep understanding may have more to do with lack of exposure than anything else.

All too often, exposure to mathematics is limited to rules that have little meaning. Teachers then pass these rules on to students. For example, how mathematics is taught in grade 3 influences students' understanding of mathematics in later years. If a teacher says "multiplication always makes bigger" as a way to help young learners differentiate between multiplication and division, this meaning for multiplication becomes worthless when students encounter multiplying with fractions in fifth grade. The rule applies to problems like 3 × 4 where the factors are whole numbers but not for problems like ¾ × 4. The product of ¾ × 4 is 3; it is less than the factor 4. This is an example of what Karen Karp, Sarah Bush, and Barbara Dougherty (2014) refer to as *rules that expire*. Providing rules that work in the short term that cannot be applied in the long term is counterproductive to supporting students with meaningful school mathematics experiences. Teachers must attend to precision when teaching concepts in mathematics, or students will learn incorrect information. Students will need to later unlearn those misconceptions—and unlearning a concept is much more difficult than learning it correctly the first time. This happens when teachers are not afforded the opportunity to develop a deep understanding of the mathematics they teach.

This book is our response to requests from teachers, coaches, supervisors, and administrators who understand the need to know mathematics for teaching but who don't know how to reach a deeper level of content knowledge or to support others to do so. First and foremost, the book provides guidance for refining what it means to be a teacher of mathematics. To teach mathematics for depth means to facilitate instruction that empowers students to develop a deep understanding of mathematics. This can happen

1

when teachers are equipped with strong mathematics content knowledge—knowledge that covers the conceptual and procedural understanding of mathematics and knowledge that is supported by a variety of strategies and tools for engaging students to learn mathematics. With these elements as a backdrop, this book can be used to go below the surface in core areas of mathematics.

Second, coaches, supervisors, and administrators benefit from the content and perspectives provided in this book because it offers a source that supports guidance and mentoring to enhance teachers' mathematics content knowledge and their knowledge for teaching mathematics. They can particularly benefit from this book as a resource for helping them recognize expected norms in mathematics classrooms.

Here, we will set the stage for what you will learn from this book along with the rationale for why it is important for you to learn it. First, we provide some of the reasons why teachers need to understand mathematics with depth. Next, we share the structure of each chapter along with a description of what you will experience through that structure. Finally, we present ways that you will be able to use this book as an individual or within a collaborative team.

A Call for Making Sense of Mathematics for Teaching

Often, teachers are not initially aware that they lack sufficient depth of mathematical understanding or that this depth of understanding is critical to being equipped to guide students' mathematical development. What we have found is that engaging in tasks designed to contrast conceptual and procedural solution processes provides a window into the gap left by teaching mathematics without understanding.

Procedural skill includes the ability to follow rules for operations with a focus on achieving a solution quickly, while *conceptual understanding* includes comprehension of mathematical ideas, operations, and relationships. The procedure for dividing a whole number by a fraction, such as $4 \div \frac{1}{5}$, is one that most teachers can execute without much thought, yet the conceptual understanding needed to compose a word problem and draw a picture to solve the same problem might be less accessible. Thus, the contrast between typical solution processes and those that develop conceptual understanding highlights the need to truly know mathematics in order to teach it.

As a team, we provide large-scale professional development workshops for school districts across the United States and beyond. We often begin our presentations by engaging participants in a short mathematical activity to set the stage for the types of mind-shifting approaches necessary to teach for depth. One such activity involves estimating the results of operations with fractions without actually performing the operation first. Consider the problems in figure I.1.

Participants most often experience success with the first four examples. However, they are lulled into a rhythm that is interrupted when they call out 2½ as an estimate for 1⅞ – ½. This response helps participants understand why they constantly need to remind students to take note of the operation. When many similar examples are used in succession, thinking often stops and procedures are instead performed with automaticity.

Estimate the result of each problem provided here without writing anything down or using an algorithm.

$$\frac{1}{2} + \frac{2}{5}$$
$$\frac{2}{6} + \frac{3}{11}$$
$$2\frac{1}{3} + \frac{6}{7}$$
$$3\frac{4}{5} + 1\frac{1}{3}$$
$$1\frac{7}{8} - \frac{1}{2}$$
$$\frac{4}{5} \times \frac{1}{2}$$
$$1\frac{3}{7} \times \frac{3}{5}$$

Figure I.1: Fraction estimation challenge problems.

The greatest pause occurs when participants encounter the multiplication problems. They have difficulty estimating $\frac{4}{5} \times \frac{1}{2}$ because applying the algorithm of multiplying the numerators then the denominators is so deeply engrained. They do not think of $\frac{4}{5} \times \frac{1}{2}$ as being close to $1 \times \frac{1}{2}$ for a reasonable estimate of $\frac{1}{2}$. Why is thinking about estimation—rather than strictly using the algorithm—so important if teachers are successful with applying the algorithm? Teachers, and those who support teachers, need to be comfortable modeling learning behaviors sought after in students. Students must be able to check the reasonableness of their answers to computations with fractions. The ability to estimate is part of the checking process. Estimation with fraction operations is not accomplished by performing the operation and then finding a benchmark fraction that is close to the answer. Rather, it is based on an understanding of the operation and an application of number sense and extending that idea to operations involving fractions (Dixon & Tobias, 2013).

When we address estimation with fraction computation with participants, they are often at a loss for a process to replace the use of the standard algorithm for multiplying fractions. (This standard algorithm might be better named the U.S. standard algorithm because there are other algorithms standard to other countries. In this book, *standard algorithms* will refer to the most common U.S. standard algorithms unless otherwise noted.) They might experience success with a problem similar to $\frac{4}{5} \times \frac{1}{2}$ because once they think to use 1 as an estimate for $\frac{4}{5}$, the problem is accessible. However, they do not know how to estimate products with factors that are not close to whole numbers such as 1 or fractions such as $\frac{1}{2}$.

Consider the last problem in the sequence in figure I.1. How would you estimate the product of $1\frac{3}{7} \times \frac{3}{5}$? A close estimate would be to find $1\frac{1}{2} \times \frac{1}{2}$. Maybe you would think of finding one group of $\frac{1}{2}$ and then adding $\frac{1}{2}$ of a group of $\frac{1}{2}$ for an estimate of $\frac{3}{4}$. In contrast, perhaps you would be tempted to change $1\frac{3}{7}$ to an equivalent fraction greater than 1. The latter strategy indicates an attempt to apply the standard algorithm and does not necessarily indicate a deep operational sense with multiplying fractions.

Teachers who do not have this sense may miss opportunities to develop it in their students. They must also understand how content is developed from one year to the next, use effective mathematics practices to build mathematical proficiency in all students, and incorporate tasks, questioning, and evidence into instruction.

Understanding Mathematics for Teaching

How does one develop fraction sense? Development of fraction sense happens best when there is an opportunity to apply fraction concepts and skills in a variety of contexts. Even if *you* have this understanding, how do you help your fellow teachers or the teachers you support develop the same? Questions such as these led us to create our mathematics-content-focused professional development institutes and the accompanying follow-up workshops, in which teachers implement new skills and strategies learned at the mathematics institutes. Conversations during the follow-up workshops provide evidence that teachers benefit from knowing the mathematics with depth, as do the students they serve. After all, discussing how to make sense of fraction operations within teacher teams is a powerful way to develop a deep understanding.

We begin each follow-up workshop with a discussion of what is going well at the participants' schools and what needs further attention. Their responses to both queries reaffirm our need to focus on teachers' pedagogical content knowledge. A typical response regarding what is going well includes a discussion about how teachers are now able to make connections between the topics they teach. For example, teachers discuss the connections they are able to make when teaching multidigit multiplication and finding area. They might explore a problem like 4×127 using an area model early in their discussion of multiplying multidigit numbers. They can then reconnect to that idea when they discuss finding areas of rectangles by choosing a rectangle with dimensions of 4 units by 127 units and make the connections explicit. Teachers report that, in past years, they taught these two content areas as separate topics, making no connections to the importance of flexible understanding across mathematics, as though the topics existed in silos, completely separate. They taught without coherence. With a deeper understanding of their content, however, they note that they are able to reinforce earlier topics and provide rich experiences as they make connections from one topic to the next. Similarly, coaches report that their deeper mathematics understanding is useful in helping teachers attend to these connections during planning and instruction and within the formative assessment process. The formative assessment process includes the challenging work of evaluating student understanding throughout the mathematics lesson and unit. Teachers need a deep understanding of the mathematics they teach to support a thoughtful process of making sense of student thinking and being confident to respond to students' needs, whether those needs include filling gaps, addressing common errors, or advancing ideas beyond the scope of the lesson or unit.

Through the mathematics institutes and workshops, participants realize the need for additional professional development experiences, but providing this level of support can be challenging for schools and districts. This book is our response to this need. We've designed it to support stakeholders who want a review as well as to address additional topics. Our approach herein is informed by our extensive experience providing professional development throughout the United States as well as internationally and is supported by research on best practices for teaching and learning mathematics.

Engaging in the Mathematical Practices

As teachers of mathematics, our goal for all students should be mathematical proficiency, regardless of the standards used. One way to achieve mathematical proficiency is to "balance *how* to use mathematics with *why* the mathematics works" (National Council of Supervisors of Mathematics [NCSM], 2014, pp. 20–21, emphasis added). Mathematical proficiency involves unpacking the mathematics embedded within learning progressions, developing and implementing an assortment of strategies connected to mathematical topics and the real world, being able to explain and justify mathematical procedures, and interpreting and making sense of students' thinking (Ball, Thames, & Phelps, 2008). These processes are well described by the eight Standards for Mathematical Practice contained within the Common Core State Standards (CCSS) for mathematics (National Governors Association Center for Best Practices [NGA] & Council of Chief State School Officers [CCSSO], 2010).

1. Make sense of problems and persevere in solving them.

2. Reason abstractly and quantitatively.

3. Construct viable arguments and critique the reasoning of others.

4. Model with mathematics.

5. Use appropriate tools strategically.

6. Attend to precision.

7. Look for and make use of structure.

8. Look for and express regularity in repeated reasoning.

The Mathematical Practices describe the ways that mathematically proficient students solve problems and engage in learning mathematics. What does this mean to you and your students? Since the Mathematical Practices truly describe how *students* engage with the mathematics, your role becomes that of facilitator, supporting this engagement. Think about $1\frac{3}{7} \times \frac{3}{5}$. If your goal of instruction is for students to estimate the product, in what ways should students engage with this task? If you want them to think of $1\frac{3}{7}$ as close to $1\frac{1}{2}$ and $\frac{3}{5}$ as close to $\frac{1}{2}$ and then to multiply those factors, making sense of the structure of multiplication would be appropriate. Finding $1\frac{1}{2}$ groups of $\frac{1}{2}$ is accessible by understanding that it results in the same product as finding one group of $\frac{1}{2}$ and an additional $\frac{1}{2}$ of another group of $\frac{1}{2}$. This thinking can be described symbolically as $1\frac{1}{2} \times \frac{1}{2} = (1 + \frac{1}{2}) \times \frac{1}{2} = (1 \times \frac{1}{2}) + (\frac{1}{2} \times \frac{1}{2})$. This structure is actually that of the distributive property of multiplication over addition, something that might be missed without an emphasis on Mathematical Practice 7, "Look for and make use of structure." How should teachers facilitate this sort of discussion with students so that the teachers are not doing all the telling (and thinking)? It requires instruction that acknowledges the value of students talking about mathematics and using mathematics to communicate their ideas.

When the mathematics content and the Mathematical Practices are addressed in tandem, students have the best opportunity to develop clarity about mathematics reasoning and what it means to do mathematics successfully.

Emphasizing the TQE Process

As part of the professional development material in this book, we include videos of grades 3–5 classroom episodes (and occasionally grades extending from this grade band) in which students explore rich mathematical tasks. Classroom videos from grades before and after grades 3–5 provide the opportunity to highlight the importance of prerequisite concepts and skills as well as links to the mathematics on the horizon. One of the included videos shows grade 1 students in order to highlight strategies that young learners explore as they focus on sums within 20. This video allows teachers in the intermediate grades to connect to those strategies when students are solving problems involving multidigit addition and subtraction. In presenting these videos, we emphasize three key aspects of the teacher's role—(1) tasks, (2) questioning, and (3) evidence—which make up what we call the *TQE process*.

Our emphasis on the TQE process helps define a classroom that develops mathematics as a focused, coherent, and rigorous subject. Thus, we uphold the following tenets.

- **Teachers with a deep understanding of the content they teach select *tasks* that provide students with the opportunity to engage in practices that support learning concepts before procedures; they know that for deep learning to take place, students need to understand the procedures they use.** Students who engage in mathematical tasks are also engaged in learning mathematics with understanding. Consider grade 3 students who are making sense of basic multiplication facts. The order of the presented facts is important to address a specific learning goal. For example, if the goal is for students to make sense of a doubling strategy as a means to determine a fact other than by rote, students might be presented with facts like 2 × 6 and 4 × 6 then 2 × 7 and 4 × 7. Students would then identify a pattern in the pairs of facts as a way to see the value in applying the doubling strategy. Once students identify the pattern, they can be led to see why doubling a factor results in doubling the product. These students are making sense of patterns in computation as a way of determining basic facts. Thus, this scenario provides insight into a classroom where carefully selected tasks support deeper learning.

- **Teachers who have a deep understanding of the content they teach facilitate targeted and productive *questioning* strategies because they have a clear sense of how the content progresses within and across grades.** For instance, in the grade 3 example, teachers would facilitate discussions around strategies for multiplying basic facts that focus on the application of properties of operations such as the distributive property of multiplication over addition when solving 7 × 8. Teacher questioning encourages students to use relational thinking strategies by thinking 7 × 8 = (5 + 2) × 8 = (5 × 8) + (2 × 8). They know that this is important for later work with multiplying multidigit numbers with understanding, foreshadowing concepts in algebra.

- **Teachers who have a deep understanding of the content they teach use *evidence* gained from the formative assessment process to help them know where to linger in developing students' coherent understanding of mathematics.** In the grade 3 example, teachers know that it is important for students to apply the associative and distributive properties as strategies and that these strategies are more valuable than a strategy based on skip counting. They look for evidence that students are using strategies based on properties of operations appropriately to make sense of basic facts.

Throughout the book and the accompanying classroom videos, we share elements of the TQE process to help you as both a learner and a teacher of mathematics. In addition, we ask that you try to answer three targeted questions as you watch each video. These questions are as follows:

1. How does the teacher prompt the students to make sense of the problem?

2. How do the students engage in the task; what tools or strategies are the students using to model the task?

3. How does the teacher use questioning to engage students in thinking about their thought processes?

Next, we describe the structure of the book to help guide your reading.

The Structure of Making Sense

To address the mathematical content taught in the intermediate grades, each chapter focuses on a different overarching topic. For instance, chapter 1 covers place value in relation to addition and subtraction. Chapter 2 then explores multiplication and division. Chapter 3 takes a look at fraction concepts, and chapter 4 covers fraction operations. Chapter 5 examines geometry, and chapter 6 closes with a focus on measurement. These topics represent the big ideas for the intermediate grades. Each chapter concludes with a series of questions to prompt reflection on the topic under discussion.

We end the book with an epilogue featuring next steps to help you and your team make sense of mathematics for teaching and implement this important work in your school or district.

To further break down each overarching topic, each chapter shares a common structure: The Challenge, The Progression, The Mathematics, The Classroom, and The Response.

The Challenge

Each chapter begins with an opportunity for you to engage in an initial task connected to the chapter's big idea. We call this section The Challenge because this task might challenge your thinking. We encourage you to stop and engage with the task before reading further—to actually *do* the task. Throughout the book, we alert you to the need to stop and do tasks with a *do now* symbol (see figure I.2).

Figure I.2: *Do now* symbol.

The presentation of mathematical ideas in this book may be different from how you learned mathematics. Recall being asked to estimate the product of $1\frac{3}{7} \times \frac{3}{5}$. This task may test your understanding of the mathematical topic being explored. You might eventually be asked to draw a picture to find the product, something you may or may not have tried in your own mathematics learning. Tasks in these sections focus on reasoning and sense making, since the rules of mathematics are developed through connections to earlier mathematical experiences rather than through procedures presented without meaning.

Since one purpose of this book is to engage you as a learner *and* teacher of mathematics, the tasks we ask you to explore support this goal. As a student of mathematics, you will consider how you learn mathematics. As a teacher of mathematics, you will explore how this newly found understanding could be the impetus for making sense of mathematics for teaching.

The Progression

Mathematics content knowledge is not enough. According to NCSM (2014), teachers must also "*understand how to best sequence, connect, and situate the content they are expected to teach within learning progressions*" (p. 24, emphasis in original). This means teachers need to know both the mathematics for their grade level and the mathematics that comes before and after their grade level—how the mathematics progresses over time.

Thus, each chapter highlights a progression of learning for a big idea. These progressions identify how learning develops over multiple years and highlight the importance of making sense of each building block along the way. The sequences defined by the progressions help the learner—and the teacher—make sense of the big idea in question. Understanding how content progresses provides avenues for supporting both the learner who struggles and the learner who needs enrichment.

Our placement of topics within grades was informed by the Common Core State Standards for mathematics (NGA & CCSSO, 2010). However, our discussion of how the mathematics is developed within the progressions was not limited by this interpretation. We do not refer to specific content standards from the Common Core in an effort to expand the discussion to include *all* rigorous mathematics standards, including those found outside of the United States. Note that because learning progressions develop over time, there will be occasions when this book addresses topics that reach into primary grades or middle school.

The Mathematics

There is much talk about rigor in instruction these days, but what does *rigor* mean in the context of teaching and learning mathematics? A misnomer is that it means *hard* or *difficult*. Rather, *rigor* refers to the need to incorporate all forms of thinking about mathematics—including concepts, procedures, the language of mathematics, and applications—in the teaching and learning process. However, this raises several questions. What does this actually look like in instruction? What teacher actions expose all students to rigor? How do you balance rigor reflected by reasoning and sense making with the ability to recall multiplication facts?

Problems in a rigorous classroom build students' deep understanding of mathematics. Consider 8×7. You know the product; you know it without needing to think. Yet what path do teachers use to bring students to this level? All too often it begins and ends with memorization. Teachers use flash cards and games and spend time each day on practice, leaving some students able to recall the facts and some unable to recall the facts. Is this an example of teaching with rigor? The answer is no.

Importantly, rigor includes making sense of strategies based on properties of operations. Sense making should precede a focus on memorization, rules, and procedures. This is where teaching might get uncomfortable. You may not have been taught the strategies as a student or see the connections. Thus, within The Mathematics section in each chapter, you will unpack the big ideas so the mathematics is explicitly connected to ways of making this knowledge accessible and rigorous for your students. For example, in using the "doubling strategy" to find the product of 8×7, you might apply the associative property or the distributive property, depending on how you determine the product. Exploring mathematics in this way develops a deep personal understanding of mathematics. As you develop this understanding, procedures and algorithms will make sense, and you will be able to explain and justify them (NCTM, 2014). Through this process, we will support you in developing the knowledge to promote students' procedural fluency, which is defined as "skill in carrying out procedures flexibly, accurately, efficiently, and appropriately" (Kilpatrick, Swafford, & Findell, 2001, p. 116).

Many of the tasks throughout this book can be characterized as high-cognitive-demand tasks, which are "tasks that require students to think conceptually and that stimulate students to make connections that lead to a different set of opportunities for student thinking" (Stein & Smith, 1998, p. 269). Consideration for the understanding, creation, selection, and implementation of high-cognitive-demand tasks is vital for effective mathematics learning (Dixon, Adams, & Nolan, 2015). While including tasks that are high and low cognitive demand supports a balance of conceptual understanding and procedural fluency, the cognitive demand of tasks often declines during instruction when the cognitive complexity of the task is not maintained (Kisa & Stein, 2015). How will you maintain the challenge of tasks through your actions? In this section and throughout the book, we provide you with excerpts from mathematics lessons so you can build a shared understanding of what mathematics instruction can look like in classrooms. In addition, we emphasize one or more of the best-aligned Mathematical Practices that support the learning of the relevant mathematics content. This is important regardless of whether you are teaching using the Common Core State Standards for mathematics. It describes good teaching and learning of any mathematical content.

The Classroom

In what ways do you support student learning in the mathematics classroom? For instance, do you encourage student discourse? Doing so allows you to consider what students are talking about and how you will respond to their talk. Your approach to student talk—and many other classroom aspects—helps determine the type of classroom learning community you and your students develop together. This classroom learning community is critical to the development of students' deep mathematical understanding.

The Classroom sections provide videos and extensive descriptions of what happens in engaging mathematics lessons. In order to assist you in thinking about how classrooms that develop mathematical understanding should look, each chapter includes two video episodes. These short videos show students exploring one task from the big idea of that chapter and one task from a related big idea. When you see the play button, please stop and watch the video. Included with the icon is the accompanying web address and a Quick Response (QR) code for you to access the video.

www.solution-tree.com/Using_Place_Value
_Understandings_to_Model_Decimals

We consider the accompanying videos to be a further investment in our effort to support the teaching and learning of mathematics. You will have the opportunity to see the topics we write about in the book in action. For instance, when we discuss about how to massage a task so that it engages students, elicits student talk, and uncovers students' errors, we then follow up by capturing the essence of these actions in real classrooms. This modeling of good mathematics teaching provides opportunities for teachers to discuss what is happening in their own classrooms with the same mathematics content. It is not always possible for teachers to leave the classroom to observe a fellow teacher engaged in mathematics instruction. Thus, these videos help fill this gap and also provide a context for teachers to try an approach to mathematics teaching as modeled in the videos.

You must also consider the classroom expectations set for students. For instance, what are the rules for students answering questions? These rules should be established and made explicit for students so they know what you expect of them when they work on tasks. Also, how do students work together on tasks? Students can benefit greatly from collaborative experiences in mathematics, but they need to know how to best collaborate with each other. In many instances, the student who is confident and right most of the time does most of the talking. Thus, helping students monitor and regulate their discourse is valuable for the mathematics learning experience. As illustrated in the classroom videos, we encourage three classroom norms for every mathematics classroom.

1. Explain and justify solutions.

2. Make sense of each other's solutions.

3. Say when you don't understand or when you don't agree.

The classroom norms need to support the active thinking of students rather than solely relying on the thinking of teachers, as is so often the case in teacher-centered classrooms. This point is true when students work on their own as well as when students work together. You should always provide students the opportunity to share their strategies and make sense of the thinking of other students in order to be sure they understand mathematics with depth.

The structure of the classroom needs to support the thinking and learning of the students, and different tasks may require different structures. Some tasks may include questions that help students make connections; other tasks may not need such support. One model that is often discussed in many schools and districts is the gradual release of responsibility, commonly described as the teaching practice where the teacher models ("I do"), then the class practices together ("We do"), and finally the students practice independently ("You do") (Fisher & Frey, 2003). Although this method is appropriate at times, we advocate for methods that include focus on the *students* making sense of and reasoning with mathematics. An alternative approach for mathematics is what we call *layers of facilitation*.

1. *I facilitate the whole class* to engage in meaningful tasks through questioning.

2. *I facilitate small groups* to extend the learning initiated in the whole-group setting.

3. *I facilitate individuals* to provide evidence of their understanding of the learning goal.

This change in teacher role focuses on the teacher as a facilitator of knowledge acquisition rather than as a transmitter of knowledge. As you read the text and as you watch the videos, you will notice our focus is largely on implementing layers of facilitation, but it is important to recognize that there are some topics and mathematical content that need to be taught following the gradual release of responsibility model. It is important for you, as the teacher, to determine when to apply this model. Keep in mind that students will benefit from opportunities to have a more participatory role during instruction whenever possible.

The Response

How do you respond when students struggle? What do you do when students express misconceptions? It is important to use student errors as springboards for learning; the errors and the gaps in prerequisite knowledge that lead to those errors inform your everyday instruction as well as your response to intervention (RTI) process within a Multi-Tiered System of Supports (MTSS).

Again, consider how students approach 8×7. Perhaps they use their recall of the fact, or maybe they need to use other strategies to determine the product. Think about questions you could ask in order to gather information about students' thinking processes, both when they have the correct answer as well as when they do not. When your students answer 64, how can you help them examine their thinking and correct their mistake without simply giving them the correct answer? One approach would be to ask questions to support the efforts of your students and encourage them to think of errors as beneficial in order to learn mathematics with depth. This is an area where your own depth of mathematical understanding is critical to help your students develop their thinking.

It is essential to explore your students' reasoning and sense making and break down that thinking in order to rebuild their understanding of mathematics. Effective teachers understand what models and strategies best support students in ways that allow them to connect their current thinking with the learning goal of the task. You can then use the evidence of the level of students' understanding you gather to inform your response both during and after instruction.

Now that you understand what is to come in the following pages, here's how we suggest you approach the book.

How to Use This Book

Collaborative teams of teachers can use this book to explore mathematics content and engage in discussions about teacher actions that will help bring mathematics to life for students. In fact, the entire TQE process is best accomplished by a collaborative team that works together to address the four critical questions—the guiding force of the professional learning community (PLC) culture (DuFour, DuFour, Eaker, & Many, 2010).

1. What do we want students to learn and be able to do?

2. How will we know if they know it?

3. How will we respond if they don't know it?

4. How will we respond if they do know it?

This book is an optimal tool for your collaborative team in a PLC culture. Although it is grade-band specific, it also provides support for vertical (across grades) discussions and planning. There are many topics in this book that can be addressed in your grade-level team or in your vertical team, including the Mathematical Practices. While the Mathematical Practices are not grade specific, how students engage with them can be expected to vary from grade to grade, and you can benefit from grade-specific as well as vertical discussions about them.

Our expectation is that individuals or collaborative teams will be able to use this book by reading the chapters in order. Within each chapter, we help you develop clarity about the mathematical content and its progression. Teachers often have questions about the sequence of mathematics content in mathematics texts and other resources—sometimes the sequence is aligned with authentic progressions and sometimes not. Thus, you can use this book as a resource to understand how background and underlying knowledge of mathematics support further understanding and how to best align mathematics curriculum with the progression of the content.

We hope this book and the accompanying videos will be your go-to source for a deep dive into relevant mathematics content, effective pedagogical actions, appropriate classroom norms, meaningful assessment, and collaborative teacher team efforts. Our goal is for this resource to connect the good work of mathematics teaching that you are already facilitating with the goals of improving mathematics teaching that you aspire to attain.

Place Value, Addition, and Subtraction

Place value and the operations of addition and subtraction on whole numbers, with a connection to decimals, are important topics in grades 3–5 mathematics instruction. In this chapter, we focus on creating a deep understanding of the base ten number system and place value to assist in developing an understanding of invented and standard algorithms. You will explore how to use manipulatives such as base ten blocks to build students' understanding of how to compose and decompose numbers in order to help with the process of regrouping. We also include multiple strategies for developing fluency to add and subtract within 1,000, which will lead to success with the standard algorithm.

The Challenge

In the first task (see figure 1.1), consider how to add two three-digit numbers using an invented algorithm. Imagine that you don't yet know the standard algorithm of lining up the addends vertically, adding the ones and regrouping if necessary, then adding the tens, and so on. As with all tasks in this book, take the time to work the task out before reading on. The time you take with the task makes the text that follows more meaningful.

> Add the following in three different ways.
>
> 257 + 138

Figure 1.1: Add multidigit numbers in three different ways.

If you found it difficult to come up with three different ways to add 257 + 138, it is likely you were only taught to add such problems in one way, using the standard algorithm. If you figured out a different way, you probably came up with it on your own and did not reflect back on experiences with alternative algorithms from elementary school. Students who are encouraged to derive their own invented strategies are better able to build their number sense rather than just their memorization skills. Figure 1.2 illustrates a student's response to the problem from the task in figure 1.1; try to make sense of the student's thinking.

How does this method compare to the methods you chose? Perhaps you had fewer or more steps. How would you explain the method used? Assessing students' work involves a close examination of students' processes. If this were your classroom, would you have stopped the student anywhere in the process before allowing him to continue?

A student begins by writing on the board:

200 + 100 = 300

50 + 30 = 80

The student pauses and continues to write:

7 + 3 = 10

300 + 80 + 10 + 5 = 395

so, 257 + 138 = 395

Figure 1.2: Student's response to 257 + 138.

You may have thought that the student was on the correct path after seeing the first and second step and then worried that he confused the tens and ones—adding 7 ones to 3 tens for a sum of 10 ones—in the third step. Assuming the student was in error, how did he end up with the correct solution? Sometimes students just get lucky. Was there another strategy at play?

Hopefully you can see that when the student added 7 + 3, he was not confusing place values but was breaking apart the 8 ones into 3 ones and 5 ones so that the student could add 7 + 3 to make a ten. If you had stopped the student to caution him against confusing place value, then you would never have seen him use the excellent strategy of making a ten. However, this make-a-ten strategy is not taught in grade 3. It is taught in grade 1. If first-grade teachers don't see the value in this strategy for future work leading to adding with regrouping, they may not emphasize this important strategy. If third-grade teachers don't realize their students have been taught this strategy, they may fail to capitalize on it.

It is also important to think about how content is developed from one year to the next, and how mathematical understanding builds on itself, so that you then build on opportunities to reinforce the development of number sense. For instance, in the discussion of the task in figure 1.1 (page 13), you encountered the make-a-ten strategy, which is a first-grade concept. To effectively make sense of mathematics for teaching, you must understand how numbers are developed in the progression from kindergarten to grade 5. These foundational ideas for the early grades are important to gain a sense of students' early experiences with these concepts.

The Progression

In this book, the development of place value and the ability to use that knowledge to add and subtract whole numbers and decimals are based on the idea that solving problems in context can assist in sense making. Allow students to use manipulatives to help build understanding of place value, and encourage them to invent algorithms based on their understanding of the base ten number system. This conceptual understanding should be built before introducing the standard algorithm. Following is a progression for building an understanding of place value, addition, and subtraction. As shared in the introduction, because of the nature of this content, our description of a progression includes content from kindergarten through grade 2 rather than content that resides exclusively in the 3–5 grade band.

- Represent numbers as 10 ones and some more ones.

- Make sense of addition and subtraction.

- Represent and solve problems involving addition and subtraction.

- Apply relational thinking strategies and properties of operations to add and subtract.

- Add and subtract 10.

- Make sense of place value through hundreds.

- Use rounding as a strategy for estimation.

- Add and subtract within 1,000 fluently.

- Explain and justify use of the standard algorithms for addition and subtraction.

If you teach topics in the correct sequence, students have opportunities to make connections that may not be made if, for example, place value concepts are not interwoven into operations. Although many addition and subtraction concepts and operations are a focus of kindergarten through grade 2 (see *Making Sense of Mathematics for Teaching Grades K–2* [Dixon, Nolan, Adams, Brooks, & Howse, 2016]), in grade 3 the focus turns to fluency of addition and subtraction within 1,000. Grades 4 and 5 make the connection between addition and subtraction of whole numbers and adding and subtracting fractions and decimals.

Kindergarten Through Grade 2

Number concepts start in kindergarten with counting and cardinality (a measure of the number of elements in a set). This work is supported by both perceptual and conceptual subitizing (recognizing how many without counting), which will be explored in more detail later in this chapter. Next, place value is introduced. Kindergarteners represent two-digit numbers as 10 ones and some other ones. They also solve addition and subtraction word problems within 10 and become fluent with addition and subtraction within 5.

Students in grade 1 continue to solve word problems involving adding and subtracting, now within 20; this work also includes word problems that require adding three numbers. Students make sense of the equal sign and use relational thinking strategies to make the process of adding and subtracting more accessible. Properties of operations (such as the commutative and associative properties of addition) are used to help students create strategies for addition.

The work from kindergarten is extended from thinking of two-digit numbers as 10 ones and some other ones to thinking of two-digit numbers as 1 ten and some other ones in grade 1. Addition within 100 is also explored; however, in grade 1 it is limited to:

- Adding a two-digit number to a one-digit number
- Adding a two-digit number and a multiple of 10

Focus on addition should be grounded by the use of concrete models and drawings as well as strategies based on place value, properties of operations, and relating addition and subtraction. Students will be able to mentally find ten more or ten less than a number and subtract multiples of 10.

In grade 2, students solve one- and two-step word problems involving addition and subtraction within 100. The structure of these problems will be discussed in further detail later in this chapter. The place value investigations in grade 2 extend to numbers in the hundreds, as this will lead directly to adding multi-digit numbers. Much of the work in grade 2 is based on the progression of being able to add and subtract fluently using many strategies, such as those based on place value, properties of operations, drawings, and concrete models, to name a few. This progression begins with fluency within 20, moving to fluency within 100, and finally using strategies to add and subtract within 1,000. Second-grade students should also have memorized all of their basic addition and subtraction facts (which are facts with one-digit addends).

Grade 3

The work in grade 3 is focused on building fluency with addition and subtraction within 1,000. As in previous grades, fluency should rely on strategies based on place value, properties of operations, and relating addition to subtraction. Students solve two-step word problems using all four operations. Students estimate to check solutions so they can respond to the question: "Is that answer reasonable?"

Grade 4

Becoming fluent with the standard algorithm for addition and subtraction is part of the work in grade 4. This fluency is still grounded in place value concepts since the algorithms rely on adding and subtracting the values in like places. Fluency with addition and subtraction is used to assist students in inventing strategies and algorithms for multiplication (repeated addition) and division (repeated subtraction) that are based on place value concepts as well.

Grade 5

In grade 5, students extend their understanding of the structure of the base ten number system to decimals. The strategies used for adding and subtracting whole numbers are used to add and subtract decimals by understanding that the values in like places must be combined. The similarities of algorithms are discussed as well as the pitfalls of using the algorithm with decimals—for instance when decimals with different numbers of places after the decimal point need to be added or subtracted, like the example 24.6 – 3.04. The structure of the place value system leads to understanding that decomposing decimals is the same process as with whole numbers. Decimal numbers build on the same ten-to-one relationship used with whole numbers.

The Mathematics

Place value, addition, and subtraction are topics embedded in much of the content in grades 3–5. Making sense of the concepts and procedures involved with these topics will assist you in supporting students who struggle and in understanding the mathematics that is built on these concepts. While much of this work is first explored in kindergarten through grade 2, the ideas are applicable to the mathematics instruction of students in the intermediate grades. Here you will explore the mathematics involved in place value, addition, and subtraction in grades 3–5, which includes unpacking word problem structures, modeling addition and subtraction word problems with equations, using basic fact strategies, adding multidigit whole numbers, subtracting multidigit whole numbers, and comparing adding and subtracting multidigit whole numbers to decimals.

Unpacking Word Problem Structures

Word problems are extremely important in making sense of mathematics, especially when the emphasis is on beginning with conceptual understanding before mastering procedures. Students make sense of mathematics by exploring it in real-world contexts. This is especially true when they develop number sense with adding and subtracting. Be intentional about providing students with word problems to solve and even having them write their own word problems. Explore this yourself prior to reading further by writing your own word problems according to the directions in figure 1.3. After you write these word problems, set them aside. You will refer to them later after exploring word problems more deeply.

Write two word (or story) problems: one addition and one subtraction.

Figure 1.3: Word problem task.

In this section, you will make sense of structures of word problems. The focus is primarily on addition and subtraction problems. We provide a deeper discussion of multiplication and division word problems in chapter 2. To begin, you will explore addition and subtraction word problems by unpacking the set of word problems provided in figure 1.4. We've adapted these problems from *Children's Mathematics: Cognitively Guided Instruction* (Carpenter, Fennema, Franke, Levi, & Empson, 2015), which provides an in-depth look at word problems and how they relate to Cognitively Guided Instruction (CGI). Rather than attempting to replicate their excellent work, we use it to support the continued development of your knowledge of the mathematics you teach with respect to problem structures. In order to fully appreciate the experience of unpacking these problems, copy the problems provided in figure 1.4 and cut them out along the dotted lines.

Copy and cut out the individual problems. Then sort them in any way that makes sense to you.

Alex has 7 red pencils and 8 blue pencils. How many pencils does she have?	Alex had 15 pencils. She gave some to Jessi. Now she has 7 pencils left. How many pencils did Alex give to Jessi?	Alex has 7 pencils. How many more pencils does she need to have 15 pencils altogether?	Alex has 15 pencils. She has 7 more pencils than Jessi. How many pencils does Jessi have?
Alex has 15 pencils. Jessi has 7 pencils. How many more pencils does Alex have than Jessi?	Alex had some pencils. She gave 7 pencils to Jessi. Now she has 8 pencils left. How many pencils did Alex have to start?	Alex has 15 pencils. Seven are red and the rest are blue. How many blue pencils does Alex have?	Alex had some pencils. Jessi gave her 7 more pencils. Now she has 15 pencils. How many pencils did Alex have to start?
Alex had 15 pencils. She gave 7 pencils to Jessi. How many pencils does Alex have left?	Jessi has 7 pencils. Alex has 8 more pencils than Jessi. How many pencils does Alex have?	Alex had 7 pencils. Jessi gave her 8 more pencils. How many pencils does Alex have altogether?	

Figure 1.4: Word problem sorting task.

Visit go.solution-tree.com/mathematics for a free reproducible version of this figure.

How did you sort them? Did you make a group that represented addition and another that represented subtraction? This is a very common approach. How did you determine the operation? Exploring choices for sorting problems provides a window into how you think about word problems. A common way to sort them is through the use of key words, such as *altogether*, *how many more*, and *left*. However, key words can be misleading and should not be stressed during instruction. Consider the two problems in figure 1.5. Notice how the use of key words leads to the proper operation. *Altogether* indicates addition in the first problem, and *how many more* indicates subtraction in the second problem.

1. Emma has 8 key chains. Calvin has 9 key chains. How many key chains do they have altogether?
2. Emma has 8 key chains. Riley has 15 key chains. How many more key chains does Riley have than Emma?

Figure 1.5: Key words in word problems.

Problems like these cause a false sense of security and might lead you to think that key words are always helpful. The result is the all-too-common poster on the classroom wall that has words for addition and words for subtraction and is often accompanied by chants like, "altogether means add." Then students encounter problems like this:

> Emma has 8 key chains. How many more key chains does she need to have 13 key chains altogether?

In this example, following key word instruction leads to an incorrect answer.

Students who are taught to rely on key words will get this problem wrong because they will see *altogether* as the last word in the problem, indicating they should add 8 and 13. However, students who have been taught through engagement in Mathematical Practice 2, "Reason abstractly and quantitatively," will likely be successful with this problem because they will be more able to reflect on the questions, "What is the problem asking?," "What do I know?," and "What do I need to do to answer the question?"

These questions are aligned with the kind of thinking that occurs when instruction is focused on reading comprehension. According to research, students do not typically apply their reading comprehension skills when they are solving mathematics word problems. Students often do not consider those strategies or replace them with key-word strategies once they realize they are solving mathematics word problems (Clements, 2011). Be intentional about supporting students to use reading comprehension strategies to make sense of mathematics word problems.

One useful strategy is to have students act out the story in the word problem. This is easier to accomplish when the story involves action. *Action* does not necessarily refer to movement but rather that something happens to an initial quantity in the problem. Consider the following problems in figure 1.6. Both problems include movement, but only the first problem involves action.

1. There were 7 sharks swimming around. Eight more sharks joined them. How many sharks are there now?

2. There were 7 sharks and 8 barracudas swimming around. How many fish are there altogether?

Figure 1.6: Action and nonaction word problems.

Acting out the first problem with countable objects would involve beginning with seven sharks and then adding eight sharks to the seven that were there at the start. With the second problem, the sharks and the barracudas are already there so there is nothing to do to act out the problem. This is an important distinction for students who are beginning to make sense of solving addition and subtraction word problems.

Now revisit your sorted cards. Which of the cards represent action? Look at the cards carefully and re-sort the eleven word problems in figure 1.4 (page 17) so that there are two piles, one with action problems and one with nonaction problems.

It is likely that you have five action problems and six nonaction problems. This is actually not correct, but don't worry about that for now. Set the nonaction problems aside and further sort the action problems into two piles, those that represent joining situations and those that represent separating situations.

If you had five action problems to start, you probably have two joining problems and three separating problems. Of the two joining problems, which would be easier for students to solve? It is likely that you chose this problem.

> Alex had 7 pencils. Jessi gave her 8 more pencils.
> How many pencils does Alex have altogether?

Which would be the easiest separate problem? It is likely that you chose this problem.

> Alex had 15 pencils. She gave 7 pencils to Jessi.
> How many pencils does Alex have left?

In both of these problems, the result of the action is the unknown quantity. In the joining problem, a student might solve it by starting with counters to represent the seven pencils Alex had to start, then adding eight counters to represent the pencils Jessi gave Alex. The answer would be the result of this action and could be determined by counting all of the counters. These problem types are *result unknown* problems and are named join (result unknown) and separate (result unknown) respectively (Carpenter et al., 2015).

The unknown quantity is used to name the other action word problems as well. If you identified two action problems, the remaining action problem is likely a *start unknown* problem and is named such because the initial quantity, or the quantity at the start of the action, is what is unknown.

> Alex had some pencils. Jessi gave her 7 more pencils. Now she has 15 pencils. How many pencils did Alex have to start?

The corresponding separating problem also has the initial quantity unknown.

> Alex had some pencils. She gave 7 pencils to Jessi. Now she has 8 pencils left. How many pencils did Alex have to start?

In both of these problems, the action itself is known, as is the result of the action. What is unknown is the initial quantity, or the start of the problem. These problems are referred to as *start unknown* problems (Carpenter et al., 2015).

The last of the action problems, if you sorted five action problems, has the unknown in yet another location. The start is known, as is the result. What is unknown is the action that must occur to solve the problem. The action of the problem is referred to as the *change*. Therefore, the following problem is referred to as a *change unknown* problem (Carpenter et al., 2015).

> Alex had 15 pencils. She gave some to Jessi. Now she has 7 pencils left. How many pencils did Alex give to Jessi?

If you originally sorted five problems into the action pile, what seems to be missing from the problems? Did you identify a join (change unknown) problem? You likely placed it in the nonaction pile when you were sorting action and nonaction problems. Look for it now. You probably missed it earlier because the action is actually implied in the problem. The action is described by the pencils Alex needs to get to have fifteen pencils altogether.

> Alex has 7 pencils. How many more pencils does she need to have 15 pencils altogether?

So there are six action problems and five nonaction problems.

The nonaction problems consist of problems that represent comparison situations and those that do not. The noncomparison problems are very similar to the action problems in that there are two distinct sets of quantities known. They are different in that the quantities are "already there" so no action is described or implied in the problem; there are two parts and a whole, and both parts are there from the start whether known or unknown. These can be referred to as *part-part-whole* problems (Carpenter et al., 2015). With these problems, either the whole is unknown or a part is unknown (see figure 1.7).

Part-Part-Whole (Whole Unknown)

Alex has 7 red pencils and 8 blue pencils. How many pencils does she have?

Part-Part-Whole (Part Unknown)

Alex has 15 pencils. Seven are red, and the rest are blue. How many blue pencils does Alex have?

Figure 1.7: Part-part-whole word problems.

The last three problems from the nonaction group are the *compare* problems. These problems are different from the others in that sets are not joined together or separated but rather, as the name implies, compared. There are three different potential unknown quantities: the difference, the greater quantity, and the lesser quantity. Match each problem to its label before reading on.

Figure 1.8 provides the three compare problems labeled by their unknowns. However, in each case, the question begins with, "How many more pencils does . . ." The question *could* have been worded, "How many fewer pencils does . . ." Thus, both of those versions are included for each problem type. Notice the similarities and differences between problem types.

	Difference Unknown	Greater Unknown	Lesser Unknown
"How many more?"	Alex has 15 pencils. Jessi has 7 pencils. How many more pencils does Alex have than Jessi?	Jessi has 7 pencils. Alex has 8 more pencils than Jessi. How many pencils does Alex have?	Alex has 15 pencils. She has 7 more pencils than Jessi. How many pencils does Jessi have?
"How many fewer?"	Alex has 15 pencils. Jessi has 7 pencils. How many fewer pencils does Jessi have than Alex?	Jessi has 7 pencils. She has 8 fewer pencils than Alex. How many pencils does Alex have?	Alex has 15 pencils. Jessi has 7 fewer pencils than Alex. How many pencils does Jessi have?

Figure 1.8: Compare problems.

Both problem types ("How many more?" and "How many fewer?") determine the same unknown quantity; however, students typically find one more direct than the other depending on the unknown quantity.

It is important to provide students with access to a wide variety of problem types. However, it is typical for teachers to use the easiest problem types during instruction. Those are the join (result unknown) and separate (result unknown) problems. To help identify the problem types used during instruction, a completed set of problem types, including those covered in figure 1.8, is provided in figure 1.9 (page 22).

Notice that the action problems, consisting of join and separate problem types, are in the upper section. The nonaction problems, consisting of part-part-whole and compare problem types, are in the lower section. Row labels describe the problem type, and column labels describe the unknown quantity.

Return to the addition and subtraction word problems you wrote as part of figure 1.3 (page 17). What problem types did you write? If you wrote join (result unknown) and separate (result unknown) word problems, then you will need to be careful to provide students with other problem types during instruction, as these are the simplest problem types and provide a limited window into addition and subtraction in context.

		Result Unknown	Change Unknown	Start Unknown
Action	**Join**	Alex had 7 pencils. Jessi gave her 8 more pencils. How many pencils does Alex have altogether?	Alex has 7 pencils. How many more pencils does she need to have 15 pencils altogether?	Alex had some pencils. Jessi gave her 7 more pencils. Now she has 15 pencils. How many pencils did Alex have to start?
	Separate	Alex had 15 pencils. She gave 7 pencils to Jessi. How many pencils does Alex have left?	Alex had 15 pencils. She gave some to Jessi. Now she has 7 pencils left. How many pencils did Alex give to Jessi?	Alex had some pencils. She gave 7 pencils to Jessi. Now she has 8 pencils left. How many pencils did Alex have to start?

		Whole Unknown		Part Unknown	
Nonaction	**Part-Part-Whole**	Alex has 7 red pencils and 8 blue pencils. How many pencils does she have?		Alex has 15 pencils. Seven are red, and the rest are blue. How many blue pencils does Alex have?	

			Difference Unknown	Greater Unknown	Lesser Unknown
Nonaction	**Compare**	"How many more?"	Alex has 15 pencils. Jessi has 7 pencils. How many more pencils does Alex have than Jessi?	Jessi has 7 pencils. Alex has 8 more pencils than Jessi. How many pencils does Alex have?	Alex has 15 pencils. She has 7 more pencils than Jessi. How many pencils does Jessi have?
		"How many fewer?"	Alex has 15 pencils. Jessi has 7 pencils. How many fewer pencils does Jessi have than Alex?	Jessi has 7 pencils. She has 8 fewer pencils than Alex. How many pencils does Alex have?	Alex has 15 pencils. Jessi has 7 fewer pencils than Alex. How many pencils does Jessi have?

Figure 1.9: Addition and subtraction problem types.

Modeling Addition and Subtraction Word Problems With Equations

When students engage in Mathematical Practice 4, "Model with mathematics," they represent contexts mathematically; they "mathematize" situations. Situations can be modeled with drawings, graphs, and tables, but for the purpose of this discussion, the focus is on equations. Figure 1.10 provides two word problems to model with equations.

Write an equation to represent each word problem.

1. Some children were playing in the park. Eight more children joined them. Now there are 12 children playing in the park. How many children were playing in the park to start?

2. The pet store sells dogs and cats. The store has 18 pets to sell but only 6 dogs. How many cats are for sale at the pet store?

Figure 1.10: Modeling word problems with equations task.

How would you solve the first problem in figure 1.10? Most adults would subtract 8 from 12 to get the answer of 4. This might have led you to write the equation $12 - 8 = \underline{\quad}$ to model this word problem. While this equation can be used to *solve* the word problem, it does not represent the *situation* provided in the word problem. *Situation equations* represent the action, or implied action, of the problem. *Solution equations* can be used to *solve* the problem. The equation, $12 - 8 = \underline{\quad}$ is a solution equation but not a situation equation. The equation that represents the situation is $\underline{\quad} + 8 = 12$. This equation is both a situation equation *and* a solution equation, as situation equations can be used to find the solution as well. It is our position that the use of situation and solution equations provides a link between the structure of word problems, the equations used to model the problem, and the solution process. Considering these different types of equations supports the connection between the structure of the word problem and the process of determining a solution and making sense of the numbers, the operations, and the context of the problem.

What is the situation equation for the second problem in figure 1.10? Did you think it was $18 = 6 +$ or maybe $18 - 6 = \underline{\quad}$? Both are correct. The second problem is a part-part-whole problem and does not represent action or even implied action (even though dogs and cats move quite a bit—this is not what is meant by action). Because there is no action in the problem, the solution equations are also situation equations. For this reason, nonaction problems are ideal for exploring the inverse relationship between addition and subtraction.

Return to the action problems in figure 1.9, and write a situation equation for each of the six word problems. Take note of the placement of the unknown quantity for each problem. Once you have completed this task, compare your situation equations to those provided in figure 1.11.

Action		Result Unknown	Change Unknown	Start Unknown
	Join	Alex had 7 pencils. Jessi gave her 8 more pencils. How many pencils does Alex have altogether? $7 + 8 = \underline{\quad}$	Alex has 7 pencils. How many more pencils does she need to have 15 pencils altogether? $7 + \underline{\quad} = 15$	Alex had some pencils. Jessi gave her 7 more pencils. Now she has 15 pencils. How many pencils did Alex have to start? $\underline{\quad} + 7 = 15$
	Separate	Alex had 15 pencils. She gave 7 pencils to Jessi. How many pencils does Alex have left? $15 - 7 = \underline{\quad}$	Alex had 15 pencils. She gave some to Jessi. Now she has 7 pencils left. How many pencils did Alex give to Jessi? $15 - \underline{\quad} = 7$	Alex had some pencils. She gave 7 pencils to Jessi. Now she has 8 pencils left. How many pencils did Alex have to start? $\underline{\quad} - 7 = 8$

Figure 1.11: Action problems with corresponding situation equations.

Notice that the unknown quantity naming the word problem (result unknown, change unknown, and start unknown) also describes the location of the unknown in the situation equation.

Nonaction problems do not have specific situation equations, as discussed with the second problem in figure 1.10. Write at least two equations that could be used to model each nonaction word problem in figure 1.9. Once you have completed this task, compare your equations to the samples provided in figure 1.12 (page 24).

Nonaction	Part-Part-Whole		**Whole Unknown**		**Part Unknown**	
			Alex has 7 red pencils and 8 blue pencils. How many pencils does she have? $7 + 8 = \underline{\quad}$ $8 + 7 = \underline{\quad}$		Alex has 15 pencils. Seven are red, and the rest are blue. How many blue pencils does Alex have? $15 = 7 + \underline{\quad}$ $15 - 7 = \underline{\quad}$	
	Compare		**Difference Unknown**	**Greater Unknown**	**Lesser Unknown**	
		"How many more?"	Alex has 15 pencils. Jessi has 7 pencils. How many more pencils does Alex have than Jessi? $15 - 7 = \underline{\quad}$ $7 + \underline{\quad} = 15$	Jessi has 7 pencils. Alex has 8 more pencils than Jessi. How many pencils does Alex have? $7 + 8 = \underline{\quad}$ $\underline{\quad} - 8 = 7$	Alex has 15 pencils. She has 7 more pencils than Jessi. How many pencils does Jessi have? $15 - 7 = \underline{\quad}$ $\underline{\quad} + 7 = 15$	
		"How many fewer?"	Alex has 15 pencils. Jessi has 7 pencils. How many fewer pencils does Jessi have than Alex? $15 - 7 = \underline{\quad}$ $7 + \underline{\quad} = 15$	Jessi has 7 pencils. She has 8 fewer pencils than Alex. How many pencils does Alex have? $7 + 8 = \underline{\quad}$ $\underline{\quad} - 8 = 7$	Alex has 15 pencils. Jessi has 7 fewer pencils than Alex. How many pencils does Jessi have? $15 - 7 = \underline{\quad}$ $\underline{\quad} + 7 = 15$	

Figure 1.12: Examples of situation equations for nonaction problems.

The equations for the compare word problems can be used for both the corresponding "How many more?" and "How many fewer?" problems because the situation does not change, just the perspective. Exposing students to nonaction problems provides the opportunity for you to see how students think about addition and subtraction in context. Are students more likely to add or subtract to solve? It also opens up opportunities for rich discussions regarding solution strategies. After students make sense of word problems, the focus turns to computation.

Using Basic Fact Strategies

How do you teach basic facts? In many instances, the teaching of basic facts is reduced to rote memorization. Although knowing facts by memory is explicitly described in the progression of adding and subtracting whole numbers, basic fact instruction should have a foundation in understanding and not just memorization. The understanding of basic addition fact strategies can start with subitizing (to recognize how many without counting). This understanding allows students to recognize numbers as well as number pairs. These two skills are known as *perceptual subitizing* and *conceptual subitizing*. When you show the dot plate (a paper plate with circular stickers arranged on it) with five dots arranged like pips on a die and you recognize automatically that there are five dots, you are using perceptual subitizing (see figure 1.13).

The difference between perceptual and conceptual sub-itizing is that conceptual subitizing uses an additional step. Once a quantity is recognized automatically, another action is applied. You can use dot plates to support this thinking. When you combine the five dots in figure 1.13 with three dots in another color (see figure 1.14), you are using conceptual subitizing—you are combining the three dots with the five dots to determine that there are eight dots without having to count each individual dot or to count on from one set of dots to combine the total number of dots together.

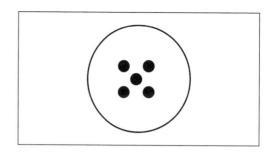

Figure 1.13: Perceptual subitizing of 5.

Showing students dot arrangements can support early childhood counting as well as build a foundation for basic addition fact strategies. Dot plates and conceptual subitizing can help students recognize number pairs for 5 and 10, supporting the make-a-five and make-a-ten strategies, as well as representing properties such as the commutative property of addition (see figure 1.15, for examples).

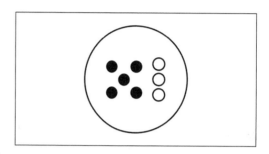

Figure 1.14: Conceptual subitizing of 8.

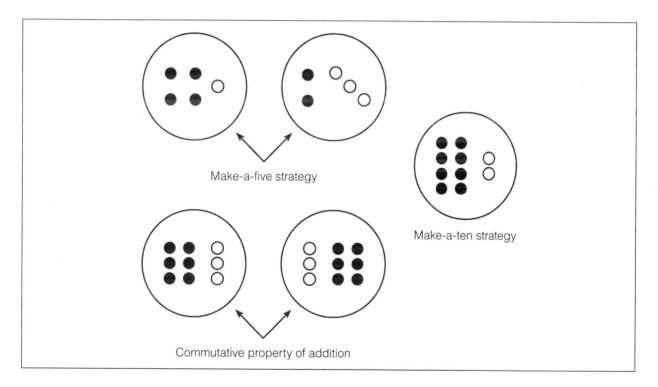

Make-a-five strategy

Make-a-ten strategy

Commutative property of addition

Figure 1.15: Connecting dot plates to strategies and properties.

In the early grades, students use the doubles strategy to assist in adding. The doubles strategy can be reinforced with dot plates. Students can also use dot plates to notice that all sums of doubles are even and consecutive sums have a counting-by-two pattern (see figure 1.16, page 26).

| 1 + 1 = 2 | 3 + 3 = 6 | 5 + 5 = 10 | 7 + 7 = 14 | 9 + 9 = 18 |
| 2 + 2 = 4 | 4 + 4 = 8 | 6 + 6 = 12 | 8 + 8 = 16 | 10 + 10 = 20 |

Figure 1.16: Doubles addition table.

Once the doubles strategy has been mastered, the learning of basic facts can be extended to adding near doubles. Most teachers recognize these strategies by the names *doubles plus one* or *doubles minus one*; for example, when adding 8 + 9 you can think 8 + 8 and then add one more. Using the term *near doubles* allows for flexibility in the use of these strategies (see the task in figure 1.17).

Use a near-doubles strategy to add 5 + 7.

Figure 1.17: Near-doubles strategy for addition task.

The problem in figure 1.17 does not fit into one of our previously defined strategies. How did you use a near-doubles strategy? Would your students struggle to come up with a similar strategy? Figure 1.18 provides two possible solution strategies for the problem in the task in figure 1.17.

| **Doubles plus two:** | **Doubles minus two:** |
| If I know 5 + 5 = 10, then 5 + 7 = 5 + 5 + 2 = 12 | If I know 7 + 7 = 14, then 5 + 7 = 7 + 5 = 7 + 7 − 2 = 12 |

Figure 1.18: Flexible near-doubles strategies.

What other strategies might students use to solve 5 + 7? Perhaps you thought of the make-a-ten strategy. Using the make-a-ten strategy provides the foundation for adding numbers whose sum is greater than 10 and leads to multidigit addition.

How can the skills learned through explorations with basic fact strategies help when adding multidigit numbers within 1,000? Can making a ten really help when you get to numbers that large? By using Mathematical Practice 7, "Look for and make use of structure," you can see how the structure of making a 10 is similar to making a 100 or 1,000—skills learned in earlier grades reinforce concepts for multidigit addition and subtraction. The strategies explored in the rest of the chapter will help you connect multi-digit operations and the importance of place value and other concepts learned in earlier grades. According to Matthew Larson et al. (2012), "Helping students use their prior knowledge to enable them to recognize what is new and different in their learning is a key element of scaffolding instruction" (p. 183). This point is important to remember when attempting to intervene with students experiencing difficulty with mul-tidigit operations. Many times, their difficulty with multidigit operations can be traced back to a lack of conceptual understanding regarding basic facts.

Adding Multidigit Whole Numbers

Find the sums of the problems in figure 1.19 to begin an investigation of multidigit addition.

Find the sums of the following addition problems by using the make-a-ten strategy.

96 + 64   87 + 35

Figure 1.19: Problems using a make-a-ten strategy to add multidigit numbers.

How did you begin your work on these problems? Did you want to go directly to the standard algorithm? Why? This happens most often when the focus is on getting the correct solution rather than giving attention to the specific requested process. If you have not had much experience in using invented strategies, problems like these can be challenging. You could have written the addends for 96 + 64 in expanded form as in figure 1.20.

After it is written in this form, it is easier to notice that the ones digits make a ten. Figure 1.21 shows how the problem can be rewritten using the associative and commutative properties of addition to illustrate this use of the make-a-ten strategy.

96 + 64

= (90 + 6) + (60 + 4)

Figure 1.20: Expanded form of 96 + 64.

Although decomposing the numbers into an expanded form was helpful with the first problem, it may not be an efficient strategy for all problems of this type. In solving the second problem (87 + 35), you may have noticed that the ones place of the addends doesn't add up nicely to 10. Figure 1.22 illustrates one way the numbers can be decomposed to make a ten.

96 + 64

= (90 + 6) + (60 + 4)

= (90 + 60) + (6 + 4)

= 150 + 10

= 160

Figure 1.21: Adding 96 + 64 using associative and commutative properties of addition.

Take a moment to explain each step in the solution process provided in figure 1.22. The make-a-ten strategy was actually used twice in this solution. Can you identify both instances of its use? First, it was used to make the next ten (90) by decomposing 35 into 3 + 32 and adding the 3 to the 87 to get a sum of 90. Then, the strategy was used again to make a hundred or 10 tens when 32 was decomposed to 10 + 22 and 10 was added to 90 to get a sum of 100.

87 + 35

= 87 + 3 + 32

= 90 + 32

= 90 + 10 + 22

= 100 + 22

= 122

Figure 1.22: Adding 87 + 35 using the make-a-ten strategy.

Because creativity and reasoning are stifled when given a prescription or rule for solving problems, it is important to use the standard algorithm (or any algorithm) as just another strategy, depending on the context and type of problem. Allowing students to engage in a productive struggle with these types of problems before knowing the procedures means they are building understanding of addition and subtraction beyond just rote memorization of steps.

Strategies for addition that we highlight next include open number lines for addition, operations using partial sums, and the standard algorithm for addition. Keep in mind that the strategies shown in this section and other sections of this chapter, as well as in the entire book, are not exhaustive lists. These strategies should act as a springboard to allow students to be creative and invent their own strategies and algorithms.

Open Number Lines for Addition

Number lines can be useful for learning the counting sequence, comparing the size of numbers, and representing operational thinking. However, using a precisely scaled number line for multidigit addition and subtraction problems can be cumbersome in grades 3–5, depending on the size of the numbers. An open number line can remove the restrictions of a number line drawn to scale. Use an open number line to find the sum for the problem provided in figure 1.23.

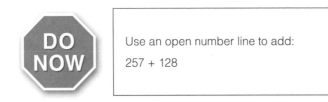

Use an open number line to add:

257 + 128

Figure 1.23: Task using an open number line to add multidigit numbers.

The number line provides a tool to record your thinking as you use invented counting strategies to add and subtract (or even multiply) numbers. When students use this tool, they should be encouraged to move away from counting-by-one strategies and replace those with strategies based on making tens or hundreds. See figure 1.24 for one way an open number line can be used to add for the problem in figure 1.23.

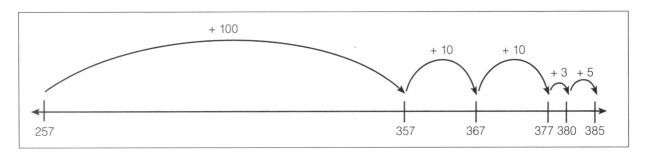

Figure 1.24: Adding 257 + 128 using an open number line.

How was the open number line used to find the sum in figure 1.24? Is this the way you used it? Make note of the similarities and differences between the process in figure 1.24 and the way you did it. If asked to find the sum for the same problem in a different way using an open number line, how would you do it differently?

Consider the representation in figure 1.25; how is it different from the strategy used in figure 1.24?

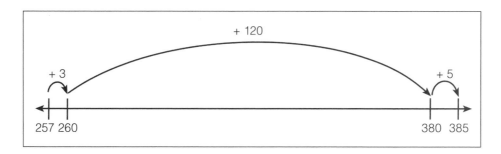

Figure 1.25: Solving 257 + 128 using an open number line (a second method).

The first solution relies on adding 100 more to a number and then adding tens, eventually making a ten to compute the final result. The second solution uses the make-a-ten strategy to begin with and then adds multiples of 10. Both solutions allow you to see connections to previous addition strategies. A strength of the open number line is that it encourages multiple solution strategies.

Partial Sums Strategy

The partial sums strategy is often referred to as the break-apart strategy. Multidigit numbers are decomposed using expanded notation as a means to add parts of the sum in succession, which results in the overall sum of the task. Figure 1.26 displays the strategy.

Using expanded notation, 149 can be thought of as 100 + 40 + 9 and 286 as 200 + 80 + 6. You can add the following partial sums: 100 and 200 to get 300, 40 and 80 to get 120, and 9 and 6 to get 15. Finally, the actual sum is determined by thinking, 300 + 120 = 420 and 420 +15 = 435. Notice how this method avoids regrouping but rather uses procedures more closely associated with counting strategies. This is not the case with column addition.

```
   149
 + 286
   300

   120
 +  15
   435
```

Figure 1.26: Partial sums model for 149 + 286.

Column Addition

For the column addition strategy, you write the problem in a place value chart. Record the values for each place in its own column. Figure 1.27 demonstrates this strategy.

As you can see from figure 1.27, you get 15 ones from adding the ones and you record the 15 ones in the ones column. Moving along to the tens, 4 tens plus 8 tens is 12 tens, record 12 tens in the tens column.

Finally, adding 1 hundred and 2 hundreds results in 3 hundreds, which is recorded in the hundreds column. After all sums are recorded in their appropriate columns, the next step is to determine if any trades need to be made. Trades are required when there is more than one digit in any one place. If there are any

hundreds	tens	ones	
1	4	9	
+ 2	8	6	
3	12	15	
3	13	5	→ Trade 10 ones for 1 ten
4	3	5	→ Trade 10 tens for 1 hundred

Figure 1.27: Column addition strategy for 149 + 286.

trades to be made, they occur below the first entries as you see in figure 1.27 (page 29). Notice that the 15 ones in the first line represent 10 ones (1 ten) and 5 ones; this observation allows you to trade the 10 ones for 1 ten, increasing the number of tens by one.

Many teachers have an issue with this strategy, as you are placing more than one digit in a place value column. However, this is a common error with the standard algorithm as well. Using column addition might help students who make this error with the standard algorithm focus on the process of regrouping and ultimately resolve the error on their own. The choice of column addition allows you to consider how to represent sums and place value in a careful and considered manner and possibly use this error as a springboard for learning.

Standard Algorithm for Addition

The last addition strategy you will explore is the standard algorithm. We take the position that standard algorithms serve as just another strategy to be used when appropriate, depending on the problem at hand and the context in which the problem is set. Take a moment to write out the language you would use to find the sum for the addition problem in figure 1.28 using the standard algorithm. Then read the directions back to yourself aloud.

> Write down the language you would use to perform the following addition problem using the standard algorithm.
>
> $$237$$
> $$+189$$

Figure 1.28: Standard algorithm for addition task.

How did your directions sound when you read them back to yourself? Did you notice yourself making any incorrect statements? You probably sounded very similar to the following four steps.

1. Seven plus 9 is 16. Put down the 6 in the ones place and carry the 1, writing it above the 3.

2. One plus 3 plus 8 is 12. Put down the 2 and carry the 1—write it above the 2.

3. Add 1 plus 2 plus 1 to get 4. Put down the 4.

4. Your answer is 426.

These steps should be familiar to you; it was the way most adults were taught as children. Will any of these statements cause students confusion? How can you describe the steps for the standard algorithm to ensure that place value concepts are supported? You must talk about the process so that students can make connections between concepts of place value and the steps involved in the standard algorithm. As teachers of grades 3–5, it is important to use students' prior knowledge of place value to help them make sense of algorithms.

In the steps provided, only the first part of the first step maintained the place value of the problem; after that, all the addition was reduced to single-digit addition. Reducing all addition to single-digit addition makes it seem that place value doesn't matter when performing operations. It essentially indicates that place value actually gets in the way of multidigit addition and that all previous lessons that may have reinforced the importance of place value can be discarded. For example, in step 2, the reference to 12 is not correct. The direction should be to add 3 tens and 8 tens then 1 ten more from regrouping the ones place, to create 12 tens. Directions such as those just listed lead students to adopt inappropriate language and undo their understanding of place value. The digits in 12 no longer have a value; they are just two digits sitting next to each other. Additionally, the use of the word *carry* implies the same thing. It is important to apply Mathematical Practice 6, "Attend to precision," with the language used when teaching this and any strategy.

The following steps describe an appropriate way to explain the standard algorithm (see figure 1.29). Notice how the reference to parts of numbers (digits) always refers to them in relation to their place value.

---

1. When you add 7 ones and 9 ones, you get 16—that is, 16 ones. Trade 10 ones for 1 ten, and you will have 1 ten and 6 ones. Record the 1 ten above the tens column and the 6 ones in the answer space of the ones column.

$$\begin{array}{r}{}^{}{}^{1}{}^{} \\ 2\,|\,3\,|\,7 \\ +\,1\,|\,8\,|\,9 \\ \hline ||\,6 \end{array}$$

2. Three tens plus 8 tens plus 1 ten is 12 tens. Trade 10 tens for 1 hundred, and then you have 1 hundred and 2 tens. Record the 1 hundred above the hundreds column and the 2 tens in the answer space for the tens column.

$$\begin{array}{r}{}^{1}{}^{1} \\ 2\,|\,3\,|\,7 \\ +\,1\,|\,8\,|\,9 \\ \hline |\,2\,|\,6 \end{array}$$

3. Two hundreds plus 1 hundred plus 1 hundred is 4 hundreds. Record the 4 hundreds in the answer space for the hundreds column.

$$\begin{array}{r}{}^{1}{}^{1} \\ 2\,|\,3\,|\,7 \\ +\,1\,|\,8\,|\,9 \\ \hline 4\,|\,2\,|\,6 \end{array}$$

Figure 1.29: Explaining the standard addition algorithm.

Think about the different language and representation in each set of written steps. In the revised set of steps in figure 1.29, the mathematics language is precise and appropriate, and each step is mathematically sound.

Because of the nature of this algorithm, students will not usually invent this strategy; instead, you will provide direct instruction on its use. This is an appropriate place for the gradual release of responsibility model of, "I do, we do, you do" described in the introduction. However, you should introduce the standard algorithm for addition as another strategy and build on prior experiences involving place value and invented algorithms.

Subtracting Multidigit Whole Numbers

Subtraction is more difficult than addition for most people. The task in figure 1.30 challenges you to find multiple ways to subtract whole numbers.

Subtract in three different ways.

325 – 71

Figure 1.30: Subtracting whole numbers in three different ways task.

Was your first strategy the standard algorithm? If so, then you are among most people who attempt a task like this. Did you struggle with finding another method? If you have not been exposed to different methods, or if your understanding of subtraction has been strictly based on procedures, it is difficult to come up with multiple methods. Did you adapt any strategies learned from the preceding addition section to help you with other strategies?

Compare your methods to the following strategies provided in this section: open number lines for subtraction, equal compensation, flexible grouping, trade-first subtraction, and the standard algorithm for subtraction. As a new strategy is introduced, ask yourself if it matches one of your strategies. If it does not match, how do the strategies differ? We also challenge you to find strategies of your own to subtract multidigit numbers.

Open Number Lines for Subtraction

How can an open number line extend your understanding of multidigit subtraction? Consider figure 1.31.

 Subtract 253 – 137 with an open number line. If possible, challenge a colleague to complete the same task and compare your number lines when you are finished.

Figure 1.31: Multidigit subtraction with an open number line task.

How did you begin your work with the open number line? Did you *count up, count back,* or *take away* to subtract? Are you not sure which one your picture represents? Although the jumps that you made on your open number line might have been different, the structure you used should match one of the three solution strategies provided in figure 1.32. See if you can distinguish between the three methods.

How did you match the open number line examples to each of the strategies? You should be able to see that solution A is counting up. It is the only method that actually has you going to the right on the number line, which means you are counting up the number sequence. With the counting-up method, you start with the second number (subtrahend) and you figure out what jumps to take to reach the first number (minuend). In this case, the jumps totaled 116; therefore it takes a jump of 116 to get from 137 to 253, so 253 – 137 = 116.

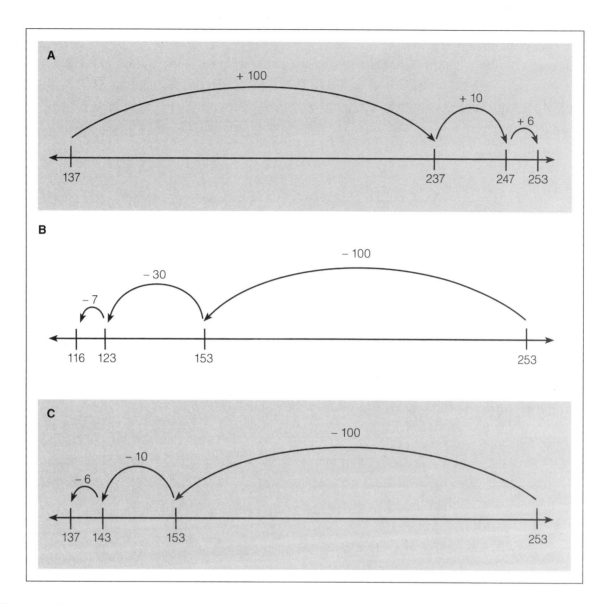

Figure 1.32: Counting up, counting back, or takeaway using an open number line.

It is more difficult to figure out the difference between solutions B and C. Solution B seems to be counting back, but in fact it actually represents take away because you are starting with 253 and taking away 137 to reach the originally unknown result of 116. Solution C is counting back—it is similar to counting up, but with this strategy you start with 253 on the number line and you need to figure out how much you have to count back to reach 137.

Throughout this process, which Mathematical Practices were you engaged in? The discussion for this activity supported your engagement in Mathematical Practice 7, "Look for and make use of structure," because you were examining similarities and differences between strategies and how they represented subtraction on the open number line.

Equal Compensation

Equal compensation is another strategy that can be used to subtract multidigit numbers. This strategy relies on your ability to subtract multiples of 10 and 100 from a given number. A concept crucial to making sense of the equal compensation strategy is that the *difference* between two numbers is the *distance* those numbers are apart on a number line. The subtraction problem 54 – 38 can be visualized by the picture in figure 1.33.

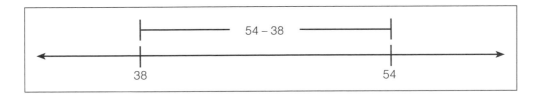

Figure 1.33: Visualization of subtraction as distance on a number line.

After you understand that the difference between 54 and 38 is the same as the distance along the number line, you can visualize moving both numbers on the number line in the same direction by the same number of units—the distance between them will remain the same. Imagine shifting both numbers two units to the right. Would the distance between the numbers still be the same? Yes. See figure 1.34 for a visualization of shifting both numbers two units to the right.

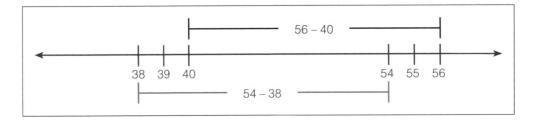

Figure 1.34: Using a number line to visualize equal compensation.

Taking advantage of your ability to subtract multiples of 10, you probably see the solution to the problem of 56 – 40 easier than the solution to the problem 54 – 38. When you apply this strategy, you are using relational thinking because you know that 54 – 38 = 56 – 40. Applying relational thinking strategies is useful as they can help you simplify computations. Using equal compensation allows you to manipulate the problem to create a relationship that is easier to compute. Not everyone will choose to compensate equally the same way; however, as long as you ensure that the distance never changes, the differences will always be the same.

Flexible Grouping

Another strategy for subtraction is called flexible grouping. This strategy is reliant on a good foundation of place value. When asked how many tens are in 436, what would you say? Many adults would say three tens, since there is a 3 in the tens place. However, the correct answer is 43 tens. Consider how to subtract 82 from 436 with the thought that there are 43 tens in 436.

Take 2 ones from 6 ones, leaving you with 4 ones. Record the 4 in the ones place. Now, subtract 8 tens from 43 tens, leaving you with 35 tens, which is the same as 3 hundreds and 5 tens (see figure 1.35).

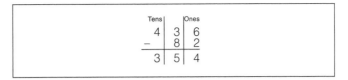

Figure 1.35: Subtracting 436 – 82 by tens and ones.

This strategy is known as flexible grouping. It is useful in that it reinforces the understanding of place value. Consider the problem in figure 1.36. Subtract using flexible grouping, prior to reading on.

Figure 1.36: Multidigit subtraction task.

You may see 203 as 20 tens and 3 ones. In order to subtract 8 ones from 3 ones in this problem, it is still necessary to regroup. However, now, rather than needing to determine how to regroup with a 0, you need only to regroup 20 tens as 19 tens so you have 19 tens and 13 ones. Next, subtract 8 ones from 13 ones to get 5 ones, and subtract 6 tens from 19 tens to get 13 tens for a solution of 135. Is this what you did? If not, make note of the differences between this process and the process you used.

Take some time and think about how you would talk someone else through the problem using the standard subtraction algorithm. How did you describe changing 203 to 1 hundred, 9 tens, and 13 ones? If your language included "borrow" or, worse, "borrow sugar from next door," think about ways this language can create misunderstandings for students. This language is sometimes used by teachers to explain subtracting. Teachers might say, "You can't subtract 8 from 3, so you have to go next door to borrow sugar. But no one is home, so you have to go to the next house."

This type of storytelling will lead to considerable place value errors and does not support mathematical understanding. When the teacher "goes next door to borrow sugar" does he or she indicate that the house next door is ten times as large as the house in the ones place? The house in the hundreds place must be one hundred times as large! A more efficient way to approach this particular problem is to use the flexible grouping strategy. It supports an in-depth understanding of place value. However, even if the traditional algorithm is used, proper place value language must be modeled in the solution process. Mathematical Practice 6, "Attend to precision," is reinforced in completing this problem using appropriate place value language. Additionally, Mathematical Practice 7, "Look for and make use of structure," is supported as you make use of the structure of the ten-to-one relationship of place value.

Trade-First Subtraction

Trade-first subtraction is a strategy similar to the standard subtraction algorithm; however all trades are conducted prior to subtracting. Refer to figure 1.37 (page 36).

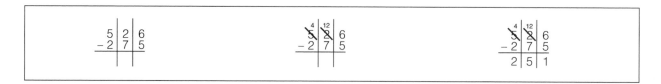

Figure 1.37: Trade-first strategy for 526 – 275.

In the trade-first strategy, the problem is placed into a place value table. Begin by trading in each of the columns where there is a need to regroup, as shown in figure 1.37. There are enough ones to subtract 5 ones from 6 ones; however, there are not enough tens represented to subtract 7 tens from 2 tens. As a result, you will trade 1 hundred for 10 tens, which will give you a total of 12 tens, leaving 4 hundreds. Once all trades have been made, execute the problem, resulting in 2 hundreds, 5 tens, and 1 one, which is 251. Use of this strategy supports understanding of the standard algorithm. Notice how the language did not indicate that "you could not subtract 7 from 2" but rather that there were not enough tens to subtract 7 tens from 2 tens. This is because you *can* subtract 7 from 2—you will get –5. This is another example of attending to precision with proper use of language when describing mathematical procedures.

Standard Algorithm for Subtraction

The approach to developing understanding of the standard subtraction algorithm is the same as the standard addition algorithm. Introducing it as another strategy is best in order to build on students' prior experiences with models and invented strategies to make sense of the algorithm. As this strategy is developed, the reasoning for each step should be recorded. An important aspect of this strategy, as with any strategy, is attending to the use of appropriate place value language. Use what you learned in this chapter to complete the task in figure 1.38.

> Record the language that you use to perform the subtraction problem using the standard algorithm.
>
> $$\begin{array}{r} 436 \\ -\ 82 \\ \hline \end{array}$$

Figure 1.38: Subtraction using the standard algorithm task.

At this point, you may be questioning the language that you have used your whole life to subtract. How does the language you were taught reinforce or diminish place value understanding? It is important to pay close attention to your language. This is reflected in Mathematical Practice 6, "Attend to precision." How might you have to change your language to be more precise? The language in the following dialogue (figure 1.39) is correct in terms of place value and proper regrouping of numbers. How does your language compare to that of the language in the examples that follow? It is important to record the steps along the way to make a connection between the steps and what is being said.

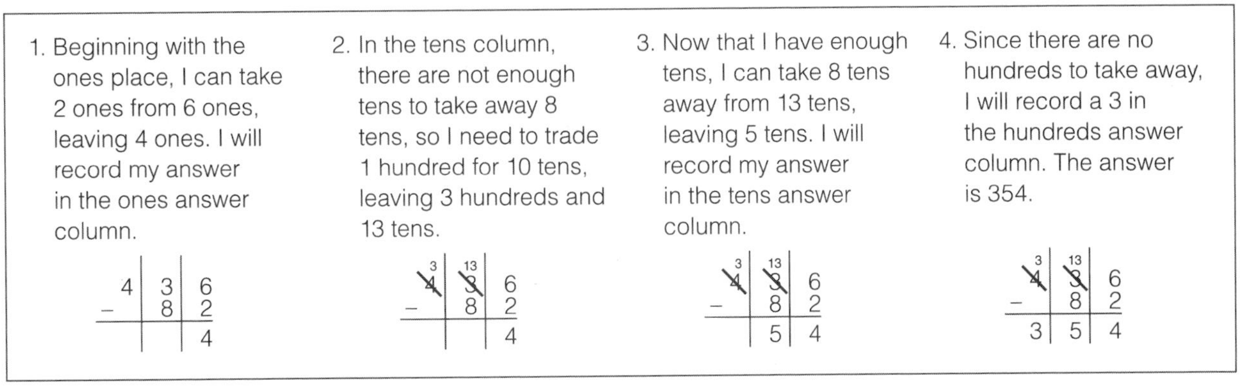

1. Beginning with the ones place, I can take 2 ones from 6 ones, leaving 4 ones. I will record my answer in the ones answer column.

$$\begin{array}{r|r|r} 4 & 3 & 6 \\ - & 8 & 2 \\ \hline & & 4 \end{array}$$

2. In the tens column, there are not enough tens to take away 8 tens, so I need to trade 1 hundred for 10 tens, leaving 3 hundreds and 13 tens.

$$\begin{array}{r|r|r} {}^3\!\!\!\!\diagup\!\!4 & {}^{13}\!\!\!\!\diagup\!\!3 & 6 \\ - & 8 & 2 \\ \hline & & 4 \end{array}$$

3. Now that I have enough tens, I can take 8 tens away from 13 tens, leaving 5 tens. I will record my answer in the tens answer column.

$$\begin{array}{r|r|r} {}^3\!\!\!\!\diagup\!\!4 & {}^{13}\!\!\!\!\diagup\!\!3 & 6 \\ - & 8 & 2 \\ \hline & 5 & 4 \end{array}$$

4. Since there are no hundreds to take away, I will record a 3 in the hundreds answer column. The answer is 354.

$$\begin{array}{r|r|r} {}^3\!\!\!\!\diagup\!\!4 & {}^{13}\!\!\!\!\diagup\!\!3 & 6 \\ - & 8 & 2 \\ \hline 3 & 5 & 4 \end{array}$$

Figure 1.39: Using the standard subtraction algorithm strategy for 436 – 82.

The process of recording each step—and the reasoning for each step—is crucial to understanding this strategy. Another crucial part of this algorithm is the use of appropriate place value language.

Comparing Adding and Subtracting Multidigit Whole Numbers to Decimals

When adding and subtracting decimals, you can use similar strategies because of the consistent ten-to-one relationship in our base ten number system. When using the standard algorithms, it is important to keep in mind that you need to add or subtract like places. Filling in a number with zero may be helpful to clarify place value. For example, when attempting to add 4.5 + 2.03, a common incorrect solution is 6.8. Can you see how a student might end up with that incorrect solution? By changing the problem to 4.50 + 2.03, it is easier to see which digits are in like places.

Standard algorithms for addition and subtraction follow the same methodology with whole numbers as they do with decimals; however, you must pay careful attention to language to ensure accuracy and precision. Using models to assist in the recording of these steps can be helpful; however, the models used will be similar to those used in the development of addition and subtraction concepts with whole numbers. Confusion can occur if you are not careful to redefine these models throughout the development of understanding.

The Classroom

While reading this chapter and completing the tasks, you have had a chance to challenge your previous understandings of addition and subtraction beyond memorization. Your attention is now directed to observing how these strategies look in the classroom. Watch each video as it is presented in its entirety before reading further.

In the first video, primary-grade students are working with a word problem that models 7 + 8. You might wonder how a video of primary-grade students is related to the work of intermediate-grade instruction. The strategies explored in first grade with single-digit addends are the same strategies students use when adding and subtracting multidigit numbers. In this video, students use counters, ten frames, and whiteboards and markers to represent their thinking regarding adding two quantities. As you watch the video, focus on the students. How are the students making sense of the problem? What strategies do students use to determine the solution?

www.solution-tree.com/Using_the
_Make-a-Ten_Strategy_With_Addition

Notice that the students use many different strategies to solve this problem. The first student in the small group begins the discussion with the teacher by identifying how he assigns each type of prize a different color counter, making sure that he is representing the problem accurately. He then presents his addition strategy as "counting all," where he includes all of the counters in determining the sum. The student places seven counters in one ten frame and eight counters in the other one. This indicates how this student is thinking about these values as separate and is not necessarily connecting how to use the ten frame to help organize his thinking about place value. While this is not an indication that the student cannot use this strategy, it does indicate that he is not representing it in this instance.

In the second round of small-group work, a student demonstrates a decomposition strategy that allows her to make a ten by pulling 5 from each of the two addends. Her diagram clearly represents her thinking and her ability to make a ten. This may not have been a strategy that you would predict a student would use, which illustrates that it is important to investigate the strategies and reasoning that were not anticipated in planning. You must consider all methods that students use and check to be sure they are mathematically accurate.

Next, the teacher asks a student to explain another student's strategy; this student describes a different make-a-ten strategy. She discusses how 3 can be used from the 8, which when combined with 7, makes 10. As there are still 5 remaining from the 8 (she took 3 from it to make the 10), this is added to the 10 and gives a sum of 15.

The teacher notices that the other student in this group has 8 + 7 represented on her whiteboard, so she asks her for her strategy. At this point, you might expect to hear another fact strategy. However, the student describes how she added the two numbers and states that she "counted" to determine the sum of 15. Finally, the student who comes to the board in the later part of the task also uses a make-a-ten strategy to determine the sum. These strategies show how important the role of listening—for both learners and teachers—is to develop a deep understanding of mathematics. It is also important that the task supported multiple ways to represent thinking and that the lesson was designed for students to learn strategies from one another, an important instructional strategy for students and teachers at all grade levels.

Now turn your attention to a grade 5 class where the focus is on making sense of place value with decimals by representing decimals using base ten blocks. The teacher sets up tasks to allow for class discussion regarding common errors and the flexible use of the whole. Watch the video in its entirety before proceeding.

www.solution-tree.com/Using_Place_Value
_Understandings_to_Model_Decimals

What did you think about the use of instructional time? The teacher used it to bring about class discussion instead of giving or telling students the answers. While watching the video, did you find yourself drawing models or reaching for base ten blocks to model the decimal number—even though base ten blocks are typically used for whole numbers? If you were asked to model 1.34 with base ten blocks, would you do it the same way as the students? You would need to consider which piece would represent the whole. If you chose to use the flat as the whole, the way the students do, can you think of another way to represent 1.34 with base ten blocks? This question is not asked of the students, but you should always emphasize flexible use of the whole and encourage students to explain their choices. This is seen later in the video when students are asked to model a number in the thousands. An argument can be made that students are engaging in Mathematical Practice 5, "Use appropriate tools strategically," even though the teacher provided the tool, because the students need to determine *how* to use the tool so that it is useful in this context.

The teacher then asks the students to model 2.05. A point should be made here that careful planning for the lesson occurred in selecting and sequencing the tasks. There is a reason that the number 2.05 is used here—can you see why the lesson progresses in this way? The teacher has planned for tasks that lead to common student errors. A theme in this book is to not shy away from common errors; on the contrary, common errors should be brought to the forefront of the lesson and used as springboards for learning. After the teacher allows a student to successfully explain one way to model 2.05, the teacher points the class's attention to a common error that has occurred. He says, "I saw someone who modeled it using 2 flats and 5 rods." The act of pointing out common errors and bringing them to the attention of students allows students to experience productive ways to reason through those errors. The teacher allows a student to explain why the model is incorrect, and the student indicates that the manipulative used to represent the hundredths is really representing tenths. Although the video did not show an elaboration of this explanation, to ensure that the class understands why the flats and rods can't be used, the students can be led to the discussion that it only takes 10 rods to make 1 flat (in this case the whole) and to represent 2.05 you need the 5 units to represent $\frac{1}{100}$ of the whole. Notice how the teacher allows students to respond to the error in a safe environment where errors are a point of learning and not a disgrace. Building a classroom culture in which errors are thought of as useful experiences is an important aspect of student learning and engagement.

The video continues with the teacher asking the class to represent 1.236. Notice how he engages the students in their thought process by asking, "So what do you guys have?" He is not as interested in the representation of the number as he is in the representation of the whole, thus he leads the students in a discussion about the block they chose to represent the whole. He asks the student what block represents 1 in their current model and what block represented 1 in the previous model. One student uses his previous knowledge of place value with whole numbers to point out the ten-to-one relationship in adjacent digits to justify why the model he uses is accurate. At this point in the lesson, the class gets a chance to listen to the reasoning of flexibility with representing a whole. In this case, it is because the manipulatives do not allow the students to have the flat be the whole since there would not be the correct manipulative to represent a thousandth. The student explains this by saying, "The thousandths are even smaller than the small cubes." Throughout this lesson, the teacher is intentionally focusing students' attention on the structure of the ten-to-one relationship inherent in place value. In so doing, he is supporting students to engage in Mathematical Practice 7, "Look for and make use of structure."

TQE Process

At this point, it may be helpful to watch the first video again (page 38). Pay close attention to the tasks, questioning, and opportunities to collect evidence of student learning. Some of the strategies the primary-grade students used with this task might help intermediate grade students who struggle with addition. The TQE process can help you frame your observations. Teachers who have a deep understanding of the mathematics they teach:

- Select appropriate *tasks* to support identified learning goals

- Facilitate productive *questioning* during instruction to engage students in Mathematical Practices

- Collect and use student *evidence* in the formative assessment process during instruction

The *task* in this lesson provides the opportunity to determine different ways that students add 7 + 8. While the learning goal focuses on the different strategies for adding to get a sum greater than 10, the task begins with a story problem. This allows the students to make sense of the addition problem in a meaningful way. By selecting the addends of 7 and 8, the teacher could expect many different strategies from the students, including counting all, counting on, make a ten, doubles plus one, and doubles minus one. Selecting a task that includes multiple strategies connects addition with Mathematical Practice 7, "Look for and make use of structure." Understanding the value of grouping ones into tens foreshadows the grouping of tens into hundreds and hundreds into thousands. The prerequisites to the structure of place value are important for students to grasp for later work with number.

The use of *questioning* in this lesson helps students deepen their understanding of the learning goal. The teacher asks questions that are open ended so students can share their thinking. The teacher also uses wait time to give students the opportunity to make sense of her questions, and she is patient when students provide explanations of their thinking. Some of the questions the teacher asks require students to provide more detail in their explanations. These questions help the teacher determine how well students are making sense of the task. When the teacher asks one student to explain how another student uses the ten frame, it allows the teacher to see how one student interprets a strategy different from her own work. This encourages students to learn the strategies that others are using. The teacher uses questions to focus on the learning goal, exploring different strategies for adding 7 and 8.

The teacher collects *evidence* of student learning throughout the lesson. Note how she listens carefully to each student response and often turns to another student to see if he or she understands the explanation. The teacher also asks questions to probe student thinking, such as "Can you show me how you did that?" and has students explain other students' strategies by asking questions such as "Can you explain to me what you think she did?" The responses provide information about each student's level of understanding, and both questions and responses are important elements of an effective formative assessment process. In order to best support student understanding, be sure to have a clear picture of how each student makes sense of problems. This will provide you the foundation to support growth along the learning progression of addition and subtraction.

The Response

Difficulty with addition and subtraction procedures usually begins with an underlying deficit in number sense that often presents as a lack of understanding of the base ten number system. Students need time to make sense of place value and the ten-to-one relationship inherent in this system. Depth of understanding of the base ten place value system is represented by the ability to flexibly use and rename numbers—important components of number sense. If you ask a student to break apart the number 37 and the only response the student can express is "3 tens and 7 ones," the student may have a deficit in understanding place value. Students who have strong number sense and who take advantage of the flexibility that the base ten number system affords are able to rename 37 in other ways, depending on how they need to use the number to compute, such as:

- 2 tens 17 ones
- 1 ten 27 ones
- 0 tens 37 ones
- 3 tens 5 ones 2 ones
- 2 tens 8 ones 9 ones

The ability to flexibly rename numbers is essential to being able to understand and use the standard algorithm for subtraction. When students know how to rename numbers, they don't have to "go next door to borrow some sugar."

Students can also struggle with strategies for multidigit addition and subtraction if they don't have a strong foundation with basic facts. A student's inability to use an open number line or invent algorithms can be inhibited by not being able to rely on recall of basic facts. If a student's attention is taken up with trying to recall a fact they have not memorized, then there is less attention available to attack the problem at hand. One of the challenges with a student who is not able to recall basic facts is how to best support the student in developing this recall. Often, teachers attempt to solve this by having students try to memorize the basic facts with flash cards. However, if basic facts are not taught with a true understanding of strategies and operations, students will eventually forget the facts they have attempted to memorize and have nothing to fall back on to assist in the recall of those facts.

Interventions for students who struggle should be grounded in conceptual understanding and invented strategies so students can make sense of the operations and use strategies to support the ability to solve problems. While memorization is an important skill for placing an abundance of information in long-term memory, memorization of mathematical procedures without understanding or the ability to adapt procedures to new situations provides little support in problem-solving situations.

Another pitfall you should help students avoid is the repetitive use of a single strategy, whether invented by the student or not. For example, for an addition problem that uses two addends, starting with one addend and counting on using the second addend is a foundational and very useful strategy. Counting on is a strategy that can work in every addition problem context no matter how large or small the numbers. However, while this is a strategy that can be used in every addition context, it may not be the most efficient strategy for every addition problem. For example, counting on may work efficiently for 12 + 9, but it would be cumbersome to apply to 49 + 67. Hence, you will want students to learn how to make decisions about which strategies are most beneficial for applying in a given problem situation.

The mathematics content and skills to come rely heavily on students' understanding and application of addition and subtraction strategies. Hence, it is critical to attend to the challenges that students experience with addition and subtraction. This might be a better way to support struggling learners as opposed to drilling basic facts during intervention time.

Reflections

1. What do you feel are the key points in this chapter?

2. What challenges might you face when implementing the key ideas from this chapter? How will you overcome them?

3. What are the important features for developing an understanding of place value, addition, and subtraction, and how will you ensure your instruction embeds the support needed for these features?

4. Select a recent lesson you have taught or observed focused on place value, addition, or subtraction. Relate this lesson to the TQE process.

5. What changes will you make to your planning and instruction based on what you read and considered from this chapter?

CHAPTER 2

Multiplication and Division

Exploring tasks with and without context allows you to consider different reasoning strategies that lead to solutions. The progression of learning with multiplication and division begins with single-digit factors and builds to multidigit facts, including knowing and applying the standard algorithms for multiplication and division. Throughout this chapter, you will apply a deep understanding of meanings of multiplication and division to strategies for determining basic facts, using approaches for invented and alternative algorithms for multidigit multiplication and division, and making sense of standard algorithms.

The Challenge

The initial task (see figure 2.1) brings attention to varied strategies for multiplying multidigit numbers.

Multiply 12 × 15 in three different ways.

Figure 2.1: Task to multiply multidigit numbers in many ways.

How did you respond to this task? It is likely you first used the standard algorithm to see that the product is 180 and then you paused as you tried to think of other ways to multiply. As an adult, you may find it difficult to think beyond the standard algorithm because that is what you were taught and what you remember. Now the expectation is that students should be able to use invented algorithms to solve problems. That means you need to become comfortable with them as well. Thinking of multiplication as groups of objects might help you reason with this problem more flexibly. How might this thinking help you make sense of 12 × 15? Note that the focus is not just on getting a correct product through a procedure but also on understanding the problem conceptually.

In the United States, there is a convention that assigns the first factor to represent the number of groups and the second factor to represent the number of objects in each group. This makes sense as students tend to think about multiplication in this groups-of-objects format in their early work around this topic. We follow that convention. Therefore, 12 × 15 represents 12 groups with 15 objects in each group. Since the goal is to find the total number of objects in 12 groups with 15 objects in each group, one way to think about it is to break apart the groups. How might finding 10 groups of 15 help? You can determine the total of 10 groups of 15 using mental computation, giving you 150. Then you only need to find an additional 2 groups of 15, which is 30. This gives a total of 180.

What if you found 6 groups of 30? How is this related to the product of 12 × 15? If you use half the number of groups, you need to use twice the number of objects in each group. In a way, you are simply combining every two groups of 15 so that all the groups have 30, but now there are only six groups.

Notice how we provide the invented strategies and the explanations and justifications for the processes used. Thinking about the meaning of multiplication as groups of objects helps students make sense of the operation and apply invented algorithms, and you should expect students to provide this level of reasoning for their strategies. Consequently, you need to be comfortable thinking in these ways as well.

The Progression

Focus on multiplication and division begins with context-embedded tasks similar to addition and subtraction. Students in grades 3–5 make sense of situations supportive of multiplication and division where the total number of objects is within 100.

Following is a progression for building understanding for multiplication and division.

- Use equal groups of objects to prepare for multiplication.

- Apply relational thinking and properties of operations to multiply and divide within 100.

- Multiply and divide within 100 using representations and word problems.

- Multiply and divide within 100 using strategies fluently.

- Multiply one-digit factors by multiples of 10 to 90.

- Make sense of multiplication and division with multidigit numbers.

- Solve multistep problems.

- Multiply with the standard algorithm fluently.

By leading with word problems, you can help students make sense of multiplication and division. They develop *operation sense*, which means they can distinguish between the four operations of addition, subtraction, multiplication, and division. Operation sense helps students develop their understandings of multiplication and division together, as related to one another, through building from single digit to multidigit factors.

Grades 1 and 2

In grades 1 and 2, students use multiple strategies to add and subtract that provide prerequisite experiences for later work with multiplication and division. For example, the use of strategies based on finding doubles will lead to multiplying by two in later grades. When students decompose numbers into tens and ones, they are learning important skills for later work with multidigit multiplication. Students explore with equal-sized groups and repeated addition to prepare for work with multiplication and division.

Grade 3

In grade 3, students use their understanding of repeated addition to develop conceptual meaning for multiplication and repeated subtraction as a model for division. Students work with equal groups, arrays, and area models to represent multiplication and division. They build a foundation for understanding multiplication and division through their work with single-digit factors and products up to 100; this eventually extends to multiplying single-digit factors by multiples of ten. Students explore patterns and use relational thinking strategies based on properties of operations to determine products. They also use strategies and facts to solve word problems of multiple types.

Grade 4

In grade 4, students extend their understanding of single-digit multiplication and division to multidigit multiplication and division. They continue to use equal groups, arrays, and area models for multiplication, building on the ideas from grade 3 and single-digit representations to multidigit representations. Consider the different ways explored for solving 12 × 15 from the beginning of the chapter. You encountered the use of a flexible understanding of decomposing and composing 12 and 15 to find the product in multiple ways. One strategy made use of the distributive property of multiplication over addition, and the other made use of the associative property of multiplication. Students use properties of operations and place value to make sense of multidigit multiplication. They also connect to their understanding of single-digit multiplication.

This progression of understanding is important to help students recognize relationships and retain their knowledge over time. In addition, they integrate this knowledge with their knowledge of other operations, as well as the order in which to complete operations, to continue developing their problem-solving skills with operations and word problems. In grade 4, students compare and contrast patterns involving addition or multiplication. Regarding division, examples include remainders, and students consider different meanings and applications for remainders depending on those contexts.

Grade 5

In grade 5, students use their knowledge of division to find quotients of up to four-digit dividends divided by up to two-digit divisors. It is important that students continue to use multiple models—such as equations, arrays, and area models—to represent their reasoning. Students' understanding of multiplication leads to fluency with the standard algorithm by the end of fifth grade.

The Mathematics

Our position is that understanding must precede memorization, which is consistent with the position of NCTM (2014). Because of this, understanding the operation of multiplication itself must precede a focus on multiplication facts. Contexts, often in the form of word problems, help accomplish this. Consider how you determined strategies for finding the product of 12 × 15. Thinking of 12 × 15 as 12 groups with 15 objects in each group helped in finding the product in flexible ways. The same is true with multiplying basic facts (facts with single-digit factors).

Here, you will explore important aspects of multiplication and division, including word problems, strategies for basic facts, and the extension of meanings for multiplication and division.

Solving Word Problems for Multiplication and Division

It is important to provide opportunities for students to explore different types of multiplication and division problems and contexts. To support the development of operation sense, these problems should occasionally be mixed in with addition and subtraction problems. Just as with addition and subtraction word problems (see chapter 1), there are different multiplication and division problem types. The main difference in structure is with the division problems, although the contexts lead to different sorts of representations with both multiplication and division.

For the purpose of distinguishing between multiplication and division problem types, again think about multiplication as describing a given number of groups with the same number of objects in each group. With this meaning of multiplication, the number of groups is known, as is the number of objects in each group. What is sought is the total. Similarly, with division, the total is known and either the number of groups or the number of objects in each group is sought. Division can be described as either representing sharing (also referred to as *partitive*) situations or measuring (also referred to as *quotitive*) situations, depending on which unknown is sought. When the number of objects in each group is sought, the problem represents *sharing division*; when the number of groups is sought, the problem represents *measurement division*. Table 2.1 illustrates the part of the problem that is given and the part of the problem that is unknown for multiplication and division structures. It might help you to think of multiplication as $a \times b = c$, where c is unknown. In the table, the unknown quantity is designated by a question mark.

Table 2.1: Multiplication and Division Problem Types

Problem Structure	Number of Groups (a)	Number of Objects in Each Group (b)	Total Number of Objects (c)
Multiplication	a	b	?
Sharing division	a	?	c
Measurement division	?	b	c

Solve the problems provided in figure 2.2 by drawing pictures. Just as is suggested for student work, your drawings should not be detailed but rather rudimentary sketches that support the situation of the problem in general terms. For example, if the context of the problem describes rows of desks, your drawing might consist of rows of dots—the important aspect of the drawing would be the rows. After you have solved the problem, identify the problem type as addition, subtraction, multiplication, or division. If the problem type is addition, subtraction, or division—include the name of the problem type. Use figure 1.9 (page 22) for addition and subtraction problem types and table 2.1 for division problem types.

What did you notice? It was probably a fairly straightforward process for you to determine which problems represented addition, subtraction, multiplication, or division; however, it might have been a little more challenging to determine the type of division. Problems 5 and 9 represent addition or subtraction with problem 5 illustrating part-part-whole (part unknown) and problem 9 providing an example of join (start unknown). Problems 2, 7, and 8 are each multiplication problems. Problems 3, 6, and 10 represent sharing division. Problems 1 and 4 represent measurement division.

Act out the problems using drawings, and then determine the specific problem type within the categories of addition, subtraction, multiplication, or division.

1. There are 36 students in the marching band. They stand in rows of 4 each. How many rows of students are there in the band?

2. Zachary bought 7 boxes of cupcakes. There are 4 cupcakes in each box. How many cupcakes did Zachary buy?

3. Bonita has a bookcase with 4 shelves. She wants to put an equal number of books on each shelf. She has 20 books. How many books should she place on each shelf?

4. A restaurant puts 4 slices of cheese on each sandwich. How many sandwiches can be made with 12 slices of cheese?

5. Marni has 32 stuffed animals. Eight of them are cats, and the rest are dogs. How many stuffed animal dogs does Marni have?

6. Taylor has 15 toys. She puts the toys into 5 bags with the same number of toys in each bag. How many toys are in each bag?

7. The students on the bus sit in 6 rows with 5 students in each row. How many students are on the bus?

8. Tam is 3 feet tall. Her father is twice as tall as she is. How tall is her father?

9. Rashid has some video games. He buys 12 more. Now he has 34 video games. How many did he have to start?

10. The house is 24 feet tall. It is 3 times as tall as the tree. How tall is the tree?

Figure 2.2: Problem type identification task.

*Visit **go.solution-tree.com/mathematics** for a free reproducible version of this figure.*

You may have noticed that you can categorize the drawings of the problems as well. Some of the drawings consisted of groups of objects while others were rows of objects. Problems 8 and 10 could be illustrated with something other than groups or rows. These problems represent multiplicative comparison contexts, wherein the groups of objects are not as clear. As Carpenter et al. (2015) note, "Multiplicative comparison problems involve a comparison to two quantities in which one is described as a multiple of the other" (p. 66). In problem 8, for example, the father's height is described as a multiplier of the daughter's height. Since the daughter's height does not represent a group of objects, the language used in the groups-of-objects meaning for multiplication is not supported.

It is important to include all of these problem types and contexts. Equal groups most closely link to earlier work with repeated addition in grade 2 and should be the first multiplication and division context used with students. Multiplicative comparison is the most difficult of these contexts. It provides helpful experiences for later work with proportional reasoning and algebraic thinking. Arrays help students make sense of fact strategies (described next) and they lead to making sense of area (see chapter 6).

Using Strategies to Make Sense of Basic Facts

After students make sense of multiplication in context, focus turns to exploring basic facts. While it is important for students to develop quick recall of their basic facts, sense making is crucial to developing algebraic reasoning strategies. When focus on fluency comes before or takes the place of focusing on fact strategies, essential learning opportunities are missed. Furthermore, if students' only access to a fact is through recall, the student is likely to make errors in computation later without realizing errors have been made. The student will lack the tools necessary to use estimates to determine if answers are reasonable.

Think of a fact students typically struggle with. Facts with factors of 6, 7, and 8 likely come to mind. Consider 8×7. How might this fact be represented, and what strategies could be used to find the solution? This fact represents eight rows with seven objects in each row. Figure 2.3 provides an illustration of an array for this fact.

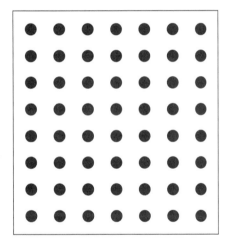

Figure 2.3: An array representing 8 × 7.

How might the array support making sense of strategies for solving 8×7? Students could add the number of dots in each row by thinking $7 + 7 + 7 + 7 + 7 + 7 + 7 + 7$. They could also add the number of dots in each column by thinking $8 + 8 + 8 + 8 + 8 + 8 + 8$. If students add seven groups of eight dots, they are actually finding 7×8 rather than 8×7. What property ensures that this provides the same product? You are applying the commutative property of multiplication whenever you change the order of the factors to think of the product in a different way. Students apply this property regularly; it is a useful and appropriate strategy for deriving basic facts from other facts they might know more quickly. As a teacher, if you change the order of the factors during teaching, you should point this action out, because the students' image of 8×7 is likely different from their image of 7×8. Think of finding fish in fish bowls. Fifty-six fish could be arranged so that there are seven fish in eight bowls (representing 8×7) or eight fish in seven bowls (representing 7×8). There is the same number of fish in each bowl, but the mental image is different.

Arrays help illustrate other properties of operations as well. Consider the distributive property of multiplication over addition. How might this property be used to find 8×7 by using other facts students might know more readily? Students typically learn their "five facts" and their "two facts" earlier than other facts. How can you break apart one of the factors in 8×7 to make use of these oft-known facts? You can think of 7 as a 5 and a 2. Figure 2.4 provides an illustration of how the array can be broken apart to make use of these more "friendly" factors.

This revised array is now two arrays. One array represents 8 × 5, and the other represents 8 × 2. Because the total number of dots hasn't changed, the two arrays combine to give the result of finding 8 × 7 because 7 = 5 + 2. This break-apart strategy can be represented symbolically as 8 × 7 = 8 × (5 + 2) = (8 × 5) + (8 × 2). It illustrates the distributive property of multiplication over addition and depends on the application of relational thinking because you need to know that the product of 8 × 7 can be represented in different ways. When students use the break-apart strategy to find a fact they don't know, they are using the distributive property.

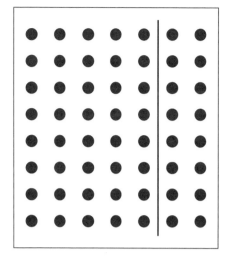

Figure 2.4: Breaking apart an array to find the fact.

How can the associative property of multiplication be used to find 8 × 7? A common use of the associative property as a fact strategy is to use doubles. What double could be used to find 8 × 7? You could find 4 × 7 and then double it. How does this make use of the associative property? If you think of 8 as 2 × 4, you would have 8 × 7 = (2 × 4) × 7. How could you change the problem so that the 4 × 7 would be multiplied first? Change the position of the parentheses: 8 × 7 = (2 × 4) × 7 = 2 × (4 × 7). Following the order of operations, you would multiply 4 × 7 to get 28, and then you would find 2 × 28. This strategy makes use of the associative property and is illustrated in figure 2.5. Notice how half of the array is covered. This strategy involves using half of the array twice.

After students make sense of strategies based on properties of operations for multiplying basic facts, they can use those strategies for other facts they don't know. Determining the strategies and justifying why they work support student engagement in Mathematical Practice 7, "Look for and make use of structure."

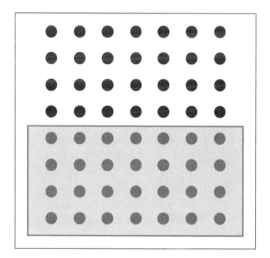

Figure 2.5: Illustrating the associative property with an array.

Make a list of facts students struggle with, and think of strategies based on properties of operations students might use to get to those facts. Which Mathematical Practice would you be emphasizing if you encouraged students to use the facts they know to determine other facts? Applying strategies to other facts engages students in Mathematical Practice 8, "Look for and express regularity in repeated reasoning." These practices also help students use what they know about multiplication facts to find division facts. Both practices are crucial in developing fluency with basic facts in meaningful ways.

Extending Meanings for Multiplication and Division

Another understanding that students develop in grade 3 is multiplying a single-digit number and multiples of ten (from 10 to 90). This process builds on students' understanding of both multiplication and place value and is a direct result of the work that students are doing with single-digit factors. How would you multiply 3 × 60? Although you may at first glance think that task is the same as 3 × 6 × 10, how would a third-grade student initially learning about multiplication see this problem? The ability to decompose one factor, such as breaking down 60 into 6 × 10, comes with experience with both multiplication and place value and provides support for continued student engagement in Mathematical Practice 7, "Look for and make use of structure."

After students make sense of multiplying single-digit factors and multiples of 10, exploration extends to multiplying single-digit and multidigit factors that are not multiples of 10. Just as with addition and subtraction, exploration of multidigit multiplication should precede the introduction of the standard algorithm. With this in mind, how might fourth-grade students who have not yet been introduced to a standard algorithm for multidigit multiplication compute 4 × 127? The task in figure 2.6 provides directions for you as you make sense of this challenge.

Describe four different ways to multiply 4 × 127 without using repeated addition or the standard algorithm.

Figure 2.6: Three-digit by one-digit multiplication task.

What strategies did you use? It is likely that you broke apart 127 into hundreds, tens, and ones or that you used other partial sums of 127 that were easier to multiply using mental computation. After you found the products of those numbers, you probably added them together to get the product of 4 × 127. Compare your strategies to those shared in figure 2.7.

$$
\begin{aligned}
4 \times 100 &= 400 \\
4 \times 20 &= 80 \\
4 \times 7 &= \underline{28} \\
&\ 508
\end{aligned}
\qquad
\begin{aligned}
4 \times 100 &= 400 \\
4 \times 25 &= 100 \\
4 \times 2 &= \underline{8} \\
&\ 508
\end{aligned}
$$

$$
\begin{aligned}
4 \times 125 &= 500 \\
4 \times 2 &= \underline{8} \\
&\ 508
\end{aligned}
\qquad
\begin{aligned}
2 \times 127 &= 254 \\
2 \times 254 &= 508
\end{aligned}
$$

Figure 2.7: Strategies for solving 4 × 127.

Were your strategies the same as those provided in figure 2.7? If not, note how they are different. How did you know if your answer was reasonable? Did you use estimation? Estimation is *not* determining the correct answer and then rounding to the nearest ten or hundred. It involves using strategies and mental computation to see if an answer is reasonable. What would a reasonable estimate be for 4 × 127? You might multiply 4 × 120 to get 480. How else might you find an estimate of the product? Discussions like this should occur frequently with students. They should come to see that finding estimates is a useful strategy in determining if an answer is reasonable. Engaging students in Mathematical Practice 3, "Construct viable arguments and critique the reasoning of others," should include the use of estimates in discussions about products and quotients.

Where might a student learn the strategy of finding 2 × 127 and then 2 × 254, and what property of operations does it illustrate? This strategy transfers from earlier work with finding doubles with basic facts. It is based on use of the associative property for multiplication.

This sense-making process is required for work with division as well. Consider the task in figure 2.8. Sense making with multidigit division should also occur before the introduction of standard algorithms. As you work on this task, think about how students who have not yet been exposed to standard algorithms for multidigit division will approach it.

Describe four different ways to divide 128 ÷ 4 without using repeated subtraction or a standard algorithm.

Figure 2.8: Three-digit by one-digit division task.

What strategies did you use? Examine the strategies provided in figure 2.9. Why do these strategies work? How might they connect to more formal algorithms for dividing?

$$
\begin{array}{ll}
120 \div 4 = 30 & 100 \div 4 = 25 \\
8 \div 4 = \underline{2} & 20 \div 4 = 5 \\
32 & 8 \div 4 = \underline{2} \\
& 32 \\
\\
100 \div 4 = 25 & 128 \div 2 = 64 \\
28 \div 4 = \underline{7} & 64 \div 2 = 32 \\
32 &
\end{array}
$$

Figure 2.9: Strategies for solving 128 ÷ 4.

When students are afforded opportunities to solve problems in ways that make sense to them, those ways might be different from how you think about the problems. Practicing with invented strategies will make you more comfortable with this process and with making sense of the solution strategies your students share.

Making Sense of Multidigit Multiplication and Division

Eventually, students transition from working with invented strategies to standard algorithms. As there is more than one standard algorithm for each operation, you will explore variations for multidigit multiplication and division here.

Multiplication Algorithms

The partial products algorithm will be developed first. Students make sense of this algorithm by connecting to base ten blocks and the area model for multiplication. You will need base ten blocks to complete the next task (figure 2.10). If you do not have access to them, you can find online versions of this manipulative to support the exploration provided in the task.

Use base ten blocks to multiply 12 × 15.

Figure 2.10: Multiplication with base ten blocks.

When students first use base ten blocks to model multiplication, they often make groups of objects. Did you make twelve groups of 15 using the blocks, or did you make an array or cover an area? If you did not make an array, do so now. Your base ten blocks will likely look something like the representation in figure 2.11.

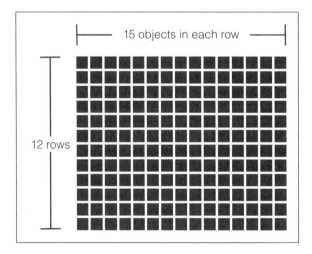

Figure 2.11: Base ten blocks as an array.

Notice that the array forms a rectangle with dimensions of 12 × 15. Rearrange the blocks making exchanges as appropriate so that the rectangle maintains its dimensions of 12 × 15 but the rectangle is filled using the fewest number of blocks as possible. This means you will exchange 10 tens for a hundred and 10 ones for a ten where possible (see figure 2.12).

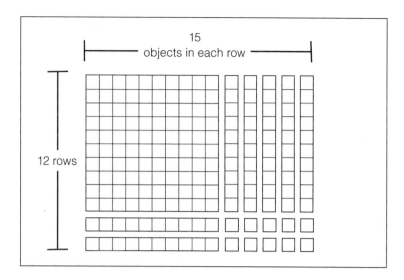

Figure 2.12: Using the fewest number of blocks to represent for 12 × 15.

Notice how the area of the 12 × 15 rectangle is filled with 1 hundred, 7 tens, and 10 ones, representing the product 180. Examine the dimensions of the rectangle as it is organized in figure 2.12. Seeing the rectangle in this way leads to work with the area model. This area model can be thought of as an *open area model* much like the open number line because proportion is not necessarily conserved as students use the model to record their thinking (see figure 2.13). Notice how the regions of the area model correspond to the regions created with base ten blocks.

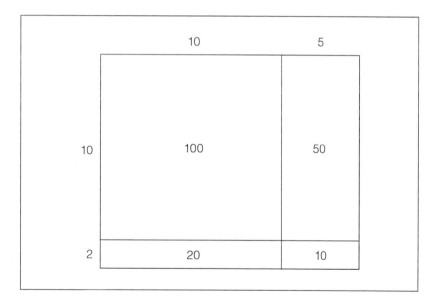

Figure 2.13: The open area model for 12 × 15.

How might you represent the dimensions of the rectangle in figure 2.13 using an expression? You could say 12 × 15 but you also might see (10 + 2) × (10 + 5). Both are correct. You might notice that the smaller rectangles add up to the large rectangle. What are the dimensions of each of those rectangles? They are 10 × 10, 10 × 5, 2 × 10, and 2 × 5. Because the areas of the small rectangles add up to the large rectangle, you can record the total area by adding its parts. You could represent this symbolically as follows:

$$12 \times 15 \quad = (10 + 2) \times (10 + 5)$$
$$= (10 \times 10) + (10 \times 5) + (2 \times 10) + (2 \times 5)$$
$$= 100 + 50 + 20 + 10$$
$$= 180$$

If you examine this process, you might see that what you have done is make sense of the distributive property of multiplication over addition with multidigit numbers. You expanded the numbers 12 and 15 to 10 + 2 and 10 + 5; you then "distributed" the 10 over the 10 + 5 and the 2 over the 10 + 5. This leads to multiplying binomials in algebra. But how does it connect to a standard algorithm? Consider the partial products algorithm used with 12 × 15 in figure 2.14.

How do the partial products in the partial products algorithm relate to the area model? They correspond to the dimensions of the smaller rectangles in figure 2.13 (page 53). When you break apart the factors 12 and 15 into 10 + 2 and 10 + 5, you can find the smaller products, or partial products, and add them together to get the targeted product. With the area model, when you break apart dimensions of the 12 × 15 rectangle, you can find the areas of the smaller rectangles and add up those areas to determine the area of the largest rectangle. Because you break apart the factors with partial products into tens and ones, and you break apart the dimensions of the rectangle into tens and ones, those smaller products and areas correspond. Making this connection explicit is crucial to help students make sense of this alternative algorithm.

	Think:
15	10 + 5
x 12	10 + 2
100	(10 × 10)
50	(10 × 5)
20	(2 × 10)
+ 10	(2 × 5)
180	100 + 50 + 20 + 10

Figure 2.14: Partial products algorithm.

When teaching algorithms to students, it is appropriate to use the gradual release of responsibility model ("I do, we do, you do"). In this way, you are demonstrating the procedures you use, and then students do them with you, before students practice the procedures on their own. When you demonstrate the procedures, be sure to connect them to prior work, such as to base ten blocks and the area model, and be sure to support the use of proper place value language. The same is true with the standard algorithm for multiplication.

Talk through the procedures you use for the standard algorithm for multiplication as you solve 12 × 15 (see figure 2.15). Notice how 12 × 15 is recorded with the algorithm: the first factor (12) is written below the second factor (15). This way of writing the factors supports the groups-of-objects meaning in the multiplication steps.

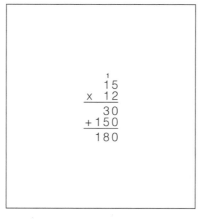

Figure 2.15: Standard multiplication algorithm for 12 × 15.

Now compare your language to that provided in figure 2.16 for the same algorithm.

Step 1

A: First multiply the ones place of the first factor by the ones place of the second factor. Two groups of 5 ones is 10 ones. Exchange 10 ones for 1 ten, and you will have 1 ten and 0 ones. Record the 1 ten above the tens column and the 0 ones in the answer space of the ones column.

```
    1
    1 5
 x  1 2
      0
```

B: Next, multiply the ones place of the first factor by the tens place of the second factor. Two groups of 1 ten is 2 tens. Add the 1 ten from the previous partial product to get 3 tens. Record the 3 tens in the answer space of the tens column.

```
    1
    1 5
 x  1 2
    3 0
```

Step 2

A: Now multiply the tens place of the first factor by the ones place of the second factor. Ten groups of 5 ones is 50 ones, or 5 tens and 0 ones. Record the 0 ones in the ones place of the answer space and the 5 tens in the tens place of the answer space.

```
    1 5
 x  1 2
    3 0
    5 0
```

B: Next, multiply the tens place of the first factor by the tens place of the second factor. Ten groups of 1 ten is 10 tens. Trade 10 tens for 1 hundred, and you will have 1 hundred and 0 tens. Record the 1 hundred in the hundreds place of the answer space.

```
      1 5
   x  1 2
      3 0
    1 5 0
```

Step 3

Add the products of the ones place of the first factor by the second factor and the tens place of the first factor by the second factor.

```
      1 5
   x  1 2
      3 0
  + 1 5 0
    1 8 0
```

Figure 2.16: Appropriate language to describe standard multiplication algorithm.

Were you precise in how you used and referred to place value? If you want students to engage in Mathematical Practice 6, "Attend to precision," you will need to be careful to model this behavior as well. Standard algorithms are efficient but are not always straightforward to describe.

Division Algorithms

Now consider division. What algorithm comes to mind when you think of multidigit division? It is probably the long division algorithm, which is provided for $632 \div 4$ in figure 2.17.

$$
\begin{array}{r}
1\,5\,8 \\
4\,\overline{)\,6\,3\,2} \\
-4 \\
\hline
2\,3 \\
-2\,0 \\
\hline
3\,2 \\
-3\,2 \\
\hline
0
\end{array}
$$

Figure 2.17: Long division algorithm.

The language typically used with the long division algorithm is not mathematically sound. Consider this common set of steps that accompanies this algorithm:

> Four goes into 6 one time. One times 4 is 4. Six minus 4 is 2.
> Bring down the 3. Four goes into 23 five times. Five times 4 is 20.
> Twenty-three minus 20 is 3. Bring down the 2. Four goes into 32 eight times.
> Eight times 4 is 32 and 32 minus 32 is zero so there is no remainder.

This language probably feels comfortable because it is familiar. You were likely taught this way; you might even teach the algorithm this way. Now consider what it really says.

"Four goes into 6"—is it a 6? No, it is 6 hundreds. Should the answer be 1? You might think the answer should be 100. However, 4 goes into 6 hundred 150 times, so that isn't right either. Then you subtract 4 (which should be 400) from 6 (which should be 600) to get 2 (which should be 200). You get the picture. Simply "adding" zeros doesn't make the language work properly ("adding" is not the correct term here, but it is frequently used). This does not account for the fact that there are 150 fours in 600 and so on.

Long division can be used to divide accurately; it is the language typically used to describe the procedure that is not mathematically accurate. This is due to the meaning of division that is implied through the language. Determining how many fours are in 632 supports the measurement meaning for division because you are seeking the number of groups of 4 there are in 632. A word problem to support this measurement meaning for division is:

> I have 632 golf balls. If I package them in boxes with
> 4 golf balls in each package, how many packages will I need?

However, the measurement meaning does not support making sense of the algorithm. Reconsider the language to support the long division algorithm in figure 2.17:

> You can think of 632 as 6 hundreds, 3 tens, and 2 ones. If you share 6 hundreds equally among four groups, how many hundreds will be in each group? There is 1 hundred in each group. You use up 4 hundreds. You have 2 hundreds left. Exchange the 2 hundreds for tens. Now you have 23 tens in all to share equally among four groups. You will have 5 tens in each group, using up 20 tens. Exchange the remaining 3 tens for ones. Now you have 32 ones. You share them equally among four groups. You have 158 in each group.

Notice how the language supports sharing among four groups. The use of sharing division is mathematically accurate with this algorithm, as is the place value language. You may also be picturing how this sharing process can be modeled precisely using base ten blocks. A word problem to support this sharing meaning for division is:

> I have 632 golf balls. If I place them into 4 bins so that there is the same number of golf balls in each bin, how many golf balls will I place in each bin?

What was needed was a shift from thinking about measurement division to thinking about sharing division. With the appropriate context and language, the abstract algorithm makes sense. When you carefully connect abstract thinking to context, you are engaging in Mathematical Practice 2, "Reason abstractly and quantitatively."

The algorithm that supports measurement division is partial quotients. It also supports flexible thinking. With partial quotients, the goal is to subtract groups of the divisor from the dividend until no more groups can be subtracted. The quotient is the number of groups subtracted in all. An important aspect of partial quotients is that you use mental computation to determine the number of groups subtracted with each step. Examine figure 2.18 (page 58) where we provide two examples of how partial quotients can be used to divide $532 \div 14$.

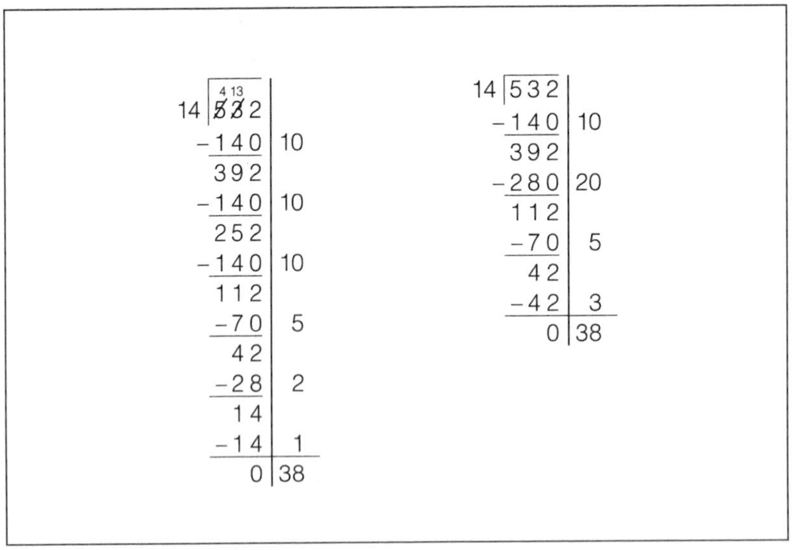

Figure 2.18: Two solutions to 532 ÷ 14 using the partial quotients algorithm.

Notice how the illustration on the left indicates that the student subtracted ten groups of 14 repeatedly until there was less than 140 left. At this point, the student subtracted five groups of 14, or 70, from what was left. How do you suppose the student knew 5 × 14 = 70? How could the student have used 10 × 14 to find the product of 5 × 14? This sort of thinking is developed when students explore number relationships and strategies for finding basic facts like the doubling strategy. When students make sense of facts by doubling, they can use those experiences to also make sense of products by halving in situations such as this.

How is the example on the right in figure 2.18 different from the one on the left? The example on the right is more efficient, as the quotient is determined in fewer steps. When students share their strategies in class, they learn from one another and become more proficient with computation. This is especially true when students are engaged in Mathematical Practice 3, "Construct viable arguments and critique the reasoning of others."

Throughout their work with multiplication and division, students build on previously learned concepts. Teachers need to provide experiences and activities that support students to make sense of the mathematics in each problem. Students should be expected to draw on their prior knowledge to unpack each task and work to connect the process to their previously held knowledge. Building on this knowledge will deepen the understanding of the operations of multiplication and division and will increase the connections students are making with these concepts.

The Classroom

Now that you have explored your own thinking about multiplication and division, and the many different ways that solutions can be represented, you will explore what this looks like in the classroom. The first classroom episode involves students making sense of a problem to determine how many people are in a marching band. Students represent the situation of seven rows of six band members. This allows students to create a model of multiplication in a real-world context. Take the time to watch the following video in its entirety, and look for how the students are making sense of the problem. Notice the different models that students create and how they explain their thinking around these models. What tools are students using? How do their models connect to the context? The best use of models becomes evident when the models align with the context of the problem. Think about how the model that a student selects represents the student's thinking about the task.

www.solution-tree.com/Modeling_Multiplication_Strategies

As students start to model this problem, some use counters, others set up an array, and still others represent groups with the same number of dots in each group. Each of these representations shows how students are making sense of the problem. It also allows you to see how students are modeling the mathematics. For instance, some students like to stay close to the context, actually thinking of each counter or each x as a member of the marching band. In setting up an array, these students are making a direct relationship between the marching band and their model. However, other students shift the model of mathematics, thinking of the problem as 7×6, making seven groups of six objects.

In the first discussion between the teacher and a student, listen to the student's thinking in his description of his model and how he solves the problem. Although the representation was an array of seven rows with six x's in each row, the student groups the rows together in order to determine the product. He groups two rows of 6 into 12, creating the addition problem of $12 + 12 + 12 + 6$. In this way, he changes the problem from a repeated addition of 7 sixes into 3 twelves and 1 six.

Students should learn a variety of strategies to solve problems, building a toolkit of strategies. Sometimes, it is beneficial to share a strategy with the class, asking different students to make sense of its different components so that all students can learn from the shared strategy. Consider how the students make sense of the teacher's statement: "I heard someone say that they used their array and they counted by fives." As students contribute different ideas toward how to make sense of this strategy and how to represent it using an equation, all students in the class are learning different ways to decompose the original 7×6 multiplication problem. The line of questioning allows the students to make sense of the strategy and link it to different multiplication facts in order to solve 7×6. This type of decomposition can be used to help students build strategies that will support improved fact fluency.

Presenting different strategies allows students to consider how breaking apart multiplication problems can lead to sense making in solving problems using multiplication. Students produce many different models, and in their explanations, they are able to make connections between a context and model. They also use their model to discuss links between the context, model, and equation. In exploring how to represent the problem, the students demonstrate Mathematical Practice 4, "Model with mathematics."

The students in the video also used different tools to make sense of this problem. Some used whiteboards and markers and others found the two-color counters to be more helpful. By providing open access to different tools and the expectation that students have a choice in using those tools, students are more likely to engage in Mathematical Practice 5, "Use appropriate tools strategically."

Be sure you have multiple goals in presenting such a lesson, as the teacher in the video did. Although the learning goal is to model and solve a multiplication problem, the teacher also wants students to see a model that would support decomposing a multiplication fact into other facts that may be more accessible to students. The available tools helped students meet that goal.

In the second video, fourth-grade students are asked to create a word problem for a division problem that includes a remainder. In fact, students must create a problem that requires making sense of the remainder in a particular way. The problem asks students to create a word problem for 26 divided by 4 that should have an answer of 7. Before watching the video, complete the task provided in figure 2.19.

 Write a word problem for 26 ÷ 4 that results in an answer of 7. Do not use the words *around*, *estimate*, or *about*.

Figure 2.19: Division in context.

How do you think fourth-grade students will approach this task? Students who have had sufficient experience writing word problems will be in a better position to respond well to this task. Also, what supports will students need to understand this problem? This task involves making sense of division and, specifically, division with remainders. As you watch the following video, consider how the students are working and what actions the teacher takes to support sense making by the students and to use the layers of facilitation (I facilitate the whole class, I facilitate small groups, I facilitate individuals).

   www.solution-tree.com/Interpreting_the
_Remainder_in_Word_Problems

Initially, the teacher's focus is on helping the students make sense of the problem. Although the students appear to understand that the solution to the division problem will have a remainder, they need to find a way to address that in the word problem so the answer to the word problem is 7. At first, the students are unsuccessful. They write word problems that represent 26 ÷ 4 but have the contextual answer of 6. The teacher calls the students back to the whole group to discuss what she is seeing. She works with the class to help them to determine that the type of problems they are creating does not meet the goal of the task. The students continue to work on the problem using the context of packaging pencils and try to find a way to obtain an answer of seven packages. The teacher calls the students back after continued efforts, and still they are struggling to meet the need for seven packages. One student offers a suggestion that will create an answer of seven by changing the conditions of the task. It's a creative proposal, but the teacher does not allow the change as it is not consistent with her learning goal.

At this point, the teacher continues to pose questions to help the class determine a way to restate the problem in order to get an answer of 7. One of the keys to this problem is how to communicate the need to have packages for all of the pencils, even if a package is not entirely filled. The wording of the problem provides a context to have rich discussions about how to achieve a specific goal provided by a context. One way the teacher is able to move the conversation forward is by understanding the types of division models that are possible. Originally, the students create *sharing division* problems, ones that look to share the pencils with a specific number of groups. Because of the teacher's understanding of the types of division problems, she is able to scaffold student thinking to help them consider *measurement division* models, which will allow them to create problems that meet the goals of the task.

TQE Process

At this point, it may be helpful to watch the second video again. Pay close attention to the tasks, questioning, and opportunities to collect evidence of student learning.

The TQE process can help you frame your observations. Teachers who have a deep understanding of the mathematics they teach:

- Select appropriate *tasks* to support identified learning goals
- Facilitate productive *questioning* during instruction to engage students in Mathematical Practices
- Collect and use student *evidence* in the formative assessment process during instruction

The teacher begins the lesson by explaining that this *task* is a little different. She anticipates that this task will be challenging, so she prepares the students accordingly. She is intentional about choosing a task that will provide opportunities for students to engage in Mathematical Practice 1, "Make sense of problems and persevere in solving them," and Mathematical Practice 2, "Reason abstractly and quantitatively." Her expectation is that the students are the ones who need to make sense of the problem and build a context. If you first model the problem for the students, which might be an expectation if you are considering the use of gradual release, then the thinking is taken from the students and is instead done by you. By placing the thinking in the hands of the students rather than providing a model for the students to emulate, the teacher in the video uses the initial discussion to support the students in making sense of the problem.

In the video, the teacher is very careful about the *questioning* that she uses and how she guides student thinking without taking over the process, ensuring that students retain the control over the way they are making sense of the problem. In considering how you monitor and support productive talk in the classroom, whether in small groups or as a whole group, consider the impact that your questions and reactions have on students. Think about how you support productive talk in your classroom. How do you ensure that the students are doing the thinking? Similarly, in what ways do you see the teacher in the video supporting student engagement with the task? How does she foster student thinking? Notice how she works to make the talk productive, even as the students are struggling with the task. The key is how the scaffolded questions are created and how they remain open ended while giving students the guidance to think about what should come next.

The teacher gathers *evidence* as part of the formative assessment process while she is teaching. Pay attention to the type of information the teacher is collecting to help guide her actions during the task. Imagine circulating around the classroom and noticing the challenge that students are having in creating the proper word problems. Observe how the teacher does not give a hint as to her thinking—her responses remain open ended and her facial expressions do not reveal whether a student is correct. At this point, it is typical for teachers to swoop in with their capes on to save the day as they rush to help the students and solve the problem. When this occurs, learning opportunities are lost. You may have felt that this is what the teacher in the video was going to do when she brings the class together. However, the teacher does not tell the students what to do; rather, she uses the gathering of the students to help them make sense of the task based on the evidence she collected by circulating the room. When she brings the class together, she does not give them an answer. Instead, she helps them achieve their goal through questioning that facilitates student thinking. It is also important to provide students processing time to achieve success with this problem. Both the scaffolding of questions and time to think through new ideas are important techniques to support students in addressing complex tasks.

The Response

How do you respond when students make mistakes with multiplication or division? Do you assume it is just a deficit in memorization of the multiplication and division facts? How do you help students use the errors as springboards to learning? Common struggles with multiplication and division often stem from misconceptions regarding the meanings of multiplication and division, not having a full toolkit of strategies to support fact fluency, and errors in understanding place value. Students may not fully understand how the place value representations in each of the factors of a multiplication problem can help them make sense of the problem.

Consider the error of only multiplying 10×10 and 2×5 to determine the product of 12×15. What understanding, if any, is the student displaying? Even in the midst of displaying errors, there is still an opportunity to give attention to what students understand in the same context. How would you respond to a student who makes this error? Often the response is simply that the student needs to multiply "all the parts of the problem." However, this response does not get to the root of the error. The error is more likely that the student did not interpret 12×15 to mean 12 groups of 15. The student's response only includes ten groups of 10 and two groups of 5 and lacks ten groups of 5 and two groups of 10. Returning to concrete representations and contexts can be useful in helping students reconsider how to keep track of the groups of objects.

It is also helpful to facilitate discussions with students so they have opportunities to explain their thinking. In this case, the student uses the concept of renaming a number appropriately but may simply be putting double digit with double digit and single digit with single digit. Hearing the student's explanation or seeing the student demonstrate the process with concrete representations can help uncover what is behind the student's error.

When students struggle with multidigit multiplication or division, it can be helpful to unpack how the students consider early stages of the learning progression and to then rebuild the steps through examples and questioning that engage the students in thinking about the task using strategies rather than trying to use memorized algorithms. As you unpack students' solution processes, pay close attention to their use of addition or subtraction with regrouping as part of the multidigit multiplication or division process. These sorts of issues are often based in errors with place value, and attention to this concept will be fruitful, as opposed to maintaining an exclusive focus on memorization of basic facts for students who struggle.

What about students who have not memorized their multiplication facts? Just as it is important for students to learn multiplication facts through sense making and strategic thinking, it is important that your support be based on the same instructional technique. Working with students to consider strategies that develop understanding of multiplication facts will provide students the support to better use their understanding of multiplication. The strategies discussed in the chapter, such as doubles and the break-apart strategy, will help students understand the relationships within multiplication and division.

Reflections

1. What do you feel are the key points in this chapter?

2. What challenges might you face when implementing the key ideas from this chapter? How will you overcome them?

3. What are the important features for developing an understanding of multiplication and division, and how will you ensure your instruction embeds the support needed for these features?

4. Select a recent lesson you have taught or observed focused on multiplication or division. Relate this lesson to the TQE process.

5. What are the changes you will make to your planning and instruction based on what you read and considered from this chapter?

CHAPTER 3

Fraction Concepts

When learning and teaching fraction concepts, the ideas of partitioning, unitizing, equivalence, and comparison are introduced in first grade and continue through fourth grade to prepare students for conceptualizing operations with fractions. Word problems with the aid of visual models can provide the foundation for understanding fraction concepts in depth.

The Challenge

Use drawings to determine which student is correct in figure 3.1 before reading the discussion of the task.

A group of students was asked to solve the following problem:

Share four cookies equally among five people. How much of a cookie will each person receive?

Analyze the following student responses to determine who is correct and incorrect and why.

- Student A: Each person will receive ⅕ of each cookie.
- Student B: Each person will receive ⁴⁄₂₀ of all the cookies.
- Student C: Each person will receive ⅘ of a cookie.
- Student D: Each person will receive four pieces.

Figure 3.1: Fraction sharing task.

As shown in figure 3.2, you can start with four cookies, partition each cookie into five equal pieces, then shade one piece of each cookie to represent the amount one person will receive.

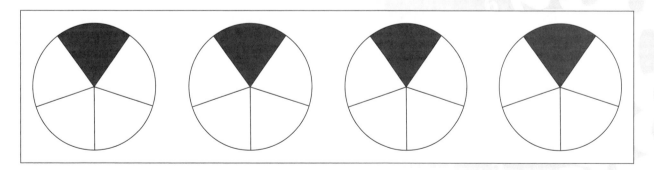

Figure 3.2: Sharing four cookies equally among five people.

Use figure 3.2 to make sense of each student's answer. You may realize that Student A's response resulted from looking at each cookie individually to find that each person receives ⅕ of each cookie. Student B used all four cookies together to say that out of twenty pieces total, each person would receive four.

Student C combined the four pieces together, which are $\frac{1}{5}$ of a cookie each, to determine that everyone receives $\frac{4}{5}$ of a cookie. Finally, Student D counted how many pieces each person receives.

Which student is correct? This question can be answered by going back to the wording of the problem. The problem asks for how much of a cookie each person receives. The only student to answer in terms of a cookie was Student C. In addition, this student correctly identified the amount of a cookie each person receives as $\frac{4}{5}$. Although Students A and B had mathematically correct responses, they did not answer the question in the problem as they incorrectly identified their whole to be each cookie (Student A) or all four cookies (Student B). Student D had what Susan Lamon (2005) identifies as a common error of counting how many pieces each person receives as opposed to answering how much of a cookie or what portion of a cookie each person receives.

Being able to name fractions is important, but fractions cannot be named without a specified whole. As shown with these students' solutions, fractions will change depending on the whole that is used. Thus, knowing the whole is more important than understanding fractions themselves, because fractions are meaningless without the whole they are based on.

The Progression

By the time students enter grade 3, they will have had experiences with partitioning circles and rectangles into halves and fourths (grade 1) and thirds (grade 2) and naming amounts as halves, thirds, and fourths (for further discussion of these ideas see chapter 5 of *Making Sense of Mathematics for Teaching Grades K–2* [Dixon et al., 2016]). They will also have explored the idea that the more equal pieces something is broken into, the smaller the pieces become, and they realize that equal shares do not imply equal shape. In grades 3 and 4, the ideas introduced in K–2 are extended with additional fraction concepts. Furthermore, in grade 4, the focus shifts to fraction operations. Following is a progression of the development of fraction concepts over grades 3 and 4.

- Partition shapes into parts with equal shares.

- Make sense of $\frac{a}{b}$ as a fraction representing the quantity formed by a parts of size $\frac{1}{b}$.

- Recognize and generate simple equivalent fractions, including those equivalent to whole numbers.

- Compare two fractions with the same numerator or same denominator.

- Explain with fraction models why a fraction $\frac{a}{b}$ is equivalent to $\frac{(n \times a)}{(n \times b)}$.

- Compare two fractions with different numerators and different denominators.

As students progress through third and fourth grade, they develop more abstract ways of reasoning about fractions. This is accomplished by first solving word problems with visual models and reasoning to make sense of the problems. Next, students use pictures to make sense of procedures for reasoning about fractions. In the last phase, students understand procedures and how to use them and no longer need the aid of a visual model. These topics are developed for students as a foundation for operating with fractions.

Grade 3

Partitioning objects into parts with equal shares extends what students investigated in first and second grade. Students explore the idea that parts do not have to be equal in shape to be equal in size. This provides them with a foundation for understanding how two different shapes can have the same area in geometry (see chapter 5).

In grade 3, students are introduced to mixed numbers and fractions greater than one. For example, when sharing five cookies equally among three people, each person will receive more than one cookie but less than two cookies. In addition, students develop understandings of defining wholes for fractions. Using the same cookie problem, the final solution is not $1\frac{2}{3}$ but $1\frac{2}{3}$ cookies or $1\frac{2}{3}$ of a cookie.

Understanding a fraction a/b as a parts of size $1/b$—or the fraction $3/5$ as three groups of $1/5$, for example—develops students' understanding of unit fractions, or fractions with a numerator of one. This further develops their understanding of wholes by exploring that fractions such as $5/5$ are equivalent to 1, which is known as *unitizing*. Finding and working with unit fractions as well as developing an understanding of fractions equivalent to 1 provide a foundation for multiplying a fraction by a whole number, such as $3 \times 1/5$ (see chapter 4).

Students in grade 3 also partition fractions into groups of unit fractions. They then learn to iterate, or "repeat," the unit fraction to develop a whole of one. For example, if given the fraction $4/5$ and asked to find $5/5$, students can break $4/5$ into four groups of $1/5$, then iterate or copy $1/5$ five times ($1/5$, $2/5$, $3/5$, $4/5$, $5/5$) to find $5/5$. It is here where students start to develop an understanding of fractions as numbers as they use linear models to locate fractions on a number line.

Grade 3 students begin work with fraction equivalence when they understand that whole numbers can be written as fractions, such as $4 = 4/1$, and as mentioned previously, fractions such as $5/5$ are equivalent to 1. Work with number lines is also extended as students find that equivalent fractions are located at the same place on the number line, and they understand, generate, and recognize simple equivalent fractions, such as $1/2 = 2/4 = 3/6$.

Students' fraction comparison strategies develop as they compare two fractions based on the same whole. At this grade level, students compare fractions with the same numerator or the same denominator. Fraction comparison strategies are explored through contexts. Students then reason through the problem with or without visual models to justify which fraction is greater or if they are both equal. They represent their solution with the symbols <, >, or =. Finally, students compare fractions without contexts and models to reason about the given fractions. Comparing fractions helps students coordinate the number of pieces with the size of each piece to develop ideas related to the "size" of a fraction. For example, when comparing $3/4$ and $3/5$, each fraction has the same number of pieces but fourths are bigger than fifths, thus $3/4$ is greater (in problems without context, the whole is assumed to be the same size). Likewise, when comparing $5/8$ and $7/8$, each fraction has the same size piece, but you have more of them in the $7/8$ than you do in $5/8$, making $7/8$ greater.

Grade 4

In grade 4, the fraction concepts of comparison and equivalence are extended as students compare fractions with different numerators and denominators. They learn about benchmark fractions, such as $1/2$. Students continue working with common numerators and denominators but may need to determine equivalent fractions to compare them. For example, when comparing $1/3$ and $3/4$, students can find a common numerator of 3 to compare $3/9$ to $3/4$, or a common denominator of 12 to compare $4/12$ and $9/12$. Using a benchmark, they can see that $1/3 < 1/2$ and $3/4 > 1/2$, thus $3/4$ is greater than $1/3$. Using a benchmark also becomes important when estimating and checking the reasonableness of solutions for fraction operations (see chapter 4).

For fraction equivalence, students use what they know about recognizing and finding equivalent fractions to develop justifications for why you "do the same thing (operation) to the top (numerator) and bottom (denominator)" to find equivalent fractions. Students explore and explain with fraction models why a fraction a/b is equivalent to $(n \times a)/(n \times b)$. They develop understanding about why dividing the numerator and denominator by the same number results in an equivalent fraction as well. This provides them with conceptual reasoning for finding common denominators when adding and subtracting fractions. In fifth grade, work with fractions focuses on fraction operations. Operating with fractions is discussed in chapter 4.

The Mathematics

What is a fraction? Where do fractions fit in the structure of numbers? A fraction is a rational number, because it describes a ratio of two numbers. In a fraction a/b, the numerator, a, describes the number of equal-size parts, and the denominator, b, indicates the number of those parts needed to make the whole. A rational number that is not a fraction can also be described as a/b, however in these instances—such as when comparing the number of boys to the number of girls in a class—a and b do not describe a part-whole relationship. While the focus of rational numbers is on fractions in grades 3–5, students' exploration of rational numbers extends to all types of ratios in grade 6 (see *Making Sense of Mathematics for Teaching Grades 6–8* [Nolan, Dixon, Roy, & Andreasen, 2016]). Here, we describe specific aspects of fraction concepts, including partitioning concepts, recognizing the whole, unitizing, creating equivalent fractions, and comparing fractions.

Partitioning Concepts

Partitioning can be introduced through fair-sharing division situations, like those we discussed with whole-number division in chapter 2. Students can draw on their previous knowledge and experience with whole numbers to explore the same problem type with fractions. Exploring these situations with contexts and having opportunities to use visual models to represent the situations help students develop the conceptual knowledge needed to define wholes for fractions, understand how fractions are represented, and move toward more abstract ways of thinking and reasoning. You'll need to anticipate the various ways students might approach sharing problems with fractions. To start exploring this, model the following sharing situations (see figure 3.3).

Represent each situation with a visual model using circles in two different ways:

Determine how much of a cookie each person gets when you:

1. Share two cookies equally among four people

2. Share four cookies equally among three people

Figure 3.3: Fair-sharing situations.

It is likely that one of the ways you shared the cookies in the first problem in figure 3.3 was by cutting each cookie into four equal parts. The other way you likely solved the problem was to partition the total amount of cookies into four equal parts (see figure 3.4).

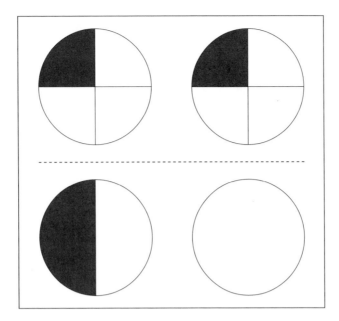

Figure 3.4: Sharing two cookies among four people.

Similar to the task presented in figure 3.1 (page 65), you need to describe the shaded amount. Looking at the first picture in figure 3.4, would you say this is ¼, ²⁄₄, or ²⁄₈? What is the whole for each solution? In this problem, you have three choices for wholes. A whole could either be just one of the single cookies, the total of two cookies, or the amount from each cookie. Using all three different wholes, what would your solution be? If you use a whole of one cookie, how much is shaded in total? You know that ¼ from each cookie is shaded; so would this mean that each person receives ¼ of a single cookie in total? In this case it does not. Although ¼ of each cookie is shaded, the shading describes the amount if the whole was each cookie individually. Because you are using one cookie as your whole, you need to find how much of a cookie each person would receive altogether. Each person would receive ²⁄₄ of a cookie when combining the shaded pieces.

What would the solution be if the whole was two cookies? Using both cookies together as the whole, there are two shaded pieces and eight pieces total in the two cookies, thus the solution would be ²⁄₈.

Which solution is correct for the problem? The problem asked for how much of *a* cookie each person receives, thus the whole is one cookie, meaning that the solution is ²⁄₄ of a cookie. Common errors such as ¼ and ²⁄₈ occur when a whole of one cookie is not used. Posing problems in which there is more than one whole to be shared provides opportunities to address this misconception. Although this problem started with two cookies, the solution was in terms of one cookie.

Having two different ways to express a *correct* solution allows students to start developing an understanding of equivalence concepts. Students can use manipulatives such as fraction circles to justify that ²⁄₄ of a cookie is equivalent to ½. Students also begin to understand unitizing ideas, such as recognizing that a fraction can be described as groups of unit fractions. For example, in the first problem you can see that ²⁄₄ is two groups of ¼. In this way, unitizing with unit fractions is introduced.

How did you solve the second problem in figure 3.3? You likely shared the four cookies among three people by cutting each cookie into three equal pieces or by giving each person one whole cookie and then sharing the last cookie among the three people by cutting that into three equal pieces (see figure 3.5).

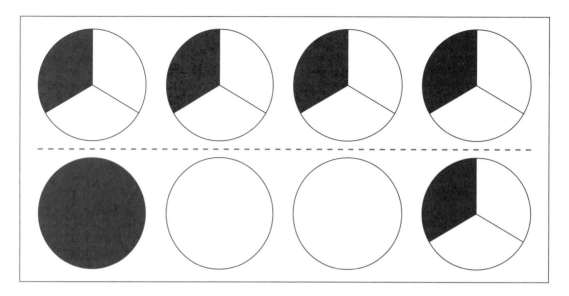

Figure 3.5: Sharing four cookies among three people.

How can you unitize using the first set of pictures in figure 3.5? Take three groups of ⅓ and combine them to get ⅔, which is one whole.

Mixed numbers and fractions greater than 1 can also be explored with sharing situations. This occurs with the second problem where four cookies are shared equally among three people. When looking at figure 3.5, the first solution can be described as four groups of ⅓ or ⁴⁄₃ cookies, and the second solution can be described as one cookie and ⅓ of another cookie or 1⅓ cookies. This illustrates that the fractions ⁴⁄₃ and 1⅓ are equivalent—both describe an amount greater than 1, and both are correct solutions to the problem.

Within each situation, the whole for each fraction was a cookie. To further develop concepts related to wholes with fractions, you can extend sharing situations. Take a moment to solve the problem in figure 3.6 before reading further.

Amanda shared three candy bars equally between her five friends so that each person received half of a candy bar as illustrated here:

Then a seventh person comes along. How much of a candy bar will *each person* need to give the newcomer so that everyone receives the same amount?

Figure 3.6: Extending fair-sharing situations.

What should Amanda and each of her friends do with their half of a candy bar? The candy bars cannot be melted back together or eaten before the seventh person can get any (well, they actually can be, but that would not be an example of fair sharing). Think about how you would have shared the candy bars equally had the original problem instead asked you to share three candy bars equally among seven people. You likely would have cut each candy bar up into seven pieces. A similar thought process can be used to share half of a candy bar among seven people.

When the seventh person comes along, each person's share can be cut into seven equal pieces (see figure 3.7). Each person then keeps six pieces and gives the seventh piece to the new person so that each person ends up with six pieces.

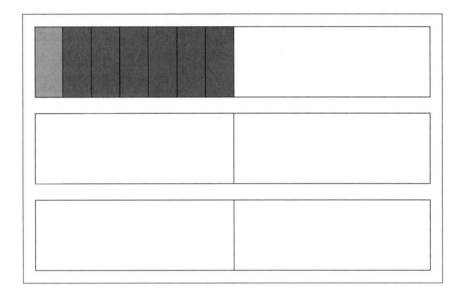

Figure 3.7: Splitting ½ of a candy bar into seven equal pieces.

How are you going to describe this amount? Look at the student solutions in figure 3.8. How would you respond to each of these solutions? Think about each solution and how a student might have used the picture to come up with each solution before continuing.

A class of students just solved the problem in figure 3.6 and generated the following solutions. For each solution, determine if that student is correct or incorrect and why.

- Student A: $\frac{6}{14}$ of a candy bar

- Student B: $\frac{1}{7}$ of a candy bar

- Student C: $\frac{6}{7}$ of a candy bar

- Student D: $\frac{1}{14}$ of a candy bar

Figure 3.8: Solution choices for the problem in figure 3.6.

You know from the problem that each person will receive six pieces of a candy bar in the end. Student A described this as ⁶⁄₁₄ of a candy bar. The answer ⁶⁄₁₄ is incorrect, but why? The question asks how much of a candy bar each person will need to give the seventh person, not how much of a candy bar each person will keep.

What about Student B's solution of ⅐ of a candy bar? What could this student have been thinking? You know that each person gives the seventh person one piece of his or her half. Because each person split his or her half into seven equal pieces, the ⅐ is actually ⅐ of a half candy bar, not ⅐ of a whole candy bar. Thus, Student B is using an incorrect whole.

What about Student C's solution of ⁶⁄₇ of a candy bar? Is this student looking at a half of a candy bar or a whole candy bar? Student C's solution is similar to how both Student A and B responded. On the one hand, the ⁶⁄₇ is describing the amount of a half of a candy bar each person keeps; therefore, the student has not answered the question of how much is given away. On the other hand, the ⁶⁄₇ is referring to half of a candy bar and not a whole candy bar; hence, the student is referring to the wrong whole. These first three solutions are common errors of either focusing on the amount each person keeps instead of the amount each person will give the seventh person or focusing on the incorrect whole of half a candy bar instead of a whole candy bar.

Now look at Student D's response of ¹⁄₁₄ of a candy bar. What whole is Student D using? When half of a candy bar is split into seven pieces, this means that a full candy bar is split into fourteen pieces. Because each person is giving away one piece of the fourteen pieces, the seventh person will receive ¹⁄₁₄ of a candy bar from each person. Thus, Student D is correct.

Defining wholes and using correct language to define wholes is crucial to be able to name fractions (Tobias, 2013). Students' ability to name fractions in terms of a whole is important because wholes can change in fraction situations, as with fraction multiplication (see chapter 4). Extending fair-sharing situations in this way will reinforce the importance of the whole. As you saw with the problem in figure 3.6 (page 70), although you worked with half of a candy bar, the solution was in terms of a whole candy bar.

Which Mathematical Practices did you engage with during this task? Because you needed to make sense of the problem yourself in order to solve the problem and you had to make sense of solutions that were different from the solution you may have gotten, you used Mathematical Practice 1, "Make sense of problems and persevere in solving them," and Mathematical Practice 3, "Construct viable arguments and critique the reasoning of others." In addition, you had to pay attention to what the whole was and use correct language to describe that whole, which is Mathematical Practice 6, "Attend to precision."

Partitioning also affords students the opportunity to develop the idea of "same size pieces," or common denominators, before formally working with fraction addition and subtraction. For example, consider figure 3.9 for a modification made to figure 3.1 (page 65). Solve the problem before continuing further.

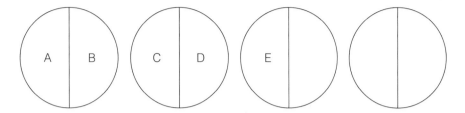

Brandon shared four cookies equally between himself and his four friends. He started by giving each person half of a cookie as illustrated here (the letters stand for which person will get that piece):

Now continue sharing the cookies for Brandon until all four cookies have been shared. How much of a cookie will each person receive?

Figure 3.9: Modifications for task to share four cookies equally among five people.

One way to share what is left is by giving each person ¼ of a cookie (see figure 3.10).

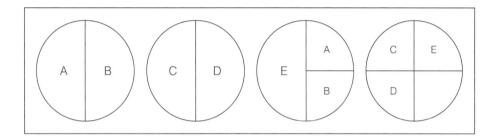

Figure 3.10: Giving everyone ¼ of a cookie.

How are you going to share the last piece? Because there are five people, you can slice the last piece into five pieces (see figure 3.11).

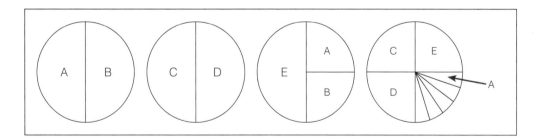

Figure 3.11: Sharing the last fourth into five.

How much will Person A receive? Think about how you name the amounts Person A is getting and how you will determine how much this is in terms of a cookie. How much of a cookie is the largest piece? ½. How much of a cookie is the second largest piece? ¼. When looking at the smallest piece, what amount is this? Is it ⅕ of a cookie? It is ⅕, but not of a cookie. When looking at the picture, you can see that it is ⅕ of ¼ of a cookie. Thus, you need to see how much of a whole cookie the smallest piece is worth.

Because the fourth is cut into five pieces, you can cut each of the other fourths into five pieces to give you twenty pieces total. Thus, the smallest piece is ½₀ of a cookie.

Students often think that the smallest piece is ⅛ of a cookie. What is their error? They are just counting how many pieces there are total without focusing on the size of each piece. Although there *are* eight pieces in the last cookie, they are not equal in size, and so they are not eighths. Stating the smallest piece is ⅛ or ⅕ reflects conceptual errors that can be brought to light with problems such as this that might not otherwise have been discussed had the problem not been altered. Thus, it is important to modify problems throughout instruction to prompt and address errors and misconceptions early so they do not carry over to later topics.

Now that you know each person receives ½ of a cookie, ¼ of a cookie, and ½₀ of a cookie, reconsider the illustration in figure 3.11 (page 73) to determine how much of a cookie each person receives in total. How are you going to combine the amounts with the pieces being different sizes? Your answer should be that you need same-size pieces. How are you going to get same-size pieces? You may have realized that you can work with the smallest piece that you have, which is ½₀. How can you convert the ½ and the ¼ into twentieths? The ½ of a cookie can be broken up into ten same-size pieces to get ¹⁰⁄₂₀, and the ¼ of a cookie can be broken up into five same-size pieces to get ⁵⁄₂₀. The remaining ½₀ of a cookie will be unchanged. The problem now will be renamed as ¹⁰⁄₂₀ + ⁵⁄₂₀ + ½₀. Combining the same-size pieces, everyone receives ¹⁶⁄₂₀ of a cookie. Notice how the focus was on the context, the cookie pieces, rather than on finding common denominators procedurally.

Recognizing the Whole

In all of the sharing situations, the solutions could not be found until you knew that the whole was one cookie or one candy bar. However, wholes can change depending on the situation, and these types of problems are important to experience as well. To explore this idea on your own, use the yellow hexagon, red trapezoid, blue rhombus, and green triangle pattern blocks to answer the following questions (see figure 3.12).

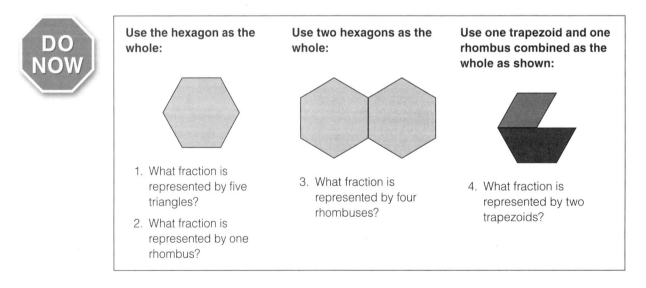

Use the hexagon as the whole:

1. What fraction is represented by five triangles?

2. What fraction is represented by one rhombus?

Use two hexagons as the whole:

3. What fraction is represented by four rhombuses?

Use one trapezoid and one rhombus combined as the whole as shown:

4. What fraction is represented by two trapezoids?

Figure 3.12: Problems to define the whole with pattern blocks.

Using the hexagon as the whole, you can compare this to the five triangles or one rhombus (see figure 3.13).

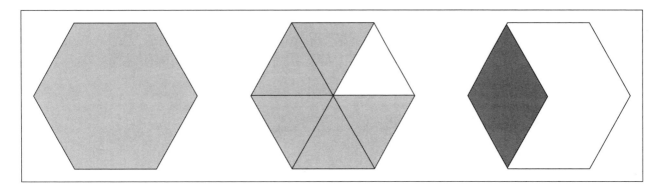

Figure 3.13: Comparing five triangles or one rhombus to a hexagon.

Students will often revert to what they know to describe things when they are uncertain. For example, students who have little experience with using symbols to represent fractions might respond to the first problem in figure 3.12 with the fractions ⅕, 5⁄1, ⅙, 6⁄1, or ⅚. How would you respond to each of these answers? Ask students to justify their responses, as this will help discussion. Are their answers correct or incorrect and why?

Only one of the answers is correct, but each of them connects to ways students are making sense of the situation. Refer to figure 3.13; you can see that ⅕ is one missing triangle and five triangles present. Similarly, 5⁄1 is the comparison of five triangles to one missing triangle. Looking at the amount that is missing—⅙ of the area of the hexagon is what you do not have. The next solution of 6⁄1 is a comparison of how many triangles it takes to fill a hexagon to how many are missing. Finally, the correct answer of ⅚ is representing the amount of area the five triangles take of the hexagon's total area.

Students often give solutions that can be explained using these types of reasoning when they try to apply whole number understandings to fractions. If students have not yet developed a fraction as a quantity, they will use whole-number ideas to describe fraction ideas because that is what they know. For example, the reasoning of one missing triangle to five triangles present to describe ⅕ will indicate that students have not yet developed an understanding of the fraction ⅕ as a quantity of something and not to be looked at as separate quantities. This sort of thinking will be supported in grade 6 when ratios are introduced. Thus, the solution to the second problem would be that one rhombus is ⅓ of a hexagon when you describe the area of the hexagon that the rhombus covers.

As previously mentioned, wholes for fractions can change. Often, the single hexagon is designated to represent the whole. It is also important to experience wholes that are greater than and less than one hexagon, which is why problems 3 and 4 in figure 3.12 are included. For problem 3, as you can see in figure 3.14 (page 76), the whole is now two hexagons, and you need to determine the fraction represented by four rhombuses.

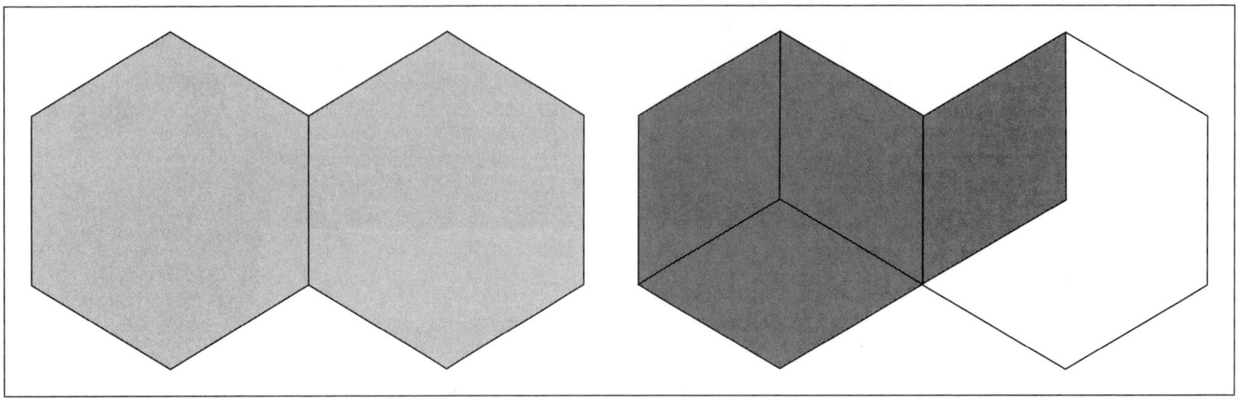

Figure 3.14: Comparing four rhombuses to two hexagons.

We've put four rhombuses together to mimic the structure of the two hexagons; however, you might erroneously think that the collection of rhombuses represents $1\frac{1}{3}$. Because two hexagons together are the whole, it takes six rhombuses to fill the whole. Because there are four rhombuses, this represents $\frac{4}{6}$ of two hexagons.

Finally, compare a whole that is a combined trapezoid and rhombus to two trapezoids (see figure 3.15).

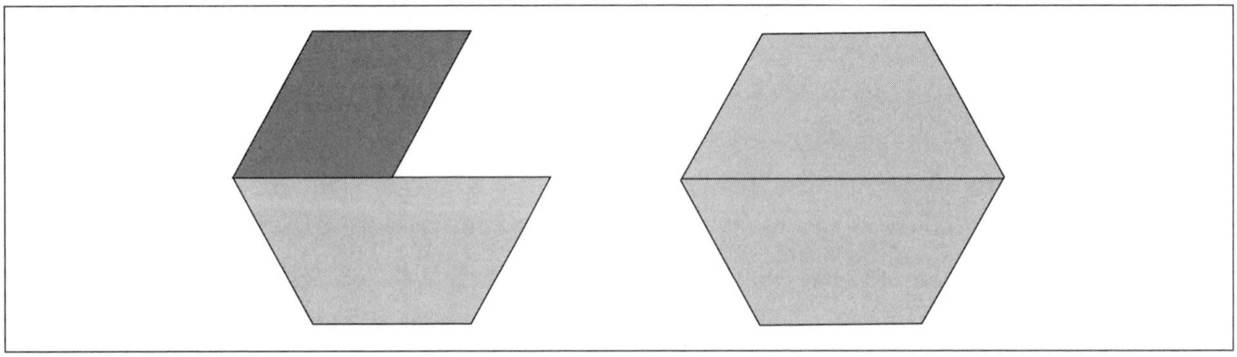

Figure 3.15: Comparing two trapezoids to a whole of a rhombus and trapezoid.

The two trapezoids make a hexagon. This can be covered with one whole and a triangle, thus the solution must be $1\frac{1}{6}$. Or is it? When you look at the whole, you can convert the trapezoid into three triangles and the rhombus into two triangles for a total of five triangles. Comparing this to the two trapezoids, which are equivalent to six triangles, you can see that the whole is five triangles and you have six triangles. Two trapezoids will represent one whole of $\frac{5}{5}$ plus one more piece of a second whole or $\frac{1}{5}$ of a second whole. Thus, the solution is $\frac{6}{5}$ or $1\frac{1}{5}$, not $1\frac{1}{6}$ (see figure 3.16).

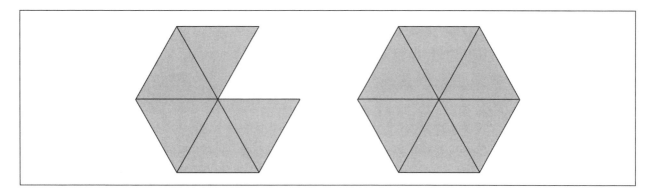

Figure 3.16: Converting to triangles.

The solution of 1⅙ is a common error that is made when wholes are changed with pattern blocks. The one in this case referred to one whole of the trapezoid and the rhombus combined. The ⅙ was ⅙ of a hexagon. Thus, the solution of 1⅙ was referring to two different wholes at once, which is why the solution was incorrect. Understanding mixed numbers in terms of wholes is a concept needed for understanding fraction operations, particularly when making sense of finding the remainder when dividing (see chapter 4).

Unitizing

Unitizing with fractions is understood when a fraction a/b is recognized as the quantity formed by a parts of size $1/b$; for example, the fraction ⅔ is two groups of ⅓. Working with unit fractions to find a whole of one is also important. Often fractions are introduced with area models and through problems where a whole is given and a part must be found, like the problem in figure 3.17.

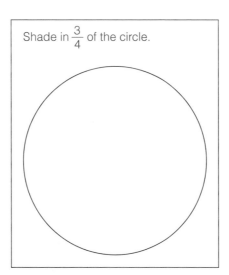

Figure 3.17: Find a part when given a whole.

Posing problems that instead ask for the whole when given the part can help develop unitizing ideas. In addition, moving away from the area model and instead working with set and linear models will further deepen your understanding of fractions as quantities. Take a moment to examine this with the problems in figure 3.18 (page 78) using two-color counters in support of the set model for fractions.

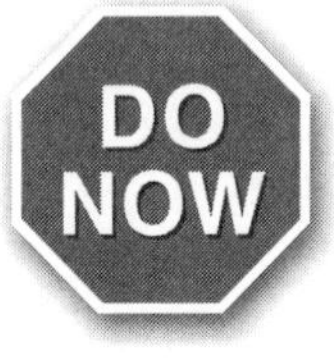

Determine the whole given the parts using two-color counters.

1. If six counters represent $\frac{2}{3}$ of the whole set, how many counters are in the entire set?
2. If eight counters represent $\frac{4}{5}$ of the whole set, how many counters are in the entire set?

Figure 3.18: Finding a whole given the part problems.

Solving the first problem, you need to start with six counters. This represents $\frac{2}{3}$ of the set. How will you find the entire set? You need to know how much is in $\frac{1}{3}$ of the entire set to find $\frac{3}{3}$ of the set, which is the entire set. How are you going to get $\frac{1}{3}$ of the entire set if the entire set is unknown? You can divide your six counters into two equal groups to find that there are three counters in $\frac{1}{3}$ of the set. Adding this to the six counters that you started with, you find that there are nine counters in the entire set (see figure 3.19).

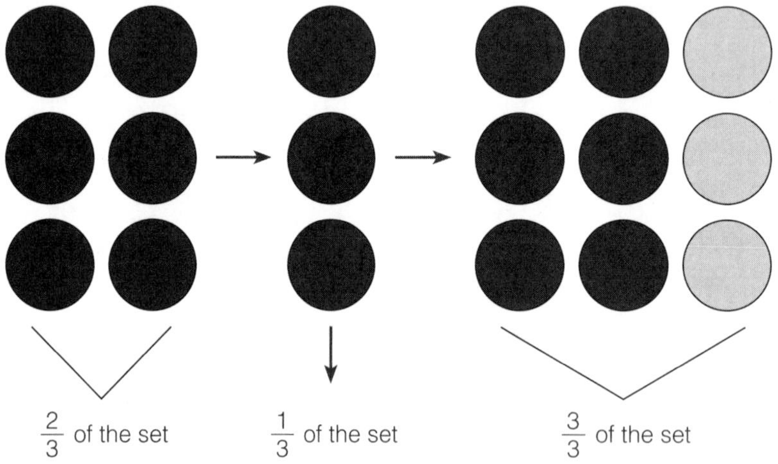

Figure 3.19: Finding the whole set when six counters is $2/3$ of the set.

Similar methods can be used to find the solution to problem 2 of figure 3.18. With both problems, a solution path is to find a unit fraction, or a fraction with a numerator of one, to find one part of the set. In problem 2 you see that $\frac{4}{5}$ is the same thing as four groups of $\frac{1}{5}$. This is then used to find the whole. In this case, $\frac{5}{5}$ of the set is ten counters (see figure 3.20).

Although these two problems allow you to engage with Mathematical Practice 8, "Look for and express regularity in repeated reasoning," you may have only paid attention to how many counters you were working with and not necessarily what fraction of the whole you were using. Linear models can be used to further extend unitizing ideas with finding a unit fraction, iterating or copying that unit fraction, and finding a whole. Before continuing, trace the number line and solve the problem in figure 3.21.

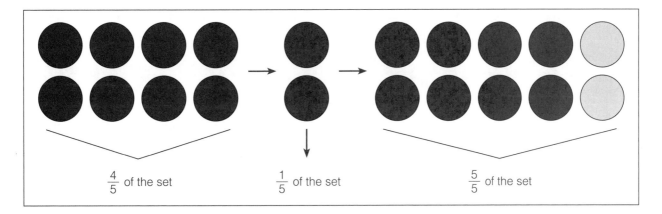

Figure 3.20: Finding the set when eight counters is ⁴/₅ of the set.

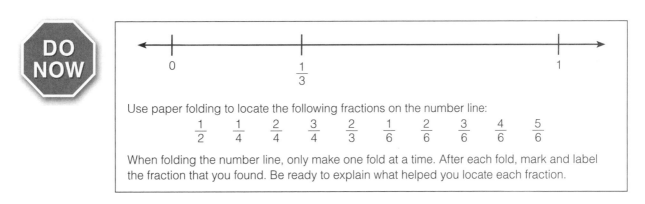

Figure 3.21: Unitizing with a linear model task.

Visit **go.solution-tree.com/mathematics** *for a free reproducible version of this figure.*

After completing the task, your number line should look something like the one in figure 3.22.

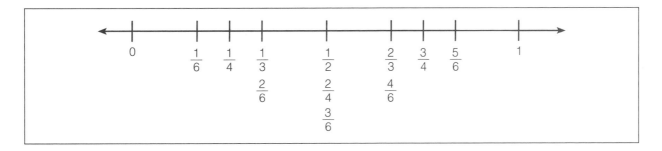

Figure 3.22: Completed number line.

The number line reinforces the idea that the length from 0 to 1 is the whole. Students may incorrectly think that the entire number line from arrow to arrow is the whole and find ½, for example, by matching the arrows on the number line instead of matching 0 and 1. Thus, the number line was purposefully made so that the distances the arrows are from 0 and 1, respectively, are not equal; otherwise students could get the correct answer from lining the arrows up, not realizing that this method is incorrect.

When folding the paper, you explore several fraction concepts. For example, to find ¼, you needed to find ½ of the distance from 0 to ½, and to find ⅙, you needed to find ½ of the distance from 0 to ⅓. When finding ¾, you may have folded to find ½ of the distance from ½ to 1, knowing that ¾ was halfway between ½ and 1.

Another concept is that the location of the fraction on the number line is how far away that fraction is from 0, with 1 being the whole. Problems like this also introduce equivalent fractions, as you see that ½, ²⁄₄, and ³⁄₆; ⅓ and ²⁄₆; and ⅔ and ⁴⁄₆ are located the same distance away from 0 on the number line. This task allows these fraction concepts to be linked together as the number line is developed.

Creating Equivalent Fractions

Equivalence concepts are important because they lay the foundation for recognizing equivalent fractions when finding common denominators for fraction addition and subtraction (see chapter 4). These ideas start with partitioning, as seen from the example in figure 3.4 (page 69) when two groups of ¼ equals ²⁄₄, which is equivalent to ½. They are further explored when unitizing with fractions on a number line, as evidenced from the paper folding activity (see figure 3.22, page 79), where ½, ²⁄₄, and ³⁄₆ are equivalent because they are equidistant from 0. Finally, these ideas are solidified as students work directly with equivalent fractions. So far, the examples to this point have focused on area models (circles, rectangles, and pattern blocks), set models (two-color counters), and linear models (number lines), with equivalence in the background. To place equivalence in the foreground, we present problems requiring the fraction kit (described in figure 3.23). Before working with these problems, make the fraction kit yourself so that you can solve the problems as intended.

Fraction Kit

Use 9 in. × 12 in. construction paper. You will need two sheets of red and one sheet of each of the following colors:

- Blue
- Orange
- Yellow
- Green

When folding, only use "hamburger" folds, with folds parallel to the shorter side. Do not use "hotdog" folds.

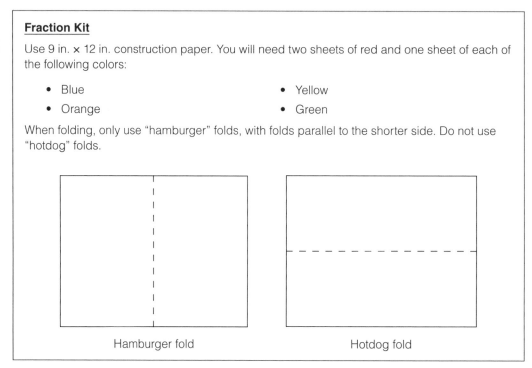

Hamburger fold   Hotdog fold

Do the following with each color:

- Red—Leave as-is.
- Blue—Fold and tear in two equal pieces.
- Orange—Fold and tear in two equal pieces. Fold and tear each of those pieces in two equal pieces.
- Yellow—Fold and tear in two equal pieces. Fold and tear each of those pieces in two equal pieces and repeat.
- Green—Fold and tear in two equal pieces. Fold and tear each of those pieces in two equal pieces and repeat twice.

When you are finished, your kit should look like this:

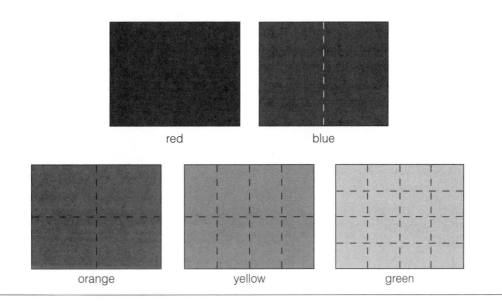

red   blue

orange   yellow   green

Figure 3.23: Fraction kit instructions.

*Visit **go.solution-tree.com/mathematics** for a free reproducible version of this figure.*

Using the fraction kit, take some time to explore the problems presented in figure 3.24.

1. If the red piece is the whole, what fraction is represented by five yellow pieces?
2. A student looked at a red whole covered with one blue piece, one orange piece, and two yellow pieces and said that one yellow piece is equal to ¼ of the whole. What might be the student's misconception?
3. How many ways can you use just one fraction kit to make 2 ½?
4. If a green piece is ¼, what is the whole?

Figure 3.24: Reasoning with the fraction kit.

When answering the questions, you should have seen that the whole can change and does not necessarily have to be the red sheet. For example, in problem 3 of figure 3.24, one way to make 2½ is to use a blue piece as the whole so that 2½ is represented by two blue pieces and an orange piece. In problem 4, if the green piece represents ¼, four of them will represent 1, which is the same size as the orange piece. Thus, when using the fraction kits with your students, you can have them explore different fractions and different wholes by varying the color for the whole. For this reason and for other reasons introduced in chapter 4, you should not label the fraction pieces with fraction names or symbols.

Now that you have explored the fraction kit, use it to focus on equivalent fractions. For the purposes of the activities in figure 3.25, the red piece will be used as the whole. Each activity can be explored with one to three people. Each person should use his or her own fraction kit.

Fraction Kit Activities

Make a game cube with the following fractions written one on each side:

$$\frac{1}{2} \qquad \frac{1}{4} \qquad \frac{1}{8} \qquad \frac{1}{8} \qquad \frac{1}{16} \qquad \frac{1}{16}$$

Activity 1: Cover the Red

1. Use the fraction game cube and fraction kits. Each person needs his or her own fraction kit.

2. Starting with the red as the whole, take turns tossing the cube and placing the corresponding piece on the red sheet.

3. Continue doing this until the red sheet is covered exactly (with no overlap).

4. While covering, exchanges must be made for a bigger color if this can be done. For example, if you toss ¹⁄₁₆ on each of your first two turns, you must exchange ²⁄₁₆, or two greens, in for ⅛, or one yellow. You will continue doing this until your board is covered with another red piece.

5. If a toss cannot be carried out, then toss again.

6. If playing with more than one person, the first person to cover the red with another red is the winner.

Activity 2: Uncover the Red

1. Begin with one red covering the other red whole game board.

2. Toss the fraction cube and remove the amount that is tossed. Exchanges must be made to remove the exact amount. For example, if you toss ¼ on your first turn, you must exchange a blue for two oranges then remove one orange.

3. Continue doing this until the red sheet is uncovered.

4. If a toss cannot be carried out, then toss again.

Figure 3.25: Fraction kit activities.

Which Mathematical Practices did you engage in during these activities? The fraction kit activities support engagement in Mathematical Practice 7, "Look for and make use of structure," and Mathematical Practice 8, "Look for and express regularity in repeated reasoning." In addition, if you record the trades you are making numerically, such as "⁴⁄₁₆ = ¼" instead of "four greens is equal to one orange," engagement in Mathematical Practice 4, "Model with mathematics," is supported. These activities can be used to lead into understanding the algorithm $\frac{a}{b} = \frac{n \times a}{n \times b}$. Examine equivalent trades that can be made with the fraction kits (see figure 3.26).

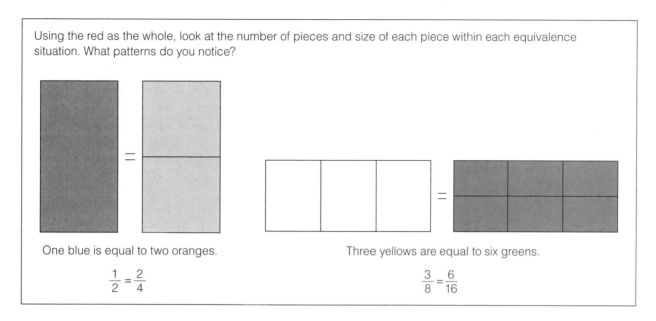

Using the red as the whole, look at the number of pieces and size of each piece within each equivalence situation. What patterns do you notice?

One blue is equal to two oranges.

$$\frac{1}{2} = \frac{2}{4}$$

Three yellows are equal to six greens.

$$\frac{3}{8} = \frac{6}{16}$$

Figure 3.26: Equivalence with the fraction kit.

You can see in the equivalence situations that the number of pieces increases as the size of each piece decreases. Looking at the first equivalence, one blue is equal to two oranges, you see that one orange is half the size of one blue. It takes twice as many oranges to fill the space needed for one blue. Similarly, when going from three yellows to six greens, each green is half the size of one yellow, thus you need twice as many greens as yellows to fill the same space.

If you look at the fraction each color is worth in terms of the red whole, you started with ½ with the blue. You need twice as many orange pieces, thus you multiply 2 × ½. But wait, because at the same time, the orange pieces are half the size of the blue piece, so you need to multiply by ½. Multiplying by 2 while simultaneously multiplying by ½ is like multiplying by ²⁄₂. Therefore, to go from one blue to two oranges you multiplied ²⁄₂ × ½. This results in a product of ²⁄₄. So the two orange pieces represent ²⁄₄. You used the same process when going from three yellows to six greens. You start with ³⁄₈ and need twice as many pieces, thus 2 × ³⁄₈. The size of each yellow is cut in half, thus you multiplied by ½. Therefore, you multiplied ²⁄₂ × ³⁄₈, which is equal to ⁶⁄₁₆ when going from three yellows to six greens.

How would you use this reasoning to explain how ¼ = ⁴⁄₁₆? Using the fraction kit and the red as the whole, how are you going to represent ¼ and ⁴⁄₁₆? The ¼ is represented by one orange; ⁴⁄₁₆ is represented by four greens. Explain the algorithm now to go from ¼ to ⁴⁄₁₆. When doing this, you can see that it takes four times as many green as orange; therefore you would multiply 4 × ¼. Since the green is ¼ of the orange, you would also multiply by ¼. This can be represented symbolically as ⁴⁄₄ × ¼ = ⁴⁄₁₆.

Comparing Fractions

Fraction comparison requires the examination of two or more fractions at the same time. When solving problems involving fraction operations, students should make use of the relative size of fractions. They should also work to understand fractions as quantities to estimate and then check the reasonableness of their solutions (see chapter 4). Before reading further, compare the following sets of fractions (see figure 3.27, page 84).

Without dividing to find decimals, determine which fraction is greater:

1. $\frac{3}{7}$ and $\frac{5}{8}$ 2. $\frac{4}{7}$ and $\frac{4}{9}$

3. $\frac{9}{10}$ and $\frac{5}{4}$ 4. $\frac{3}{8}$ and $\frac{5}{8}$

5. $\frac{6}{7}$ and $\frac{8}{9}$

Figure 3.27: Fraction comparison problems.

What strategy did you use to compare the fractions? Perhaps you started by drawing pictures only to see that the pictures for these particular fractions were too difficult to draw to compare. Was your strategy based on making sense of the fractions as numbers or based more on rote procedures? If you solved problem 1, for example, by using the method shown in figure 3.28 to determine that ⅝ was larger, you were using a rote procedure that is often used without understanding.

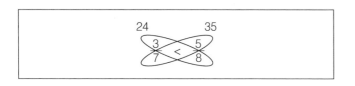

Figure 3.28: Cross multiplying to compare fractions.

In this process, 7 × 5 is multiplied to get 35, and 8 × 3 is multiplied to get 24. Because 35 is greater than 24, ⅝ is greater than ³⁄₇. This use of rote and poorly understood procedures is not a goal for instruction in grades 3–5. Although students will be able to get the correct answer with this procedure, it is likely that they will not know what this procedure means or why it works. In addition, they will not be making sense of fractions as numbers, since they are just applying a learned procedure to find the solution.

Placing comparison situations in context will allow more sophisticated ways of reasoning to develop as the fractions will now have meaning. Recall that when fractions are presented out of context, they are assumed to be from the same whole, so contexts should be considered based on this assumption. Contemplate, for example, the contexts presented in figure 3.29. Solve each problem before reading further.

Use reasoning strategies to solve each of the following problems. Avoid the use of rote procedures such as finding common denominators.

1. Salima and Nicola are racing their bicycles. Salima is ³⁄₇ of the way to the finish line, and Nicola is ⅔ of the way to the finish line. Who is closer to the finish line? How do you know?

2. Marc and Larry each bought the same type of energy bar. Marc has ⅛ of his energy bar left. Larry has ¹⁄₁₀ of his energy bar left. Who has more energy bar left? How do you know?

3. Valerie and Scott each bought a small apple pie at the grocery store. Valerie ate ⅝ of her pie, and Scott ate ⅞ of his pie. Who ate the most pie? How do you know?

4. Giselle and Paige each bought a small pizza. Giselle ate ⅚ of her pizza, and Paige ate ⅞ of her pizza. Who ate more pizza? How do you know?

Figure 3.29: Problems involving fraction comparison in context.

In problem 1 of figure 3.29, you may have found that Nicola is closer to the finish line, but how do you know? You know that Nicola is more than halfway to the finish line. What about Salima? Salima is less than halfway to the finish line. The halfway mark is the benchmark you used to compare the two fractions. Because $3/7$ is less than half, and $2/3$ is more than half, $2/3$ is greater than $3/7$.

In the second problem, who has more energy bar left? You know that both Marc and Larry have one piece left or a common numerator of one. Because the denominators are different, they each have different size pieces—so who has the larger piece? The more pieces something is broken into, the smaller the pieces become. Because Marc's energy bar was only broken into eight pieces compared to Larry's ten pieces, Marc's pieces will be larger. Thus, Marc has more of his energy bar left.

Problem 3 may seem obvious that Scott ate more. When answering how you know, you again need to refer to the number of pieces and size of each piece. Unlike problem 2, where you had the same number of pieces, you now have the same size pieces. Because Scott ate more same-size pieces than Valerie, $7/8$ of a pie is greater than $5/8$ of a pie.

Problem 4 is the most difficult of the four problems. Rather than comparing how much each person ate, you should focus on how much each person has *left*. Giselle has $1/6$ of a pizza left, and Paige has $1/8$ of a pizza left. Using the same strategy as for problem 2, you know that $1/6$ is greater than $1/8$. Giselle has more pizza left over, meaning that she *ate* less pizza than Paige. Thus, $7/8$ is greater than $5/6$ because there is less left over in $7/8$ than in $5/6$.

To recap the strategies introduced through this task, problem 1 of figure 3.29 used the idea of a benchmark. Problems 2 and 3 used reasoning with the same number of pieces or common numerators (problem 2) and same size pieces or common denominators (problem 3). We purposefully listed these three problems before problem 4 so that more difficult reasoning could be developed. For example, reasoning with common numerators was incorporated in problem 2 and applied in a different way in problem 4. Thus, you need to use the reasoning you discovered in problem 2 for problem 4. Problems 1 through 3 require you to compare the fractions provided in the problems directly, whereas in problem 4, you need to compare what was missing from each fraction. Had problem 4 been presented first, you may not have developed the reasoning strategies as intended. Go back to the problems in figure 3.27 and re-solve the problems using these reasoning strategies. You may find that you are able to think about the fractions as quantities and reason in ways that you normally would not when just applying rote procedures.

After reasoning strategies are used to compare fractions, they can be applied to ordering situations where more than two fractions are compared. For example, solve the problem in figure 3.30.

DO NOW

Order the following fractions from least to greatest using the reasoning strategies you just explored. Be prepared to justify the position of each fraction.

$$\frac{4}{5} \quad \frac{9}{8} \quad \frac{5}{11} \quad \frac{4}{7} \quad \frac{5}{6}$$

Figure 3.30: Ordering fractions task.

When ordering the fractions from least to greatest, which is least and how do you know? You may have found that $5/11$ is least. Likewise you may have found that $9/8$ is greatest. With both of these fractions, what was the strategy you used? A common response to ordering these two fractions is using a benchmark. The fraction ⁵⁄₁₁ is the least because it is the only fraction less than ½, whereas ⁹⁄₈ is the greatest because it is the only fraction greater than 1.

Knowing that ⁴⁄₅, ⁴⁄₇, and ⁵⁄₆ go in between ⁵⁄₁₁ and ⁹⁄₈, what strategies are you going to use to order them? What do you notice about ⁴⁄₅ and ⁴⁄₇? They both have a common numerator of 4. How will you order them? Because fifths are bigger than sevenths, ⁴⁄₅ is greater than ⁴⁄₇. The only fraction left to compare now is ⁵⁄₆. Will you compare ⁵⁄₆ with ⁴⁄₅ or ⁴⁄₇ and why? It makes more sense to compare ⁵⁄₆ with ⁴⁄₅ because, based on estimation, they both *seem* closer to a whole. They are both one piece away from 1, so that will help you determine a useful strategy to use. Because ⁴⁄₅ has ⅕ missing and ⁵⁄₆ has ⅙ missing, and ⅕ is greater than ⅙, which fraction is greater? Because ⁵⁄₆ has less missing, it is greater than ⁴⁄₅. Because ⁵⁄₆ is greater than ⁴⁄₅, you also know that it is greater than ⁴⁄₇. Thus, the order of the fractions from least to greatest is: ⁵⁄₁₁, ⁴⁄₇, ⁴⁄₅, ⁵⁄₆, ⁹⁄₈.

As you used strategies to compare and order fractions, you were engaged in Mathematical Practice 7, "Look for and make use of structure." We gave you problems that allowed you to see the structure of how fractions are ordered. To engage students in the same process, instruction should focus on problems in context first. In thinking about the first fraction comparison task presented to you, you likely used a rote procedure to solve the problems without reasoning about the fractions as quantities. This is similar to what students do when given problems devoid of context first. They develop a solution strategy that they know will get them the correct answer, but they don't often understand why the method works. Contrast this to the reasoning used to solve the problems in context. Each problem elicited a different reasoning strategy. More formal names for those strategies are *comparing to a benchmark, common numerators, common denominators,* and an application of *common numerators.* The fractions had meaning, thus you could think about them more as quantities and reason through what the numerator and denominator represent. After the strategies were developed, you then applied them to an ordering situation out of context. By using the reasoning strategies, the order for the fractions was probably found more quickly than had you used a rote procedure instead. Thus, the contexts became a way for you to conceptualize what the fractions represent so that you could transfer that meaning on to new fractions and more difficult situations, reinforcing the development of procedural fluency with ordering fractions.

The Classroom

Now that you have explored fraction concepts on your own, turn your attention to what this looks like in the classroom. The videos in this chapter provide ways to introduce fraction comparison to your students. The first video focuses on comparing fractions with the same numerator or the same denominator. In this video, students are asked to compare two different pairs of fractions to determine which fraction is greater. We encourage you to watch the video in its entirety before continuing further.

www.solution-tree.com/Comparing
_Fractions_Using_a_Benchmark

Now that you have had the opportunity to watch students actively engage in developing fraction comparison strategies, what are your thoughts? Consider how the teacher's goal of the lesson was supported with questioning and discussion. What kinds of questions were posed? What types of comparison strategies did the students discover? The teacher set the stage for the students to explore strategies that showcase students' conceptual understanding of comparing fractions. The teacher's intent is to use layers of facilitation (I facilitate the whole class, I facilitate small groups, I facilitate individuals) effectively to engage the whole class, small groups, and individuals in the learning experience.

Notice how the students explore the fractions in their groups to develop methods for comparing fractions. This is important: the students develop reasoning strategies to compare fractions instead of performing procedures modeled by the teacher, such as focusing on common denominators or cross multiplying. During this exploration, the students are able to generate several strategies to compare. One student suggests using models by drawing eighths and shading ⅝ in one model and ⅜ in another model to compare the two fractions. Another explains that both fractions have a denominator of 8 and that since 5 is greater than 3, ⅝ is greater than ⅜. When solving the second part of the task, one student suggests comparing ⁴⁄₉ and ⅘ to one to determine that ⅘ is greater. It is here that the teacher introduces the idea of comparing to a benchmark fraction.

It is important to note that the teacher's goal is to have the students develop a benchmark strategy for comparing fractions, specifically with using a benchmark of ½. However, the teacher is careful to not introduce this strategy until after several students share their thinking. Had the teacher introduced comparing to ½ first, students might have been quick to disregard other strategies and not develop as many strategies for comparing as they did. Although the goal of the lesson is for students to develop an understanding of comparing fractions with benchmarks, this is saved for the end of the discussion with both parts of the task.

In the second video, students are comparing fractions that have the same numerator as well as fractions with different numerators and denominators. Please watch the video in its entirety before proceeding.

  www.solution-tree.com/Comparing
_Fractions_by_Focusing_on_Numerators

Now that you have had the opportunity to watch students actively engage in developing fraction comparison strategies, what are your thoughts? Consider the tools provided for the students and ways discussion was facilitated.

Perhaps you noticed that when the class is discussing their solutions for comparing ⅕ to ⅙, not all students agree on the same answer. The teacher facilitates the discussion by having the students who think ⅙ is greater explain their reasoning first. Although ⅙ is incorrect, the teacher does not tell the students that this is incorrect. Rather, she asks someone in the class to respond. This teaching strategy supports students to engage in Mathematical Practice 3, "Construct viable arguments and critique the reasoning of others." When the student responds and then provides reasoning for why ⅕ is the correct answer, the student who had initially said ⅙ changes his answer. The teacher does not need to correct the students who have incorrect solutions. Instead, by listening to others in the class, students are able to determine the correct solution on their own.

Notice that students have fraction circles to help them solve the problems. The first problem of comparing ⅕ and ⅙ is easily solved with fraction circles as both fifths and sixths are available. However, the second problem of comparing ⅚ to ⁶/₇ cannot be solved with the fraction circles, as sevenths are not available. It is important to note that this is one way to push students' thinking forward—that is, limiting the capacity or availability of manipulatives to solve given problems. Presenting problems that cannot be solved using familiar methods requires students to develop other strategies to further deepen students' understanding of a topic.

You may have noticed that the first problem requires students to think about the amount each person ate, whereas the second requires them to think about how much is left over. Though similar reasoning is needed for both problems, students have to think backward with the second problem. You may overhear the error one student makes while the class is working in groups on the Giselle and Paige problem. The student explains to his group that Giselle ate more because sixths are bigger than sevenths. Only paying attention to the numerator, or in this case the denominator, is a common error students make when working with fractions. When leading the whole-class discussion, the teacher corrects this error by asking the students a question about the size of each person's leftover piece. The class then determines that Paige ate more because her leftover piece is smaller.

The goal of the tasks in both videos is for students to develop reasoning strategies for comparing fractions. How can your mathematics lessons engage students in making deep and meaningful connections to the content? Such engagement will be marked by the instructional choices you make to increase student involvement and sense making during mathematics.

TQE Process

At this point, it may be helpful to watch the second video again (page 87). Pay close attention to the tasks, questioning, and opportunities to collect evidence of student learning.

The TQE process can help you frame your observations. Teachers who have a deep understanding of the mathematics they teach:

- Select appropriate *tasks* to support identified learning goals
- Facilitate productive *questioning* during instruction to engage students in Mathematical Practices
- Collect and use student *evidence* in the formative assessment process during instruction

The teacher chose two *tasks* for this lesson, and the order she uses them in is crucial to meeting the lesson target. The first task provides the prerequisite understanding for the second task. The first task is relatively easy, while the second task is much more difficult. Once students make sense of the common numerator strategy with unit fractions, they are able to apply it to fractions that can be described as being one away from a whole like ⅚ and ⁶/₇. If the teacher had selected comparing ⅚ and ⁶/₇ as the initial task in the lesson, the students would likely have engaged in an unproductive struggle resulting in the teacher needing to provide too much guidance. When introducing the second problem, the teacher tells the class that she has "a challenge problem" for them. Notice that the teacher does not add "and here is a hint on how to start." Rather she places the responsibility of solving the problem on the students. The teacher's role is that of a supporter and facilitator for the students. This coupled with opportunities for students to explore the problem on their own, work in groups, and have tools available supports their engagement in Mathematical Practice 1, "Make sense of problems and persevere in solving them."

The teacher is purposeful with the *questions* she uses as well as with which students she calls on during the whole-class discussions. During the first problem she is careful to have students with both correct and incorrect answers explain their solutions. Had the teacher only called on students who were correct, students who were incorrect may not have fully understood why their thinking was incorrect. In addition, the teacher pays attention to what methods individual students and small groups are using to solve the problems; she calls on students who solved the problem with different methods to ensure that the whole-class discussion includes a variety of strategies for solving the problem. The teacher asks questions in a way that guides students to the correct solution as opposed to telling students the correct solution.

The students provide *evidence* of how they are thinking about the problems as they participate in the conversation. It is clear that some students still rely on fraction manipulatives to make sense of comparison strategies while others are able to reason using context. The teacher uses the formative assessment process throughout the lesson by listening to student responses and using questioning to support student sense making. As the students share their responses, she is able to keep track of this evidence and provide follow-up questions and responses that support the learning goals of the lesson.

The Response

Many difficulties students have with fractions stem from incorrectly applying whole-number ideas to fractions, such as $\frac{1}{6} > \frac{1}{5}$ because $6 > 5$, or that $\frac{4}{8} > \frac{3}{4}$ because $4 > 3$ and $8 > 4$. Other difficulties stem from having limited experiences with fractions. For example, students who have only used fractions in part-whole situations will say that fractions such as $\frac{5}{3}$ do not exist because you cannot take five parts when you only have three parts total. Conceptual errors, such as not understanding the importance of the whole or the need for equal-size parts, are less likely to be overcome until conceptual problems are presented during instruction. Furthermore, students often struggle with fractions because, like place value, how a digit is placed matters and students have to learn this. For instance, consider the digits three and seven. For whole numbers, 37 is different from 73. Likewise, for fractions, $\frac{3}{7}$ is different from $\frac{7}{3}$. Guiding students to notice the positioning of digits and understanding of fractional value based on this positioning is important for students' understanding of fractions.

When learning about fractions through rote memorization, problems can look like the following (see figure 3.31).

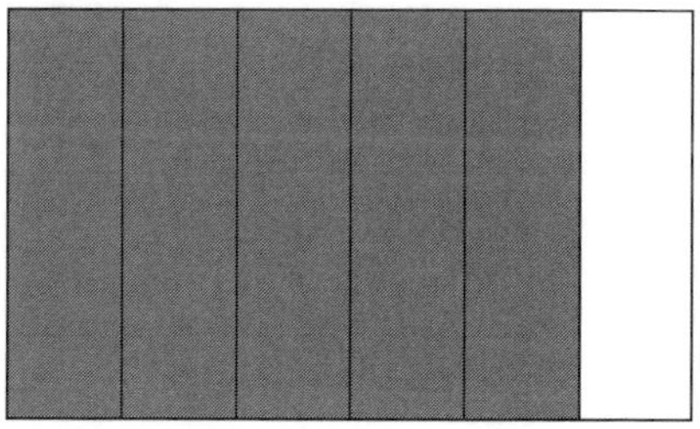

Name the fraction shaded.

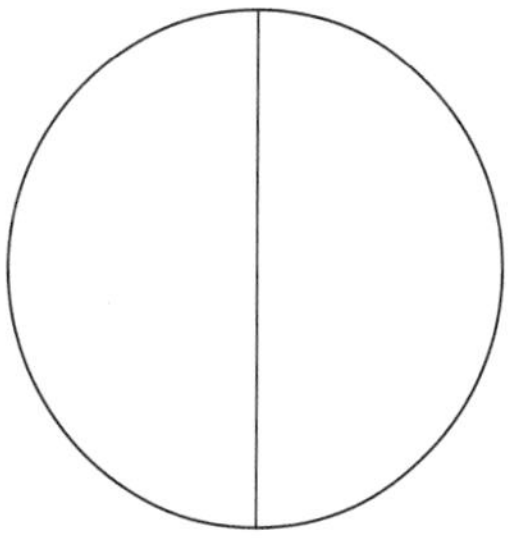

Shade ½

Figure 3.31: Naming fractions by shading.

These problems emphasize fractions without understanding since students only have to count how many pieces are shaded and determine how many pieces there are total or count how many pieces there are total and shade in how many are represented by the fraction symbol. In addition, the whole for each problem is given, thus students will not need to think about the fraction in terms of a whole. Problems such as these are not likely to help students overcome errors with fractions, as they can use counting with whole numbers to find the correct solution.

In some cases, students' errors can be linked back to their difficulties with whole numbers. For example, students struggling with understanding how ³⁄₆ is equivalent to ½ may not understand that 6 divided by 2 equals 3, which means that 3 is half of 6. If students struggle with unitizing, for example understanding how ¹⁰⁄₁₀ or 1 is ten groups of ¹⁄₁₀, they may also struggle with understanding place value concepts such as 10 tenths equals 1.

How can you tailor instruction to develop students' understandings of fractions as quantities and overcome their procedural and conceptual errors? One way to do this is through conceptually based problems presented in context, such as those provided throughout this chapter. By giving students problems where the fractions have meaning and requiring work with a variety of models to find the solution, students will develop an understanding of fractions in terms of wholes and equal-size parts. The shape of area models should vary. In other words, avoid using squares, rectangles, and circles only. When students use only these shapes, they have difficulty applying fraction concepts when shapes other than these are used. In addition, numbers should be varied so that students gain experiences with fractions less than, equal to, and greater than 1 as these concepts will provide them with a foundation for conceptualizing fraction operations. By knowing the progression for how fraction understandings develop, you can purposefully design instruction so that students continually build from what they know to develop more sophisticated ways of reasoning and thinking about fractions that might not otherwise develop if they were to just learn rote procedures.

Reflections

1. What do you feel are the key points in this chapter?

2. What challenges might you face when implementing the key ideas from this chapter? How will you overcome them?

3. What are the important features for developing an understanding of fraction concepts, and how will you ensure your instruction embeds the support needed for these features?

4. Select a recent lesson you have taught or observed focused on fraction concepts. Relate this lesson to the TQE process.

5. What changes will you make to your planning and instruction based on what you read and considered from this chapter?

CHAPTER 4

Fraction Operations

This chapter focuses on mathematics for teaching addition, subtraction, multiplication, and division of fractions with depth. You can develop students' fraction operation sense by embedding operations in context through word problems. To do so, first use visual models to solve the problems, then represent the contexts and solutions with equations, and finally, make sense of procedures for solving the equations more efficiently. Check the results through estimation to be sure solutions are reasonable.

The Challenge

The initial task in this chapter (see figure 4.1) begins this process by providing word problems to be solved with visual models. These three problems may be challenging if you have not previously explored representing fraction operations with drawings. The key is to act out the context of each problem with pictures. The discussion that follows will be much more meaningful if you make an attempt to solve each problem using a picture and then write the situation equation before proceeding.

Use a visual model to solve each problem so that the drawing represents the context of the problem. Do not simplify your answer. Then write an equation to model the situation.

1. There is ⅔ of a pie left over. Jessica ate ¾ of the leftover pie. How much of a whole pie did Jessica eat?

2. Tisa brought ¾ of a pan of brownies to school. Her friends ate ⅔ of what she brought. How much of a pan of brownies did her friends eat?

3. The park measured ⅔ of a mile by ¾ of a mile. What fraction of a square mile is the park?

Figure 4.1: Fraction multiplication in context problems.

How did you begin to solve the first problem? What shape did you use? How did you identify the part of the pie that was left over? You likely drew a circle partitioned into three equal parts and shaded two of them to indicate the pie that was left over, as illustrated in figure 4.2.

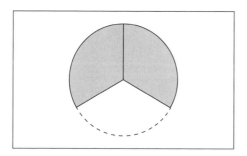

If you drew a rectangle to represent the pie, you are not representing the context of the problem with your drawing (unless you have an unusual pie dish!). Research indicates that students are more likely to use visual models like drawings or manipulatives that match the context of the problem when they are first making sense of an operation with fractions (Dixon, Andreasen, Roy, Wheeldon, & Tobias, 2011). As a teacher, you should support this process with your models as well.

Figure 4.2: Two-thirds of a pie.

So you have your circle with ⅔ shaded. Now you need to determine how much Jessica ate. She ate ¾ of what is represented by the shaded region. The two shaded pieces need to be partitioned so that ¾ of the two pieces can be determined. The most direct route is to cut each of those two pieces into two equal pieces, making four shaded pieces as illustrated in figure 4.3. If you partitioned each third into four equal pieces, you just might be forcing the picture to follow a procedure that mirrors the algorithm by creating 12 equal pieces in the whole like you do when you multiply the 3 and the 4 in the denominators of the factors in the problem.

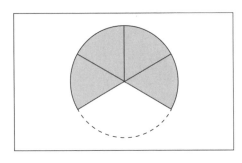

Figure 4.3: Partitioning the ⅔-size pieces to make four equal pieces.

Finding ¾ of the four shaded pieces is straightforward, but how do you name those three pieces? They need to be named in terms of the original pie. The third piece of the pie—the one that was already missing to start—needs to be thought of as two equal pieces as well. This is a place where errors are often made, and you need to remember the importance of connecting the concept of fraction—that all of the pieces in the whole have to be the same size—to this context. That means the entire pie needs to be described as equal parts—in this case six equal pieces—and Jessica ate ³⁄₆ of the whole pie, as illustrated in figure 4.4. You should leave the result in this form rather than changing it to ½, as the directions indicate that you should not simplify your result. These directions are important to follow when using visual models to solve fraction problems because if you simplify the fraction, it is no longer directly representative of your picture.

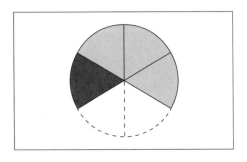

Figure 4.4: Three-sixths of the original pie is eaten.

The drawing in figure 4.4 clearly represents the context of the problem. You began with ⅔ of a pie and partitioned the two-thirds-sized pieces into two equal-sized pieces each so that there would be four equal-sized pieces. Then you shaded to indicate what ¾ of that leftover pie would be in terms of the original whole pie and determined that Jessica ate ³⁄₆ of the original pie. How do you represent this in equation form? How do you model this mathematically? Because you are finding a part of a part of a whole, you are multiplying. You know that ⅔ and ¾ need to be multiplied, but in what order? You learned in chapter 2 that although the product is the same, the order matters when you want to preserve the context of the problem, such as with situation equations. Are you multiplying ⅔ × ¾ or ¾ × ⅔?

Many teachers (and students) are quick to respond that the problem is represented by ⅔ × ¾ because ⅔ is the first factor mentioned in the word problem. However, if you think of finding groups of objects, as discussed in chapter 2, you see that you are finding a part of a group of a part of a whole. Two-thirds represents the part of the whole so you are finding ¾ of ⅔ or ¾ × ⅔. The equation to model this problem is ¾ × ⅔ = ³⁄₆. Some may model this situation as ¾ × ⅔ = ⁶⁄₁₂, but this might be overemphasizing the standard algorithm of multiplying the numerators then the denominators. The product in an equation does not need to be the result of applying the algorithm. You found the product by showing your reasoning through a picture, and if your picture resulted in ³⁄₆ of the pie being shaded, it is appropriate to record the situation equation as ¾ × ⅔ = ³⁄₆.

You may want to revisit the second problem in the task before continuing. The discussion regarding the first problem might change your response to the second. It's important to remember that experiences with the curriculum should alter how you think about future work. This is an example of moving along a learning trajectory and how carefully selected tasks and experiences with those tasks move learning forward.

In the second problem, Tisa brings ¾ of a pan of brownies to school. You probably shaded ¾ of a rectangle in a way similar to one of the two illustrations in figure 4.5—both represent the problem context. The first illustration will be used for the purpose of this discussion.

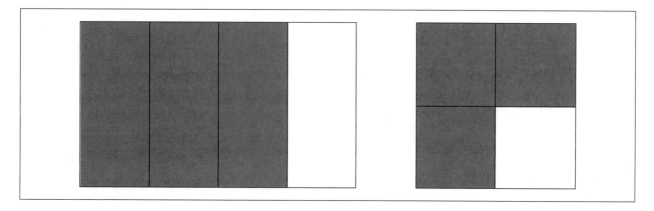

Figure 4.5: Three-fourths of a pan of brownies illustrated in two different ways.

At this point, you can differentiate between "drawing an algorithm" by following a set of procedures for visually representing fraction multiplication versus "acting out the problem" using drawings. If you partitioned each of the fourths into three equal pieces to make twelve pieces in all, you might be following a procedure, thus losing some of the value in using visual representations to build fraction operation sense. Looking at the drawings in figure 4.5, you realize that there are three pieces shaded and Tisa's friends ate ⅔ of that shaded region, or two of the three shaded pieces. It is enough to identify those two shaded pieces in terms of the whole pan of brownies to solve this problem as illustrated in figure 4.6.

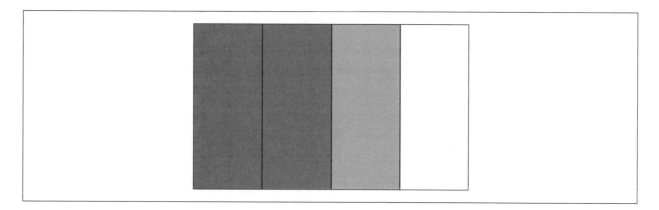

Figure 4.6: Two-thirds of ³/₄ of the pan of brownies.

With this problem, the result is represented by ²/₄ of a pan of brownies, and the operation is multiplication, since you are finding parts of parts of objects. The equation would again include one of these two expressions: ⅔ × ¾ or ¾ × ⅔. This situation describes finding ⅔ of ¾ of a pan of brownies, so ⅔ × ¾ = ⁶⁄₁₂ is the situation equation.

The third problem describes the portion of a square mile covered by a park. The visual should represent a fraction of a square, with the square designating the square mile and the darker shaded region designating the park, as illustrated in figure 4.7.

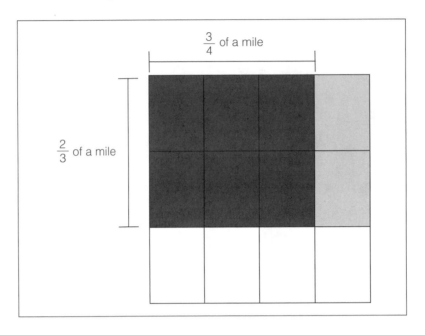

Figure 4.7: A park measuring ²/₃ of a mile by ¾ of a mile.

Note that because this problem describes a portion of an area and the entire region is a square, either dimension can serve as the base or height. Therefore, the equation to represent the situation can be either ⅔ × ¾ = ⁶⁄₁₂ or ¾ × ⅔ = ⁶⁄₁₂. The illustration would be slightly different if ¾ of the entire square mile was shaded first and then ⅔ of that shaded portion was then shaded. The problem could also be solved by shading ⅔ of the entire square mile and then ¾ of the entire square mile and finally using the area included in both shaded portions to determine the area of the park. Regardless of the slight differences in shading, the product for this situation is representative of the illustration as well as the result of performing the standard algorithm for multiplying fractions.

Which Mathematical Practices did you engage with as you explored this task? For many of you, it was likely Mathematical Practice 1, "Make sense of problems and persevere in solving them." We presented the task in a way that probably was unfamiliar to you. First, you needed to make sense of using visual models for solving fraction multiplication problems, and then you may have engaged in a productive struggle as you worked to solve them. However, you were also engaged in Mathematical Practice 4, "Model with mathematics"—this Mathematical Practice refers to "mathematizing" a situation. In each case, you began with a word problem and modeled it visually as well as with an equation. You "mathematized" the situation. You saw that how the problem was modeled depended on the context of the problem, even though the product was the same in each case. Because of this, how the problems were ordered was important; the progression helped develop understanding.

The third problem in the task most closely represents the standard algorithm, reinforcing the need to order tasks intentionally. If the goal of instruction is to move from conceptual understanding to procedural fluency, as is our position, then it would make sense to provide students with experiences visually representing solutions to problems like the first two in this task before introducing them to problems like the third one.

The Progression

The development of fraction operations in this book is influenced by our position that conceptual understanding must precede procedural fluency to build mathematical proficiency. Fraction operation sense builds on the foundation of a deep understanding of fraction concepts, as described in chapter 3. Following is a progression for the development of fraction operation sense with an understanding that a progression for fraction concepts was already followed.

- Make sense of adding and subtracting fractions with like denominators.
- Make sense of multiplying fractions by whole numbers.
- Make sense of adding and subtracting fractions with unlike denominators.
- Make sense of multiplying fractions and mixed numbers.
- Make sense of dividing whole numbers by unit fractions and unit fractions by nonzero whole numbers.
- Make sense of dividing fractions and mixed numbers.

The placement of topics within grades provides a window into how this content develops over time. Although topics related to fraction concepts are of focus in grade 3, it is in grade 4 that attention turns to fraction operations, thus we begin this progression in grade 4. Emphasis on fraction operations spans grades 4 through 6, and teachers can maintain coherence by connecting to earlier work with multiplication of whole numbers in grade 3.

Grade 4

Addition and subtraction with like denominators are explored with and without context in grade 4. The key is that students solve these problems with visual models rather than with the standard algorithm of adding the numerators and keeping the denominator. It might seem surprising that fraction multiplication is explored prior to adding and subtracting fractions with unlike denominators. However, it does make sense when it is linked back to how multiplication of whole numbers develops (see chapter 2). Multiplication of whole numbers is developed as repeated addition in grade 2 and ultimately as multiplication in grade 3. Similarly, fraction multiplication is developed as repeated addition of fractions in grade 4. This is why multiplication is limited to multiplying fractions by whole numbers like $3 \times \frac{1}{5}$. The problem $3 \times \frac{1}{5}$ can be thought of as three groups of $\frac{1}{5}$ or $\frac{1}{5} + \frac{1}{5} + \frac{1}{5}$ and can be computed using a visual model. Viewing multiplication in this way provides the link between adding fractions with like denominators and multiplication. This topic is developed further in grade 5.

Grade 5

In grade 5, work with addition and subtraction is extended to adding and subtracting fractions with unlike denominators. First, students solve problems with and without context using visual models and eventually using equations. As students solve fraction addition problems with visual models and record their results using equations, they see a pattern emerge. Once the fractions are described as equal parts of the same size whole through the process of finding like denominators, students simply need to combine the parts they have, which is indicated by the numerators of the fractions, to find the sum. Through exploration, they see that this pattern applies to fraction subtraction as well. Ultimately the goal is for students to add and subtract fractions with like and unlike denominators without the need for visual models but with understanding why the procedure they use works. Furthermore, they determine if their answers are reasonable. Estimating sums and differences is an excellent way to determine reasonableness of these solutions. Making estimates relies on an understanding of fraction concepts (see chapter 3). Students know which benchmark fractions are near the given fractions and can use mental computation to check the reasonableness of their responses (see the introduction).

Grade 5 students extend work with multiplication to multiplying fractions by fractions with and without context or equations. The task in figure 4.1 (page 91) provided opportunities for you to solve fraction multiplication word problems using visual models. You used an equation to represent the solution but not to determine the solution. Using an equation to solve typically means applying an algorithm—in this case, the algorithm of multiplying numerators and multiplying denominators to find the product of two fractions. Regardless of solution process, it is important to use estimation to check to see if the product is reasonable. For example, in the first word problem in figure 4.1, an answer of $\frac{3}{6}$, or $\frac{1}{2}$, is reasonable because $\frac{3}{4} \times \frac{2}{3}$ can be thought of as $\frac{3}{4}$ of a group of $\frac{2}{3}$ of a whole, so it is less than a whole group of $\frac{2}{3}$ but more than half of a group of $\frac{2}{3}$. Therefore, a reasonable product would be between $\frac{1}{3}$ and $\frac{2}{3}$.

Finally, fifth-grade students are introduced to fraction division but only with two specific structures. Students divide:

1. Whole numbers by unit fractions (a unit fraction is a fraction with a numerator of 1), such as with $6 \div \frac{1}{3}$
2. Unit fractions by nonzero whole numbers (they cannot divide by 0 as this quotient is indeterminate), such as with $\frac{1}{4} \div 2$

Students encounter these structures with and without context and solve the problems using visual models or equations. Solving problems like these using equations provides an excellent opportunity to begin to make sense of the "invert and multiply" algorithm for dividing fractions. This algorithm is further developed in grade 6.

Grade 6

In grade 6, students extend the work they began in grade 5 to divide fractions by fractions with and without context using visual models or equations. Students connect their previous experiences to make sense of the "invert and multiply" algorithm. They might even explore the common denominator algorithm for dividing fractions. In any case, they use estimation and their understanding of division to check the reasonableness of their results.

Throughout the progression, emphasis is on reasoning and sense making. Much of what students encounter is presented in context, through word problems. When students use algorithms, they are able to explain why those algorithms work.

The Mathematics

How do students come to make sense of algorithms like "invert and multiply"? How do teachers? For both students and teachers, the efficiency of using "invert and multiply" does not outweigh the need for conceptual understanding of fractions and divisors. Here, you will unpack the mathematics of fraction operations, providing you the background necessary to teach this topic with depth, particularly by using context, manipulatives, and visuals to develop understanding of fraction operation algorithms.

Making Sense of Fraction Operations in Word Problems

Which should come first, computation or word problems? Our position is that instruction should lead with word problems as it did with whole-number operations. Initially, students make sense of word problems by acting them out, either with manipulatives, drawings, or mental images. After students solve problems in this manner, they can represent the process they followed with symbols and operations—much like you did with the problems in figure 4.1 (page 91). Eventually, students will be able to skip the step of acting out the problem and write the equation directly. At that point, students are well on their way to developing fraction operation sense. Consider the problems in figure 4.8. Solve them by acting them out, and think about how the operation is inherent in the action of the problem. You might also find it valuable to work with members of your collaborative team and compare your solution strategies.

Use drawings to solve the following problems. Record how you represented and solved each problem using equations.

1. Carmen had ½ of a yard of ribbon. How much more ribbon does she need so she will have ⅚ of a yard of ribbon altogether?

2. Julio bought ½ of a pound of sliced turkey. He made four sandwiches with the same amount of turkey on each sandwich. How much of a pound of turkey was on each sandwich?

3. Ming plans to make 3 batches of chocolate cookies. One batch calls for ¾ of a cup of cocoa. How much cocoa will she need to make the cookies?

4. Blake and Jordan each bought the same type of candy bar. Blake ate ¾ of his candy bar, and Jordan ate ⅝ of his. How much more candy did Blake eat than Jordan?

Figure 4.8: Fraction operation word problems.

The problems in figure 4.8 represent different operations. In the first problem, you know that Carmen starts with ½ of a yard of ribbon and ends with ⅚ of a yard of ribbon. The goal is to find out how much she needs to get to have ⅚ of a yard. The drawing in figure 4.9 (page 98) shows the ½ of a yard of ribbon she has to start and her goal of ⅚ of a yard of ribbon.

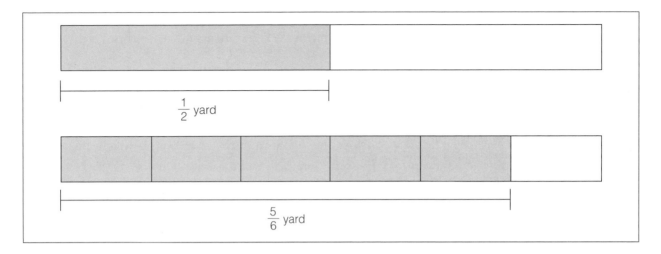

Figure 4.9: One-half yard and ⁵⁄₆ yard of ribbon.

The answer to this problem is described by what is needed to go from ½ of a yard to ⅚ of a yard. You know from your work with equivalent fractions that ½ of a yard of ribbon can be renamed as ³⁄₆ of a yard of ribbon. You can see from the drawing that if Carmen has ³⁄₆ of a yard of ribbon, she would need ²⁄₆ of a yard of ribbon more to reach her goal of ⅚ of a yard of ribbon (see figure 4.10). Although ²⁄₆ is equivalent to ⅓, it is not necessary to simplify the fraction at this point because the simplified form is not as clear in the picture.

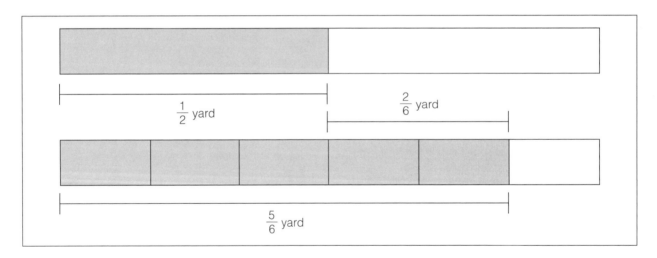

Figure 4.10: Carmen needs ²⁄₆ yard of ribbon.

The drawing is fairly straightforward, as is determining the answer. However, what situation equation would you use to represent the action in this problem? Recall from chapter 1 that while adults often think of problems in this form as subtraction problems, the structure of the problem is that of a join (change unknown) problem. The initial quantity is ½ of a yard, the change to the initial quantity is unknown, and the result is ⅚ of a yard. Therefore, the situation equation would be ½ + _____ = ⅚.

In the second problem, Julio needs to distribute his ½ of a pound of turkey evenly among four sandwiches. This is accomplished by further partitioning the ½ of a pound so that it is in four equal parts. You can use a rectangular drawing to illustrate this (see figure 4.11), where the large rectangle is one pound of turkey, so the shaded portion is ½ of a pound of turkey.

Now that there are four equal parts of turkey, the parts need to be named. Fractional parts are named as equal parts of a whole. In this case, the whole is the pound of turkey, or the largest rectangle in figure 4.11. Therefore, the remaining rectangle must be divided up into parts equal to the parts of turkey on each sandwich so that the amount of turkey on each sandwich can be described in terms of a fraction of a pound of turkey (see figure 4.12). The ½ of a pound of turkey was divided into four equal parts, so the other half of the pound of turkey also needs to be divided into four equal parts, making eight equal parts all together. Therefore, each sandwich will be made with ⅛ of a pound of turkey.

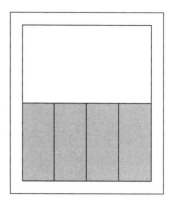

Figure 4.11: Sharing ½ pound of turkey among four sandwiches.

This problem is a sharing division problem (see chapter 2 for a discussion of word problem types for division). An equation to model this word problem is ½ ÷ 4 = ⅛. Because ½ of a pound of turkey was shared among four sandwiches, each sandwich was made with ⅛ of a pound of turkey. There was no need to rewrite this equation as a multiplication problem to solve it. The word problem helps you make sense of fraction division. In fact, word problems can help you and your students make sense of all fraction operations if you act them out.

Think of a word problem that would support measurement division. Recall from chapter 2 that when modeling sharing division with whole numbers you know the total and the number of groups but you seek the number of objects in each group. With measurement division you know the total and how much is in each group

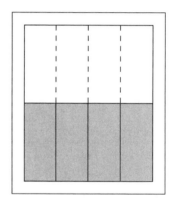

Figure 4.12: Each sandwich will have ⅛ pound of turkey.

and you seek the number of groups. When fractions are involved, you might not have whole groups or whole objects in groups; rather, you might have a part of a group and a part of an object. For example, you might have ¾ of a pound of turkey and want to know how many sandwiches you could make with ¼ of a pound of turkey on each sandwich. This is a measurement division problem because you know the total (¾ of a pound), you know how much is in each group (¼ of a pound), and you need to determine how many groups you can make (three sandwiches).

The third problem in figure 4.8 (page 97) is solved by finding three groups of ¾ of a cup of cocoa. This problem can be drawn in several ways. It is common to draw three wholes with ¾ of each whole shaded (see figure 4.13, page 100).

Your goal is to determine how much cocoa this is all together. One way is to count the number of fourths. This would result in 9/4 cups of cocoa. Another way is to make full cups by rearranging the fourths in the picture. You could use one fourth-size piece from the last cup to complete the first cup and another to complete the second cup. This would indicate that Ming needs two full cups and ¼ of an additional cup or 2 ¼ cups of cocoa.

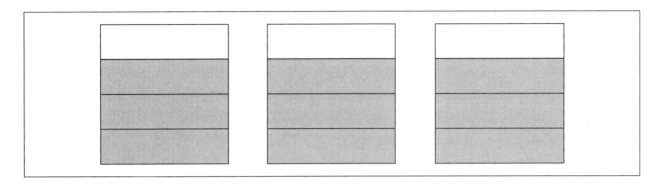

Figure 4.13: Three groups of ¾ cup of cocoa.

The equation to represent this situation is 3 × ¾ = 2¼, however, a solution equation is ¾ + ¾ + ¾ = 2¼. This problem can be solved by multiplying a fraction by a whole number or by adding fractions with like denominators. These options provide reinforcement for why these two topics are placed prior to adding fractions with unlike denominators and are in grade 4 in the learning progression.

The fourth problem in figure 4.8 (page 97) is a comparison problem, comparing the amount Blake ate (¾ of a candy bar) to the amount Jordan ate (⅝ of a candy bar). Figure 4.14 provides a visual of this comparison.

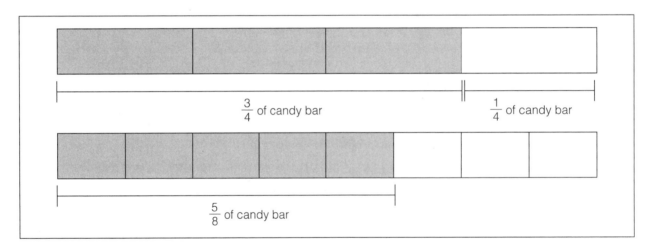

Figure 4.14: Blake's ¾ of a candy bar compared to Jordan's ⅝ .

When the ¾ of a candy bar is compared to the ⅝ of a candy bar, it is clear that Blake ate part of a fourth more. Equivalent fractions are used to describe that part in terms of equal parts of the whole. If you cut each fourth into two equal pieces, you can see that the part of the fourth representing how much more Blake ate than Jordan can be described as ⅛ of a candy bar. So, Blake ate ⅛ of a candy bar more than Jordan (see figure 4.15).

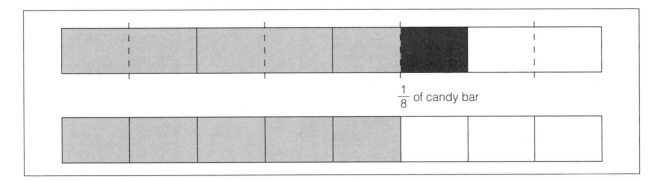

$\frac{1}{8}$ of candy bar

Figure 4.15: Blake ate ⅛ of a candy bar more than Jordan.

An equation to represent this solution process is ¾ – ⅝ = ⅛. The process was really to change ¾ to ⁶⁄₈ so that ⁶⁄₈ – ⅝ = ⅛. By recording the steps used to solve the problem in equation form, the standard algorithm for subtracting fractions with unlike denominators begins to emerge out of sense making with word problems rather than as a set of rules to be memorized. The importance of using word problems cannot be overstated. You need to be prepared to provide word problems to your students to support sense making. It might be necessary to create these word problems to support students' learning, which can sometimes be more complicated than anticipated (see figure 4.16).

Complete a word problem to support solving ⅘ – ½ that begins, "Stefan had ⅘ of a pizza left over in his refrigerator . . ."

Figure 4.16: Creating a context for ⁴⁄₅ – ¹⁄₂.

Did you write something like this?

> Stefan had ⁴⁄₅ of a pizza left over in his refrigerator.
> If he ate ½ of the leftover pizza, how much pizza does he have now?

Does this word problem make sense? At first, it may seem to make sense and match the expression ⅘ – ½ . Using drawings to act out the problem can provide additional clarity. Figure 4.17 (page 102) provides this illustration.

The illustration in figure 4.17 clearly matches the word problem, but does it match the expression? Is it modeled by ⅘ – ½? Does ⅘ – ½ = ⅖? Using the algorithm to find ⅘ – ½ requires you to find common denominators. In doing so, you could represent the expression as ⁸⁄₁₀ – ⁵⁄₁₀. However, when you perform the subtraction, you see that ⁸⁄₁₀ – ⁵⁄₁₀ = ³⁄₁₀. This is a problem because ³⁄₁₀ is not the same as ⅖! The drawing leads to the result of ⅖. How could this be?

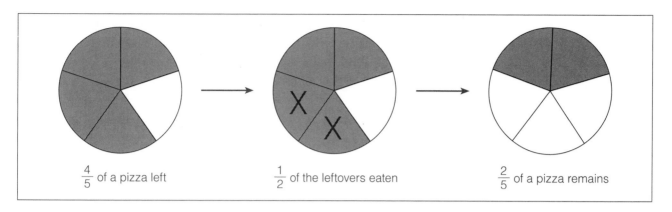

$\dfrac{4}{5}$ of a pizza left $\dfrac{1}{2}$ of the leftovers eaten $\dfrac{2}{5}$ of a pizza remains

Figure 4.17: Illustration of eating ½ of the leftover pizza.

The word problem is not correctly modeled by $\frac{4}{5} - \frac{1}{2}$ but rather it is modeled by $\frac{4}{5} - (\frac{1}{2} \times \frac{4}{5})$. There is $\frac{4}{5}$ of a pizza left over, but Stefan must eat ½ of a *whole* pizza from what is left over in order to support $\frac{4}{5} - \frac{1}{2}$. A correct word problem to support $\frac{4}{5} - \frac{1}{2}$ is:

> Stefan had $\frac{4}{5}$ of a pizza left over in his refrigerator. If he ate ½ of an entire pizza from what was left over, how much pizza does he have now?

The wording seems strange, but it supports $\frac{4}{5} - \frac{1}{2}$. The issue is that $\frac{4}{5}$ and ½ must refer to the same-size whole; $\frac{4}{5}$ of an entire pizza and ½ of an entire pizza. This issue with misrepresenting fraction subtraction is common but is less likely to occur when using comparison subtraction problems, as in problem 4 of figure 4.8 (page 97). It is also less likely to occur when the unit is more clearly defined, for example when working with yards of fabric as in the first problem in figure 4.8 rather than with pizza. (For an in-depth discussion of this common error, see Dixon et al., 2014.)

After students have made sense of fraction operations through word problems, they will benefit from additional practice solving fraction computation problems with manipulatives and drawings. Manipulatives are useful for exploring fraction operations, however they are also limiting.

Using Manipulatives to Compute With Fractions

It is important that you explore fraction operations using different manipulatives, such as construction paper fraction kits, pattern blocks, and fraction tiles. The experience will be enhanced if you actually use these manipulatives while solving the problems rather than just reading about them. We've organized the problems by manipulative to facilitate this process. Be sure to solve the problems presented in each task using the indicated manipulative prior to reading the text that follows that task.

Fraction Kits

The first manipulative-based task (see figure 4.18) uses the fraction kit you created in chapter 3.

Solve with fraction kits. Use the red as the whole for each problem.

1. $\frac{3}{8} + \frac{5}{16} = ?$ 2. $\frac{1}{3} \times \frac{3}{4} = ?$ 3. $\frac{5}{8} \div 2 = ?$

Figure 4.18: Fraction operations tasks with a fraction kit.

In the first problem, you probably began by covering ³⁄₈ of the red whole using three yellow pieces. You may have left them there and added five green pieces to represent adding ⁵⁄₁₆ (see figure 4.19).

At this point, the solution process often diverges. How did you determine the sum? You might have seen that half of the whole plus an additional ³⁄₁₆ of the whole was covered, as illustrated in figure 4.20.

Thinking back to your work with fraction concepts, you know that ½ is equivalent to ⁸⁄₁₆, and you can conclude that ³⁄₈ + ⁵⁄₁₆ is three more sixteenths than ⁸⁄₁₆, or ¹¹⁄₁₆. If you didn't use the benchmark of ½ to determine the sum, you might have exchanged the eighths for sixteenths to see that the red whole is covered by ¹¹⁄₁₆, as in figure 4.21.

What *is* important is that you use the manipulative in ways that make sense to you. Be sure to allow your students the opportunity to use the manipulatives in ways that make sense to them as they explore using visual models to compute with fractions.

At first glance, the second problem looks impossible to solve using fraction kits with the constraint that the red is the whole because there are no thirds. However, after you connect meaning to the factors, the problem becomes much more accessible. The problem, ⅓ × ¾, asks, "What is ⅓ of a group of ¾ of the whole?" It could be connected to a word problem like, "I have ¾ of a pan of brownies left over. If I eat ⅓ of the leftover brownies, how much of the entire pan will I eat?" A quick answer should be "too much." An estimate should be less than ½ because you are finding less than a half of a group of less than a whole when you multiply ⅓ × ¾. This problem is solved with the fraction kit by starting with ¾ of the whole covered and then identifying

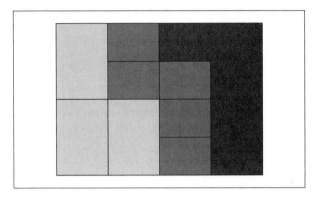

Figure 4.19: The red whole covered with three eighths and five sixteenths.

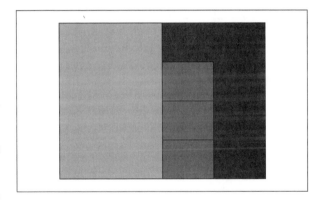

Figure 4.20: Half of the whole and 3 more sixteenths show ³⁄₈ + ⁵⁄₁₆.

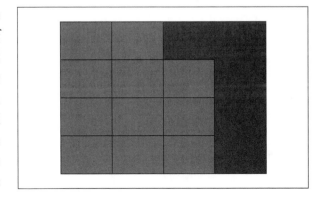

Figure 4.21: Sixteenths covering ¹¹⁄₁₆ of the whole.

⅓ of the ¾. This is ¼ of the entire pan of brownies, as illustrated in figure 4.22. You know your answer is reasonable because it is consistent with your estimate of less than ½.

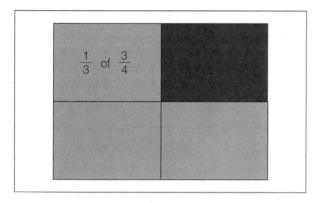

Figure 4.22: One fourth represents ¹/₃ of ³/₄ of the whole.

You may have been less tempted to follow the procedure on this problem than on the first problem in figure 4.1 (page 91). You were probably not looking for a way to represent each fourth in three equal parts. The fraction kit seems to help students and teachers look at fraction operations more intuitively. Using the fraction kits to introduce fraction operations with visual models is an excellent strategy for students to use as it helps them make sense of the operations rather than following your modeling with the gradual release of responsibility. Remember that your students are more likely to engage in Mathematical Practice 1, "Make sense of problems and persevere in solving them," if you replace the gradual release of responsibility model with the layers of facilitation (I facilitate the whole class, I facilitate small groups, I facilitate individuals) described in the introduction.

The third problem in figure 4.18 (page 103) can be solved using a sharing division context. You can imagine sharing ⅝ of a pan of brownies equally between two people. Somehow the pieces will need to be represented by an even number of pieces so that each person will receive the same amount of brownies. This can be achieved by exchanging the five eighth-size pieces for ten sixteenth-size pieces so that each person will receive ⁵/₁₆ of the pan of brownies. This is determined with the fraction kit by starting with five yellow pieces and exchanging them for ten green pieces to represent ¹⁰/₁₆ of the whole. You then share those ten pieces equally among two groups. Each group has ⁵/₁₆ of the whole, showing that ⅝ ÷ 2 = ⁵/₁₆.

Pattern Blocks

Similar to the fraction kit, pattern blocks represent an area model for fractions. However, using pattern blocks to solve fraction operations tends to feel different than solving similar problems with fraction kits. Use pattern blocks to solve the problems in figure 4.23. If you do not have easy access to this manipulative, you can find it online at virtual manipulative sites.

Solve these problems with pattern blocks. Use the hexagon as the whole for each problem.

1. $\dfrac{5}{6} - \dfrac{2}{3} = ?$ 2. $\dfrac{3}{5} \times 2\dfrac{1}{2} = ?$ 3. $3\dfrac{1}{3} \times \dfrac{1}{2} = ?$

Figure 4.23: Fraction operations tasks with pattern blocks.

You may have been able to solve the first problem in figure 4.23 without finding common denominators for $\frac{5}{6}$ and $\frac{2}{3}$. This contradicts the frequently used rule that says, "You must find common denominators to subtract." Using pattern blocks, you might have represented $\frac{5}{6}$ with five triangles and $\frac{2}{3}$ with two parallelograms and then covered the triangles with the parallelograms to find that there was one triangle left uncovered. The triangle left uncovered is $\frac{1}{6}$ of the whole, so $\frac{5}{6} - \frac{2}{3} = \frac{1}{6}$ (see figure 4.24). Exploring problems with manipulatives might cause you to rethink how you describe the process of subtracting fractions. Although finding like denominators and subtracting the numerators is an appropriate algorithm to use for fraction subtraction, it is not the only method for subtracting fractions.

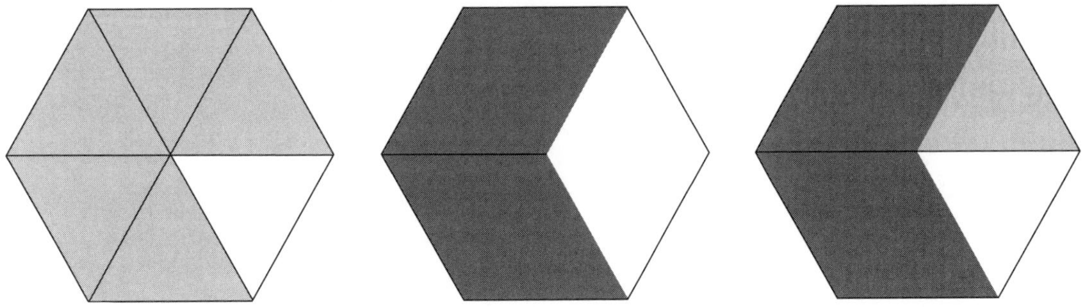

Figure 4.24: Representing $\frac{5}{6} - \frac{2}{3}$ with pattern blocks.

Multiplying $\frac{3}{5} \times 2\frac{1}{2}$, the second problem in figure 4.23, is less straightforward. What does this fraction problem mean? Thinking of it in context will help you find meaning in the operation, which is interesting, because students are often led to believe that word problems make mathematics more difficult. In this instance they actually make the problem easier to compute with a visual model. What could $\frac{3}{5} \times 2\frac{1}{2}$ represent? It could represent determining how much pie is in $\frac{3}{5}$ of $2\frac{1}{2}$ pies. This context helps you realize that the first action is to show the $2\frac{1}{2}$ pies. This is accomplished with two hexagons and one trapezoid. The next action is to split the $2\frac{1}{2}$ pies into five equal parts so that $\frac{3}{5}$ of the $2\frac{1}{2}$ can be determined. This may be challenging at first, until you realize that the $2\frac{1}{2}$ can be exchanged for five trapezoids. At this point, the solution to the problem becomes evident. Three-fifths of the five trapezoids is three trapezoids. Two of the trapezoids make up one hexagon, or one whole, so you have $1\frac{1}{2}$ as the product (see figure 4.25, page 106). This answer is reasonable because $\frac{3}{5} \times 2\frac{1}{2}$ is approximately $\frac{1}{2}$ of 3 or $1\frac{1}{2}$.

The final problem in figure 4.23 involves finding more than one group of $\frac{1}{2}$. This problem is different from others encountered so far in this chapter. You are finding three groups of $\frac{1}{2}$ and an additional $\frac{1}{3}$ of a group of $\frac{1}{2}$, 3 and $\frac{1}{3}$ groups of $\frac{1}{2}$. Three groups of $\frac{1}{2}$ can be represented with pattern blocks using three trapezoids, but how do you find $\frac{1}{3}$ of a group of $\frac{1}{2}$? One-third of a group of $\frac{1}{2}$ is found by exchanging a trapezoid for three triangles and using one of them to represent $\frac{1}{3}$ of the trapezoid. Figure 4.26 (page 106) illustrates $3\frac{1}{3}$ groups of $\frac{1}{2}$ with three trapezoids and one triangle, which are then combined to make one whole and $\frac{4}{6}$ of another whole by exchanging two trapezoids for a hexagon and one trapezoid for three triangles.

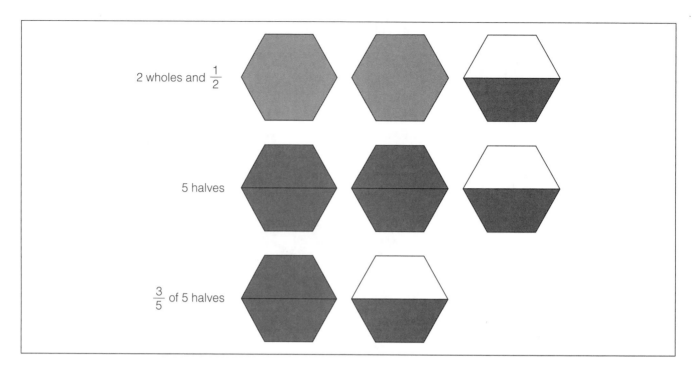

Figure 4.25: Representing ³/₅ × 2¹/₂ with pattern blocks.

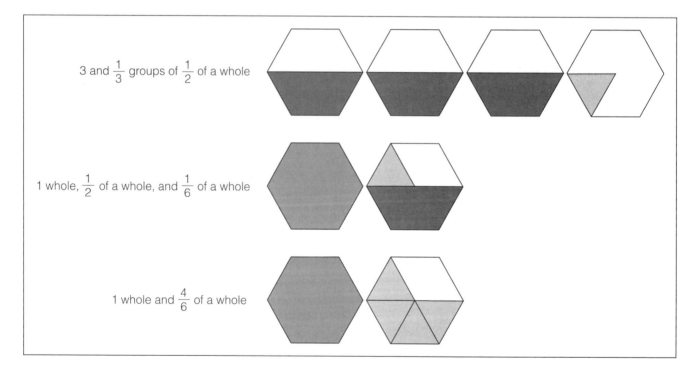

Figure 4.26: Representing 3¹/₃ × ¹/₂ with pattern blocks.

Fraction Tiles

You can use fraction kits and pattern blocks to represent the area model and fraction tiles to represent the linear model (for a conversation on fraction models, see chapter 3). Figure 4.27 provides three problems for you to solve using fraction tiles (also available online). Be sure to solve them before reading the discussion of their solutions.

Solve with fraction tiles.

1. $\dfrac{1}{4} + \dfrac{2}{3} = ?$ 2. $\dfrac{3}{4} \times \dfrac{2}{3} = ?$ 3. $\dfrac{5}{12} \div \dfrac{1}{6} = ?$

Figure 4.27: Fraction operations tasks with fraction tiles.

Fraction tiles are different from the manipulatives previously used here for fraction operations in that the pieces are labeled with their fraction names. This can be helpful in connecting work with manipulatives to adding and subtracting with algorithms. Figure 4.28 illustrates the process of adding the fractions in problem one. Fraction tiles for ¼ and ⅔ are laid out end to end. In order to name them as one fraction, those tiles are replaced with twelfth-size pieces because fourths and thirds can both be described as twelfths. That is, ¼ is equivalent to ³⁄₁₂, and ⅔ is equivalent to ⁸⁄₁₂. This process can be represented symbolically as ¼ + ⅔ = ³⁄₁₂ + ⁸⁄₁₂ = ¹¹⁄₁₂.

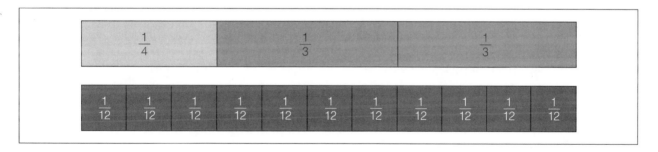

Figure 4.28: Representing ¼ + ²/₃ with fraction tiles.

Using fraction tiles for multiplication is slightly more confusing because of how the tiles are labeled. The second problem in figure 4.27 requires you to find ¾ of the length of ⅔ of the whole. Notice the change in language to support the linear model—using the attribute of length indicates that you are thinking of the manipulative as a linear model for fractions as opposed to an area model. It's important to match your language with the manipulatives you provide students. As they learn to represent fraction operations visually, the tools they have access to should connect to the context. In essence, when you are thinking about representing fraction operations in this way, *you* are engaging in Mathematical Practice 5, "Use appropriate tools strategically."

You begin with ⅔ of the length of one whole but then you need to find ¾ of that length. This is accomplished by finding a way to partition the ⅔ into four equal lengths so that you can find ¾ of ⅔. What is confusing here is that the tiles that allow you to partition ⅔ into fourths are actually labeled as sixths because they are each $\frac{1}{6}$ of the original whole length. Three of those pieces represent $\frac{3}{4}$ of the $\frac{2}{3}$ and so $\frac{3}{6}$ is $\frac{3}{4}$ of the length of $\frac{2}{3}$ of the whole, or $\frac{3}{4} \times \frac{2}{3} = \frac{3}{6}$, as illustrated in figure 4.29. Just as in the problems in figure 4.1 (page 91), the answer is not the expected solution from the algorithm or the answer in simplest terms but, instead, the answer that makes sense from the manipulatives.

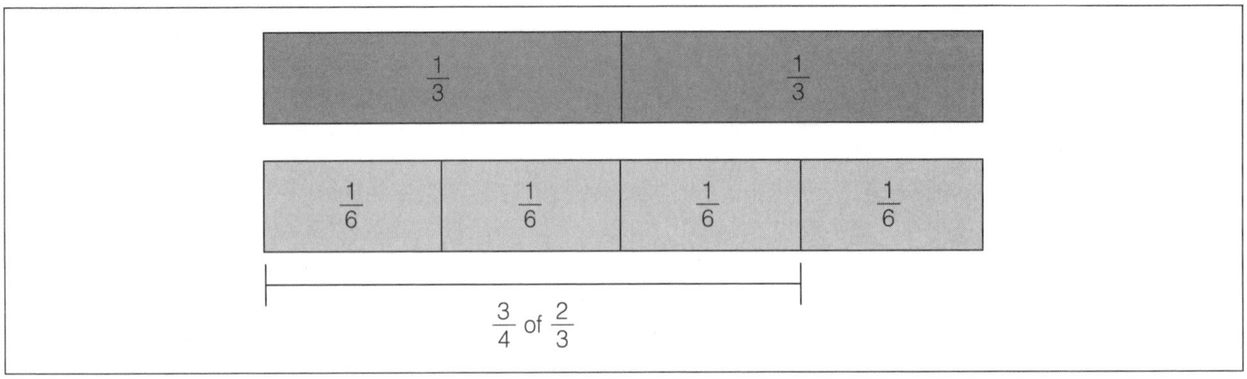

Figure 4.29: Representing $\frac{3}{4} \times \frac{2}{3}$ using fraction tiles.

In the third problem in figure 4.27 (page 107), the goal is to find how many lengths of $\frac{1}{6}$ of the whole are in $\frac{5}{12}$ of the whole. This problem could be placed into context as follows:

> You have $\frac{5}{12}$ of a stick of butter. You want to make a flavored popcorn recipe that calls for $\frac{1}{6}$ of a stick of butter for each batch. If you follow the recipe, how many batches of popcorn could you make so that you use up all the butter?

To solve this with fraction tiles, start with $\frac{5}{12}$ of the whole. Line up the $\frac{1}{6}$-length tiles along the $\frac{5}{12}$ to see how many batches of popcorn you could make with the butter you have available, and see that you could make two batches with some butter left over (see figure 4.30).

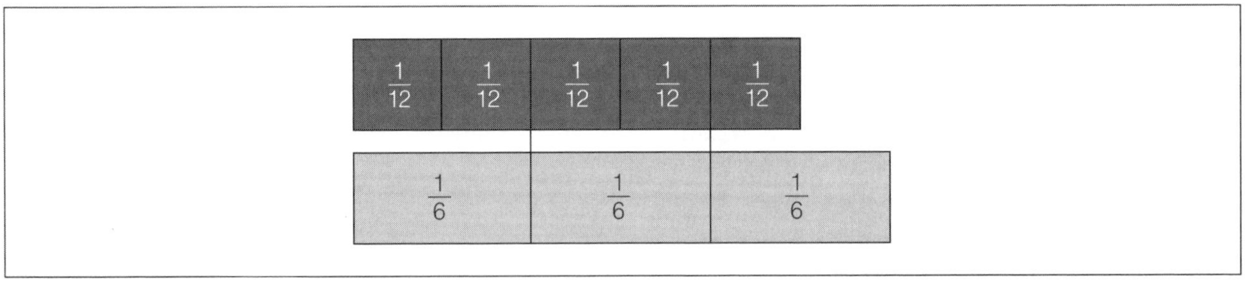

Figure 4.30: Representing $\frac{5}{12} \div \frac{1}{6}$ using fraction tiles.

What remains is determining how to handle the leftover butter. It is represented by $\frac{1}{12}$ of the whole stick, but does that answer the question? The question asked, "How many batches could you make so that you use up all the butter?" You could make two batches and $\frac{1}{2}$ of a third batch because $\frac{1}{12}$ is $\frac{1}{2}$ of the amount of butter you need to make another batch. It is $\frac{1}{2}$ of $\frac{1}{6}$, therefore, $\frac{5}{12} \div \frac{1}{6} = 2\frac{1}{2}$.

The confusion with what to do with the leftover amount is something encountered when using visual models to solve fraction division. It is not encountered when using algorithms to divide. This point of confusion will be discussed further in The Classroom and The Response sections later in this chapter. Now we turn our attention to developing algorithms.

Connecting Visual Solutions to Algorithms

While manipulatives are very helpful in many situations, they can limit the fractions used in computation. For example, if you are using a fraction kit to add fractions, you cannot add ⅓ + ½ without changing the kit because it does not have fraction pieces that describe thirds of a whole when the whole is the red piece. It is also difficult to add fifths with pattern blocks because a whole would need to be created by using more than one pattern block. Drawings allow for more freedom in using different fractions; however, some fractions can be difficult to represent, such as sevenths, because it is hard to draw seven equal pieces of a whole. Eventually, students should compute with fractions using equations rather than visuals. Make sure you connect students' experiences with visual models to their work with procedures.

The algorithm for adding fractions with unlike denominators is fairly straightforward, as long as attention is given to the language used when describing the process. Recall the cookie problem from chapter 3. After the four cookies were shared fairly among five friends following the constraints of the problem, each friend had ½ of a cookie, ¼ of a cookie, and ¹⁄₂₀ of a cookie. In order to combine these cookie parts and describe them together as part of a whole cookie, all of the parts need to be composed of pieces that are the same size (see chapter 3 for an in-depth discussion of equivalent fractions). Describing all of the cookies with equal-size pieces leaves each person with ¹⁰⁄₂₀ of a cookie, ⁵⁄₂₀ of a cookie, and ¹⁄₂₀ of a cookie. Consider the language typically used to solve this problem. It goes something like this: "Because the denominators are the same, you just add the numerators." Contrast this with language supportive of building conceptual understanding of the fraction addition algorithm: "Because the parts of the cookie are made up of pieces that are the same size, you can combine the pieces. You have ten twentieth-size pieces, five twentieth-size pieces, and one twentieth-size piece so you have sixteen twentieth-size pieces altogether or ¹⁶⁄₂₀." Using this sort of language prevents students from making the common error of adding the numerators and adding the denominators. It is interesting that using a word problem—a context—helps bring meaning to the algorithm.

Problems like number 3 in figure 4.1 (page 91) provide an excellent opportunity to make similar connections between word problems and the algorithm for multiplying fractions. If students solve several problems involving the context of area with dimensions less than one whole, they can begin to see a pattern across problems. For instance, they see that the number of parts in the whole can be found by multiplying the denominators, and the shaded region can be found by multiplying the numerators. They may even begin using this shortcut without needing to be told. These students are engaging in Mathematical Practice 8, "Look for and express regularity in repeated reasoning."

Fraction division is introduced in grade 5 with division of whole numbers by unit fractions and unit fractions by whole numbers. This entryway into fraction division allows for a meaningful development of the algorithm. Consider the problem 6 ÷ ⅓. This problem can be interpreted as representing the number of thirds in six wholes.

Solving it with a visual model might involve drawing six rectangles and partitioning each rectangle into three equal parts for a solution of eighteen parts in all or eighteen one-thirds (see figure 4.31).

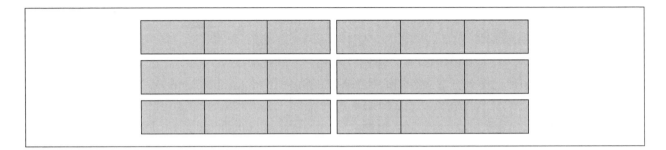

Figure 4.31: How many thirds are in six wholes?

Since each rectangle is split into three equal parts, with each part being one-third, another way of thinking about this is six groups of three one-thirds. This second way leads to the standard algorithm because you began with $6 \div \frac{1}{3}$ and changed it to 6×3 to describe the solution. Thus, $6 \div \frac{1}{3} = 6 \times 3 = 18$.

The transition from dividing whole numbers by unit fractions to dividing whole numbers by any fraction follows nicely. Consider $6 \div \frac{2}{3}$. You know that there are eighteen groups of $\frac{1}{3}$ in 6. How can that help you determine the number of groups of $\frac{2}{3}$ there are in six wholes? Because $\frac{2}{3}$ is twice the size of $\frac{1}{3}$, there would be half as many groups of $\frac{2}{3}$ as $\frac{1}{3}$. Therefore, there are nine groups of $\frac{2}{3}$ in 6 (see figure 4.32). This leads to the standard algorithm by multiplying 6×3 and dividing by two or finding $6 \times \frac{3}{2}$.

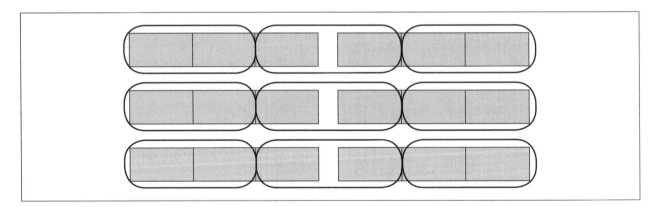

Figure 4.32: Nine groups of $^2/_3$ in six wholes.

The process of making sense of the algorithm up to this point relies heavily on Mathematical Practice 7, "Look for and make use of structure." Extending this exploration to dividing fractions by fractions is possible but is served better by using Mathematical Practice 8, "Look for and express regularity in repeated reasoning." Now use the algorithm for a wider range of division problems with both fractions and mixed numbers, and record the original expression—the expression once you "invert and multiply"—and the answer. Check the solutions by using drawings to see that the algorithm is applied successfully to the other situations.

You might be surprised to know that there is another algorithm for dividing fractions. It involves finding common denominators. After the dividend and the divisor are described as fractions with common denominators, dividing the numerators results in the quotient. Consider ⅚ ÷ ⅔. You can rewrite the expression using common denominators as ⅚ ÷ ⁴⁄₆. Now you are finding how many groups of four sixth-size pieces are in five sixth-size pieces. There is one group and ¼ of another group, or 1¼ groups, as illustrated in figure 4.33. Another way to compute this quotient is to find 5 ÷ 4, or to divide the numerators once the denominators are common. This algorithm might actually become your preferred algorithm, because it is more readily justified with both fractions and mixed numbers.

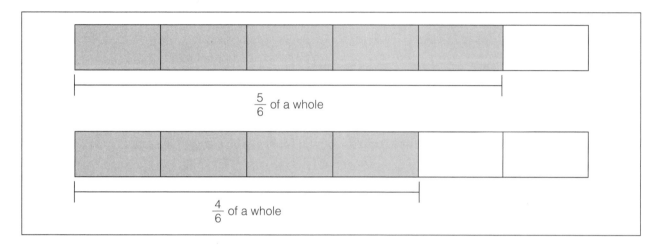

Figure 4.33: One group of four sixth-size pieces and ¼ of a group of four sixth-size pieces in ⁵⁄₆.

What is most important is that the strategies you use are accurate, generalizable in that they can be applied to all such cases, and efficient. You must be able to explain *and* justify the algorithms you use so that you can support students to do the same during instruction. The videos described next provide a window into what this looks like in the classroom.

The Classroom

Now that you have made sense of fraction operations, think about what instruction looks like when the focus is on developing conceptual understanding of operations with fractions. The included videos provide opportunities to observe students in action making sense of fraction operations.

The first video offers a window into a fifth-grade class where students explore multiplying fractions with fraction kits. Prior to watching the first video, solve the task in the video using a fraction kit so that you can compare the process you used to how the class solved the problem (see figure 4.34).

Solve the following using a fraction kit:

Susie had ¼ of a pan of brownies. She ate ¾ of what she had. How much of the original pan of brownies did Susie eat?

Figure 4.34: Fifth-grade video problem.

What did you use to represent the pan of brownies? You could have used the red piece of the fraction kit, but you also could have used a blue or an orange piece to represent the pan of brownies. How did you name the three-fourths of the one-fourth of the pan using fraction language? How might this be handled in the classroom? The fraction kit is a powerful, yet inexpensive, tool. Watch the first video before proceeding.

www.solution-tree.com/Multiplying
_Fractions_Using_a_Fraction_Kit

The teacher identifies the red piece of paper from the fraction kit as the whole to remove unnecessary confusion when representing the problem. This is so the focus remains on how to find parts of a fourth. In this way, the students can focus on finding fourths of a fourth and naming them. The students are able to use the green pieces to show three-fourths of the fourth-size piece. The difficulty is in naming those pieces in terms of the whole. This is an aspect of fraction operations that is new to students as they begin to make sense of fraction multiplication. The teacher anticipates this and is prepared to provide scaffolding as necessary. He is teaching with common errors in mind.

This is also the case in the sixth-grade class where students explore dividing a mixed number by a fraction. Prior to watching the second video, solve the problem provided in figure 4.35 using pattern blocks or drawings.

Douglas ordered 5 small pizzas during the great pizza sale. He ate ⅙ of one pizza and wants to freeze the remaining 4⅚ pizzas. Douglas decides to freeze the remaining pizza in serving-size bags. A serving of pizza is ⅔ of a pizza. How many servings can he make if he uses up all the pizza?

Figure 4.35: Leftover pizza problem.

What did you get as an answer? It is likely that you determined that Douglas could make 7⅙ servings or 7¼ servings. Which is correct? This is the topic of discussion in the sixth-grade class.

Now watch the second video before proceeding.

www.solution-tree.com/Dividing_Fractions_in_Context

Notice how the students are given time to make sense of the problem in ways that they choose. Some students draw pictures, and others use manipulatives. How does the teacher gather information regarding how students are making sense of the problem? How does she use her time while students are working? The teacher circulates the room asking questions but not indicating correctness of responses. Not only is she providing scaffolding as necessary, but she is also collecting information to use later during the whole-class discussion. She is looking for common errors as well as for students who solve the problem correctly. She knows the common errors to anticipate, so she is able to determine who has them and how to address them with the class during whole-group discussion.

The teacher begins the whole-class discussion by providing the two responses she heard from the class. At this point, the teacher does not indicate which is correct. She is engaging the students in Mathematical Practice 3, "Construct viable arguments and critique the reasoning of others." If she indicates which is correct, *she* is engaging in this practice rather than the students. Rather, the students defend their responses, and classmates critique the reasoning to unpack a common error with fraction division in a much more impactful way than having the teacher correct the students.

TQE Process

At this point, it may be helpful to watch the first video again. Pay close attention to the task, questioning, and opportunities to collect evidence of student learning.

The TQE process can help you frame your observations. Teachers who have a deep understanding of the mathematics they teach:

- Select appropriate *tasks* to support identified learning goals
- Facilitate productive *questioning* during instruction to engage students in Mathematical Practices
- Collect and use student *evidence* in the formative assessment process during instruction

The *task* for this lesson is for students to make sense of a fraction operation problem. As the students in the class have not used the fraction kits before, part of the sense making at the beginning of the class is to make sense of how to use a fraction kit to model the problem. It is important for a teacher to understand what experiences students have coming into a lesson and how that will impact their understanding of the task. The teacher establishes sense making of the manipulative and helps the students link that understanding to the task. He begins supporting the entire class to make sense of the problem, as opposed to having the students begin the task on their own. After a common way of representing the pan of brownies and ¼ of the pan is established, he again returns the sense making to the students so they can use the context of the problem to determine what to do next. Students need to make sense of the connection between the fraction kit and the brownies. An important feature of tasks involving manipulatives is to connect the manipulative to both the context of the task and the mathematics used to model the task.

The *questioning* that the teacher uses helps the students make sense of both the model and the task. The teacher anticipates that there will need to be sense making of the fraction kit and begins the class by asking about the link between the fraction kit and the task. Teacher questions and student responses link the fraction kit to the context of the story so that students can work in small groups with a common understanding of where to start with the fraction kits. In the whole-group discussion near the end of the lesson, the teacher asks another student to respond to a student question, rather than offering support himself. This provides the opportunity for students to answer questions from each other and demonstrates that the teacher is not the only person in the classroom who can provide help.

The students provide *evidence* of their learning as they participate in the conversation. After the student provides the support, the teacher checks for understanding of the first student by asking her to talk through the entire solution process. This provides evidence to the teacher that she has changed her thinking and is not simply repeating the words of the student who supported her. The teacher is supporting the student to engage in Mathematical Practice 1, "Make sense of problems and persevere in solving them." All too often, when students struggle, the teacher solves the problem for the students. Notice how, in this case, the teacher uses another student and appropriate scaffolding to help a struggling student make sense of the problem and persevere.

The Response

Typical areas of difficulty related to fraction operations occur when students use algorithms incorrectly. For example, some students may add numerators as well as denominators when adding fractions; others might forget to invert when dividing fractions. These types of errors occur when students memorize procedures. When a more conceptual approach is taken with instruction on fraction operations, the errors students make are impacted. The errors themselves are more conceptually based. Consider the multiple choice options presented in figure 4.36.

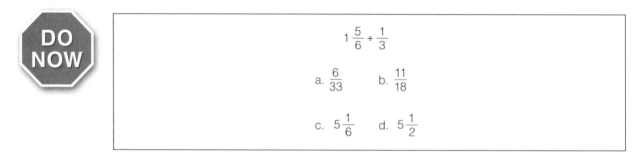

$$1\frac{5}{6} \div \frac{1}{3}$$

a. $\frac{6}{33}$ b. $\frac{11}{18}$

c. $5\frac{1}{6}$ d. $5\frac{1}{2}$

Figure 4.36: Multiple choice showing common errors with fraction division.

The correct answer is choice d. What common errors are identified by the other choices? Options a and b represent common procedural errors of forgetting to invert and inverting the wrong fraction. Choice c does not represent an error that is common to students who are taught procedurally; this is more of a conceptual error or an error with understanding concepts related to finding the solution. It is more clearly recognized by using manipulatives or drawings to solve the problem as illustrated in figure 4.37.

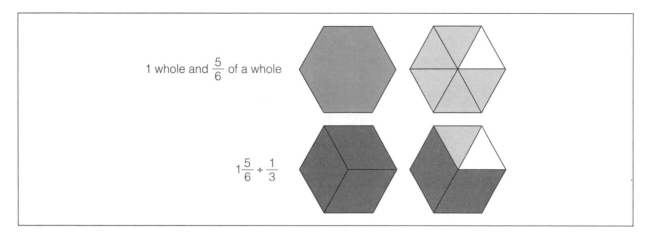

$1 \text{ whole and } \dfrac{5}{6} \text{ of a whole}$

$1\dfrac{5}{6} \div \dfrac{1}{3}$

Figure 4.37: Solving 1⅚ ÷ ⅓ conceptually with pattern blocks.

Students see that there are five groups of ⅓ of a whole in 1⅚, with ⅙ of a whole left over. These students incorrectly determine that 1⅚ ÷ ⅓ is equal to 5⅙ . They do this because they lose track of the meaning of division as finding the number of groups when the total and the group size are known. The answer should be given in terms of the group size. In this case, there are 5½ groups of ⅓ in 1⅚ rather than 5⅙ groups.

What is an appropriate response to this sort of error? What is the intervention? For errors like this, students may need to revisit the meaning of division. They should connect what they are doing with operations with fractions to operations with whole numbers through the use of context.

A measurement division word problem with whole numbers is:

> I have 12 cookies. If I want to put the cookies in bags
> so there are 3 cookies in each bag, how many bags can I make?

With this problem, you can make four bags. Notice that 12 represents the total number of objects, 3 represents the number of objects in each group, and the answer is in terms of the number of bags because the bags represent the groups. When operating with fractions, focus should be placed on keeping track of the whole. In the example in figure 4.35 (page 112), a word problem might shed light on the errors. This problem could be placed in the context of servings of pizza.

> There are 1⅚ pizzas left over from a party and a serving
> of pizza is ⅓ of a pizza. How many servings are left over?

There are five servings and ⅙ of a pizza left. This is 5½ servings so 1⅚ ÷ ⅓ = 5½ .

What is important to note is that the response to errors is not to focus on rote memorization or simply practicing procedures exclusively. The response also includes making connections to earlier work with whole numbers to further develop an understanding of the operations—in this case, fraction operations. This approach is in contrast to interventions that consist of pages and pages of worksheets with fraction computation problems devoid of context for students to perform. Practice is still important, but students often practice poorly understood procedures and sometimes even incorrect procedures when a focus on conceptual understanding is not included in the intervention.

Reflections

1. What do you feel are the key points in this chapter?

2. What challenges might you face when implementing the key ideas from this chapter? How will you overcome them?

3. What are the important features for developing an understanding of fraction operations, and how will you ensure your instruction embeds the support needed for these features?

4. Select a recent lesson you have taught or observed focused on fraction operations. Relate this lesson to the TQE process.

5. What changes will you make to your planning and instruction based on what you read and considered from this chapter?

CHAPTER 5

Geometry

The focus of this chapter is the mathematics for teaching plane and solid geometry with depth so that you and your students develop a strong foundation for the study of geometry. What you need to know about the study of geometry is sometimes beyond what you will address with students in grades 3–5. This is in large part to be sure that you do not teach rules that will expire as students learn geometry in later grades.

Geometry is the study of space, objects in space, and the movement of objects in space. School geometry includes a focus on objects with zero, one, two, and three dimensions. Consider the images in figure 5.1.

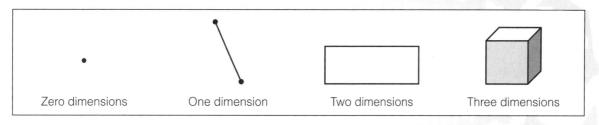

Figure 5.1: Dimensions of plane and solid geometry.

An example of an object with zero dimensions is a *point*. A point does not have dimensions such as length, width, and height. Although the geometric object of a point seems very simple, the point is quite vital to the subsequent dimensions in geometry. For instance, it takes two distinct points to create a line segment. A line segment is an example of an object with one dimension; it has length. By connecting line segments that do not exist on the same line, you can create objects with two dimensions, such as a rectangle. A rectangle has the dimensions of length and width. Zero-, one-, and two-dimensional geometry (commonly described as *plane geometry*) includes abstract representations of the real world. When you hold up an attribute block that is the shape of a rectangle and say, "This two-dimensional shape is a rectangle," you are not actually correct. The shape you are holding is actually three-dimensional because it has length, width, and height to it. Even when you draw a representation of a rectangle on a sheet of paper, the drawn lines have a thickness, even though it is quite small. It is understood, by most adults, that you are ignoring the third dimension, the height, in order to represent the rectangle in a way that makes sense in the real world.

The question becomes, how do you truly represent a two-dimensional object in a three-dimensional world? Since students use screens constantly, you can represent a two-dimensional object correctly by referring to them on a TV, computer, or smartphone. This distinction should be a topic of conversation with the students to ensure they have the same understanding of representing two-dimensional shapes in a three-dimensional environment. As for the three-dimensional world (described as *solid geometry*), students are surrounded by it. The combination of these two worlds affords students the opportunity to explore concrete objects and helps provide models that represent the abstract objects of zero-, one-, and two-dimensional geometry, which will build toward three-dimensional geometry. Hereafter, two- and three-dimensional objects are referred to as shapes.

The Challenge

You can expect that grades 3–5 students need a variety of tasks in order to acquire conceptual understanding in both plane (two-dimensional) and solid (three-dimensional) geometry. We designed the initial tasks in figure 5.2 to initiate conversation about foundational principles for studying plane and solid geometry. This task is designed to provide you experience with the type of activities that your students need in order to use the language of geometry and develop a sense of space, both in two and three dimensions. It is important for you to have the knowledge of the language and expectations in order to properly prepare your students for their next steps. The Progression will help you understand the expectations for students in grades 3–5.

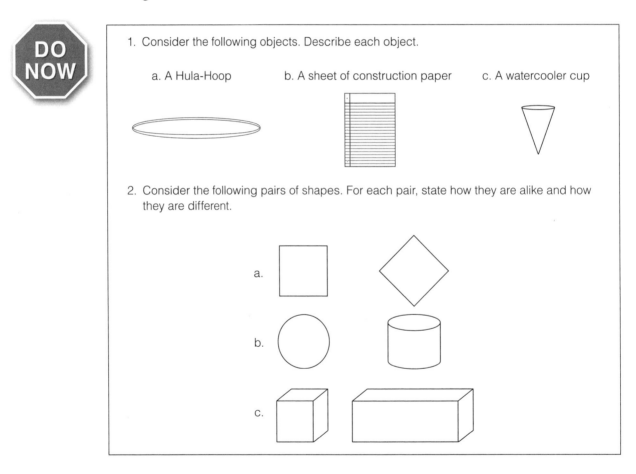

1. Consider the following objects. Describe each object.

     a. A Hula-Hoop   b. A sheet of construction paper   c. A watercooler cup

2. Consider the following pairs of shapes. For each pair, state how they are alike and how they are different.

     a.

     b.

     c.

Figure 5.2: Geometry context task.

3. Suppose you have a large, circular birthday cookie. Draw a picture of your cookie.

    a. If you want to share the cookie fairly between you and one friend, how would you cut the cookie? Draw a picture.

    b. If you want to share the cookie fairly between you and two friends, how would you cut the cookie? Draw a picture.

    c. If you want to share the cookie fairly between you and three friends, how would you cut the cookie? Draw a picture.

The first problem in the task in figure 5.2 relates to the importance of students learning to make observations about the environment and objects in their environment. Space is geometry's environment. You want students to be able to transfer their observation activity in the natural environment to observation activity in geometry's environment. Recall how you described a Hula-Hoop. Perhaps you included statements similar to the following.

- A Hula-Hoop is perfectly round.

- A Hula-Hoop is plastic.

- A Hula-Hoop has no ending or beginning.

- A Hula-Hoop has a hole in the middle.

- A Hula-Hoop looks like a big bracelet.

You might have included things a Hula-Hoop can or cannot do. For instance, you might have stated that the Hula-Hoop can roll, and it can be placed around other objects. Now recall how you described a sheet of construction paper. Perhaps you included statements similar to the following.

- A sheet of construction paper feels fuzzy.

- A sheet of construction paper does not have any lines on it.

- A sheet of construction paper is [bigger or smaller] than a page of notebook paper.

- A sheet of construction paper is all one color.

- A sheet of construction paper is shaped like a rectangle.

You might have also included things that a piece of construction paper can do or what can be done to it. For example, you might have included that the construction paper can be folded in half. This sort of observation supports future understanding of fractions and symmetry.

Finally, recall your descriptions of the watercooler cup; you may have included the following.

- A watercooler cup has one pointy end.

- A watercooler cup has a circular top or opening.

- A watercooler cup can stand up on the circular end.

- A watercooler cup can hold water or other substances and objects.

- A watercooler cup looks like an ice cream cone.

You might have also included that the watercooler cup will spin around on a table or other flat surface.

When students engage in considering how to describe these real-world objects, they link geometry concepts with their world. This engagement enables you to gather knowledge about the geometry concepts your students have already been exposed to through informal or formal geometry experiences, providing an entry point to geometry topics students are ready to explore further as they develop their observation skills. For example, a student who says that the Hula-Hoop is perfectly round has perception about the uniformity of the shape and is able to translate his or her observations to reasonable descriptions. The student's use of vocabulary such as *round* is helpful in developing the foundation for early understanding of the shape of a circle. The examples in this task can help anchor students' understanding of a variety of geometry shapes.

Deep explorations in geometry will engage students in discussions about descriptions that are meaningful to learning geometry. For instance, a student who says a Hula-Hoop is pretty is making a subjective statement; the next student who describes a Hula-Hoop might not perceive it as pretty. Engaging students in making observations about the world around them and collecting their descriptions are ways to engage all students in the study of geometry.

The second problem in the geometry context task presents another important foundational concept to studying geometry—that of making comparisons. To compare shapes, you need to apply your observation and description skills. What do you notice about the first pair of shapes? Perhaps you see that they both have four sides and are the same size. How would you name them? You would probably be quick to say that the first shape looks like a square, but what about the second shape? Students often call this shape a diamond; however, it also looks like a square—it is the same as the first shape, but it has been rotated, or turned. Making comparisons also provides an opportunity to consider how shapes share common characteristics. It is important to ensure that differences are geometrically significant. A rotated or reflected (flipped) shape will still be named the same as a shape that is in a more common orientation, like the first square in figure 5.2 (page 118). Comparisons also provide an opportunity to consider how shapes share common characteristics and provide a basis for developing definitions that include necessary distinctions. This groundwork with shapes can happen with students even before they know the names of the shapes.

Consider your work on the third task in figure 5.2 (page 118); it is a revisit of a grade 2 task because we find that students in grade 3 still need to address the concept represented by the task. Be sure you provided drawings to support your work. In this task, you should have considered how many people in total were to share the cookie. When students first read or hear this task, they sometimes neglect to do this and just share the cookie among the targeted friends. Also, when students work through this task, guide them away from spending too much time decorating and drawing the cookie. Although this is an element of the task, it is not the primary goal. What you should have is three drawings similar to those in figure 5.3.

You can expect that some might falter on the "equalness" of the parts; be as exact as possible in order to develop this early understanding of a whole divided into equal parts as the foundation for fraction understanding. The use of a circular model for this early entry into fraction understanding is very common, but the idea can also be easily addressed with a rectangular model. In grade 1, the focus might be on halves and fourths. However, in grade 2, the focus will include thirds, and in grade 3, there is an expectation to use fraction notation and language for ⅓. The summary point is to use this geometry task to support work with fractions.

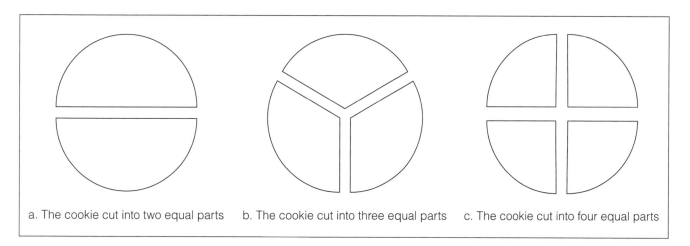

a. The cookie cut into two equal parts   b. The cookie cut into three equal parts   c. The cookie cut into four equal parts

Figure 5.3: Sharing a birthday cookie equally.

The Progression

The understanding of geometry is greatly impacted by students' engagement in geometry tasks and activities. Geometry incorporates a variety of mathematics concepts allowing students to count the number of sides, angles, faces, and vertices of a shape, as well as measure attributes of a shape such as the length of sides. Students should be able to estimate to compare the length of sides of two shapes. Additionally, geometry is related to fraction understanding, and it is also a foundation for higher levels of mathematics, such as trigonometry.

The building of fraction concepts begins in early grades when students divide rectangles and circles into halves, thirds, and fourths, as well as reasoning that the more equal pieces a shape is divided into, the smaller the size of each piece becomes. In trigonometry, unit circles and right-triangle geometry are used to calculate trigonometric ratios such as sine, cosine, and tangent. Hence, the geometry understanding students develop in K–2 and extend in grades 3–5 is very important to students' overall mathematics learning. Following is a progression of geometry content through grade 5.

- Describe, analyze, and compare nondefining attributes of shapes.
- Identify and name shapes.
- Relate shapes to one another.
- Create shapes.
- Classify shapes.
- Compose and decompose shapes.
- Identify defining attributes (such as angles, parallel lines, perpendicular lines, presence of symmetry, and faces) of shapes.

Kindergarten Through Grade 2

Students in kindergarten to grade 2 should spend time exploring geometry within the context of their environments, such as the classroom, the school, or the surrounding community. There is a myriad of shapes in the environment that you can direct students to notice. Scaffolding also helps students begin developing the skill of describing what they can see or touch. As students engage in formal learning opportunities, they use their language to share what they think or know about shapes and their presence in the environment.

In the primary grades, students learn two- and three-dimensional shapes such as circles, triangles, quadrilaterals (squares, rectangles, rhombuses, trapezoids), other named polygons (pentagons, hexagons), cubes, right rectangular prisms, right circular cylinders, spheres, and cones. Students use concrete models of these shapes in a variety of geometry learning opportunities so they build strong familiarity with the shapes, see them in the world around them, and are able to identify and name them.

Grade 3

Geometry in grade 3 extends work with two-dimensional shapes such as triangles, quadrilaterals (squares, rectangles, rhombuses, trapezoids), and other named polygons (pentagons, hexagons) by categorizing them based on their defining attributes. Concrete models of these shapes should continue to be easily accessible to students and should be used in a variety of geometry learning opportunities so that students build strong familiarity with the shapes, recognize them in the world around them, and are able to identify and name them.

Grade 3 students begin to create their own models of shapes by drawing (using points, line segments, angles, and so on), cutting from paper, molding from clay, and building with pipe cleaners. The exactness of the model might not be in place, but the early understanding of the shapes reflected in the students' models will help you assess students' understanding of the attributes of the shapes.

Grade 4

Grade 4 geometry builds heavily on previously learned geometry. For instance, it is expected that as students' general language and mathematical language mature, their command of geometry vocabulary will become stronger and more formal, representing an important connection to Mathematical Practice 6, "Attend to precision." Students should be expected to use more refined definitions that include the essential attributes necessary for a mathematically powerful definition in geometry and exclude nonessential attributes that detract from the clarity of definitions. This helps students move from *categorizing* based on defining attributes to *classifying* based on definitions.

Composing and decomposing shapes is also an important experience in grade 4 geometry. Students should have access to a variety of tools—such as grid paper, pattern blocks, attribute blocks, and construction paper—to use two or more shapes to compose a new shape and to decompose a larger shape into two or more shapes. Some of this effort should also involve visualization so that students begin developing an abstract perspective of composing shapes. Students use these experiences to make sense of lines of symmetry in shapes so they can identify shapes that are symmetric and draw lines of symmetry.

A third important feature for grade 4 geometry includes experiences where students draw and cut out shapes and identify the vertices, sides, and angles of those shapes. Students should also describe how line segments in a shape relate to each other—for example, whether a pair of intersecting lines is perpendicular or parallel.

Grade 5

Grade 5 geometry has a focus on the relationship between shapes. Students continue to use definitions to classify two-dimensional shapes. The more experiences students have exploring shapes, the more capacity students build for understanding and applying geometric concepts.

Throughout this chapter, you will engage in multiple geometric tasks. At times, the content may be outside the limits of grades 3–5; however, it is important that you know the progression of the content.

The Mathematics

The tasks throughout this section highlight the important geometry content and important actions needed to fully experience geometry. These tasks become richer and more beneficial in an environment where you have the opportunity to work collaboratively by engaging in discourse and debate. Consider flexible ways of thinking because many of the tasks can have more than one correct or appropriate response. In this section, you should work through these tasks to explore the content and the mathematics actions that will engage students in the study of geometry.

Here, you will explore aspects of geometry instruction, including understanding nondefining and defining attributes; relating attributes of shapes; sorting, defining, and classifying two-dimensional shapes; and recognizing three-dimensional shapes.

Understanding Nondefining and Defining Attributes

In geometry, it is valuable to observe and examine. Studying two-dimensional and three-dimensional geometry involves observing, touching, holding, and rotating objects and concrete models of geometric shapes. Noticing shapes and their location, positioning, and size is a foundation for studying them in a formal learning environment. In addition, observing and examining objects provides the opportunity to use language, both formal and informal, to *describe* what is noticed. Increased exposure with objects and prompts for describing them helps students develop more precise and clear language for what they notice when examining an object. For example, in the attribute train task (see figure 5.4), you will use a collection of buttons. You may collect buttons from your personal belongings or purchase a set of assorted buttons from an arts and crafts store. This informal task allows you to draw on your personal experiences, which support the development of your understanding of geometry.

Use a bag of twenty-five to thirty assorted buttons—varied in size, style, color, number of holes, and so on.

1. Sort the buttons.

2. Make a "train" of buttons so that each "car" or button in the train shares exactly one attribute with the car behind it and exactly one attribute with the car in front of it.

3. Make a "train" of buttons so that each "car" or button shares exactly two attributes with the car behind it and exactly two attributes with the car in front of it.

4. Make a "train" of buttons so that each "car" or button shares no attributes with the car behind it and no attributes with the car in front of it.

Figure 5.4: Attribute train task.

How did you do? You may have struggled at first to build the button trains, but perhaps the process to think about the button attributes became more familiar as you continued the task. The attribute train task brings observation, examination, and description together because in order to arrange the buttons, you need to observe the buttons, handle them, and develop a sorting method. The first level of the task is an open, unguided sorting activity. It addresses the notion that in geometry, you have to think flexibly and figure out more than one way of sorting shapes based on the context. This is why there isn't any guidance given for the sort. How did you sort the buttons? In other words, what rules did you create and use to sort the buttons? Your rules dictated the result of your sort, but the rules may or may not be similar to rules that others might use.

Additionally, the open sort provides important information about what you are noticing in the process of sorting the buttons. For instance, you might find that initially you attempted to sort the buttons only by the attribute or characteristic of color. This can be a valuable and productive first step of sorting and one that is most often first chosen by students. However, it is important to note that color is a nondefining attribute in geometry. This is not the approach wanted for naming shapes in geometry. For instance, according to the definition of a circle, a red circle is not different than a blue circle. Color is irrelevant to the definition of *circle*, and naming the color is subjective among the different people looking at it. Defining attributes characterize objects based on the definition of the object. Take some time and make a list of nondefining and defining attributes of the buttons. Think about more suggestions to include in figure 5.5.

Nondefining Attributes of the Buttons	Defining Attributes of the Buttons
Color	Shape
Shininess	Number of Holes

Figure 5.5: Nondefining and defining attributes of buttons.

Although nondefining attributes may not contribute to definitions, they add to the practice of observing, examining, and describing in geometry. The second and third parts of the attribute train task require you to make a train with the buttons, as shown in figure 5.6.

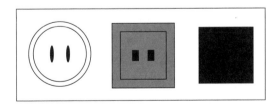

Figure 5.6: Train of buttons.

The train you created forms a line of buttons in which the consecutive buttons share one, two, and then no attributes. For example, for the case of one attribute, perhaps the first button is white, round, and has two holes; the second button is grey, square, and has two holes; the third button is black, square, and has no holes. The first button shares only one attribute with the second button, and the second button only shares one attribute with the third button. This can be a challenging task, but these tasks help clarify what you notice about the buttons by guiding you to use your descriptions of the buttons to *analyze* and *compare* the buttons. This task helps move beyond the nondefining attribute of color and guides learners to consider other attributes to show how the buttons are alike and how they are different, as well as helping learn how to analyze and compare geometric shapes. As you work through this task with your collection of buttons, you should notice things such as the number of holes in a button and whether or not the button has a shank (the elevated part of the back of the button that holds the thread). These attributes are either present or not and help determine the type of button. Think of these attributes as defining attributes. The constraints of the task guide you to use results of your observations, examinations, and descriptions to position the buttons in the train.

Which Mathematical Practices were you engaged in while solving this task? When referring to the mathematics actions that you made during this button task, you were engaged in Mathematical Practice 1, "Make sense of problems and persevere in solving them." For each set of directions, you had to make sense of what was being asked and make decisions based on your reasoning about the buttons, such as your sorting rule. The sorting rule changed according to the directions and was at times challenging; completing the task required perseverance. Mathematical Practice 6, "Attend to precision," was also evident in this task, as you had to attend to the specific detail of the buttons, particularly when you could only have no or one common attribute between consecutive buttons.

This task lends well to working in collaborative groups. As students make decisions, ask them to justify why they positioned buttons as they did. Neighboring collaborators might have some buttons in common, but they may have used them differently in the train. Hence, there might be some justifications warranted across collaborating teams as well as within a collaborating team. Ultimately, the desired outcome of the attribute train task in figure 5.4 (page 123) is to learn the difference between nondefining and defining attributes. This understanding will continue and be sharpened in the next couple of tasks. As you work through sorting activities, engagement in these practices supports your ability to reason with shapes and their attributes.

Relating Attributes of Shapes

The attribute block sorting task in figure 5.7 (page 126) makes a transition from exploring everyday objects, such as buttons, to using models of two-dimensional shapes. This transition supports a focus on defining attributes. For this example, you will use attribute blocks and two circular loops. If you do not already have attribute blocks, templates for them are available at **go.solution-tree.com/mathematics**; copy the blocks on colored paper, and cut them out. You can use a different material, such as foam paper, to make attribute blocks with a different thickness. For this particular task, you will not use the nondefining attributes of color, size, or thickness as sorting attributes. These nondefining attributes do not contribute to the definitions of the two-dimensional shapes. If you do not have circular loops, you can just draw loops on paper.

This task begins with an open sort of attribute blocks. You have the opportunity to use observations, examinations, and descriptions to sort them. After you finish sorting, consider what defining attributes you used to create your rules. For instance, defining attributes might include shape and number of sides.

Use a set of attribute blocks and two loops to complete the following:

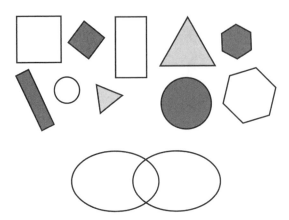

1. Sort the attribute blocks.

2. Using defining attributes, create two rules and sort the attribute blocks using two loops that do not overlap so there are blocks in each loop and there are blocks that are not in either loop.

3. Using defining attributes, create two rules and sort the attribute blocks using two intersecting loops so there are blocks in each loop that are not in the intersection of the loops, there are blocks in the intersection of the loops, and there are blocks outside of both loops.

4. Using defining attributes, create two rules and sort the attribute blocks using a loop within a loop (one inside the other) so there are blocks in the outer loop (but not in the inner loop), in the inner loop, and outside of both loops.

Figure 5.7: Attribute block sorting task.

When using tasks such as this with students, at the conclusion of the open sort process, engage in discourse about the sort to introduce new geometry vocabulary in a powerful way. With attribute blocks, color might present itself as a nondefining attribute. Discussions involving defining attributes are also important here. In addition, the use of informal language like "these shapes have three lines" can include feedback such as "yes, for shapes, we call these lines *sides*." Making note of language use during and after this sorting experience provides formative assessment data regarding geometry concepts and the definitions students are developing.

Sorting loops help present information and how different parts of the information are or are not related. Essentially, the information is present in one or more parts of the sorting loops to show how the parts are related. The outcome of using the sorting loops depends on the rules used. The second part of the task—creating two rules and sorting the attribute blocks using two loops that do not overlap (disjoint loops)—provides a case where two sets of attribute blocks share no common attributes, other than they are attribute blocks (see figure 5.8). In this case, the set of attribute blocks is described as the universal set.

This task aligns with the idea that two or more shapes can be distinct by definition and have no attributes in common, though they exist in the collection of two-dimensional shapes, as is the case with polygons with exactly three sides and polygons with exactly four sides. Note that these rules also provide some shapes that are outside of the loops, such as circles and hexagons.

The task of creating two rules and sorting the attribute blocks using two intersected loops (creating a model of a Venn diagram) provides a case where some shapes in a set of attribute blocks have something in common with other shapes in a set of attribute blocks, but not all shapes have something in common (see figure 5.9). Hence, some blocks might be present in the intersection of the two sets while other blocks would be outside of the intersection of the two sets. For example, shapes with three or four sides could be the rule for one loop and shapes with four or more sides could be the rule for the second loop. Shapes with four sides would be in the intersection of the loops, and circles would be outside both loops but in the universe.

The task of creating two rules and sorting the attribute blocks using a loop within a loop provides a case where a set of attribute blocks is entirely included in another set of attribute blocks (see figure 5.10).

One goal of the task in figure 5.10 is to draw attention to the relationship between squares and rectangles. If you have not considered that relationship, hold this part of the task for later. You can return to it after reading about it later in the chapter.

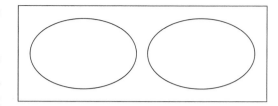

Figure 5.8: Disjoint loops.

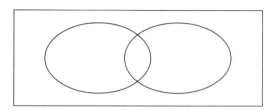

Figure 5.9: Intersected loops.

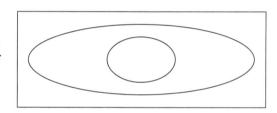

Figure 5.10: Loop within a loop.

These cases are the beginning of developing an understanding of how to *relate* shapes in geometry. How one shape relates to another shape is a large component of the content of geometry in the intermediate grades. The hands-on nature of using the sorting loops helps students explore relationships in geometry and is another context for the proper use of geometry vocabulary. As with the attribute train task (see figure 5.4, page 123), engagement in attribute block sorting (see figure 5.7) is aligned with Mathematical Practice 1, "Make sense of problems and persevere in solving them," as well as Mathematical Practice 6, "Attend to precision." Take some time to think about how you engaged in these practices while completing this task.

Sorting, Defining, and Classifying Two-Dimensional Shapes

In the next task (see figure 5.11, page 128), you will use a set of cards displaying a variety of two-dimensional shapes. We have provided these shape cards in figure 5.12 (page 128). Copy them and cut them out along the boundary lines to form rectangular cards that contain the shapes.

DO NOW

1. Sort the shape cards into polygons and nonpolygons.
2. Define **polygon**.
3. Sort the simple polygons into triangles, quadrilaterals, and other polygons.
4. Name each type of triangle.
5. Classify the triangles.
6. Sort the quadrilaterals.
7. Name each type of quadrilateral.
8. Classify the quadrilaterals.

Figure 5.11: Shape cards sorting task.

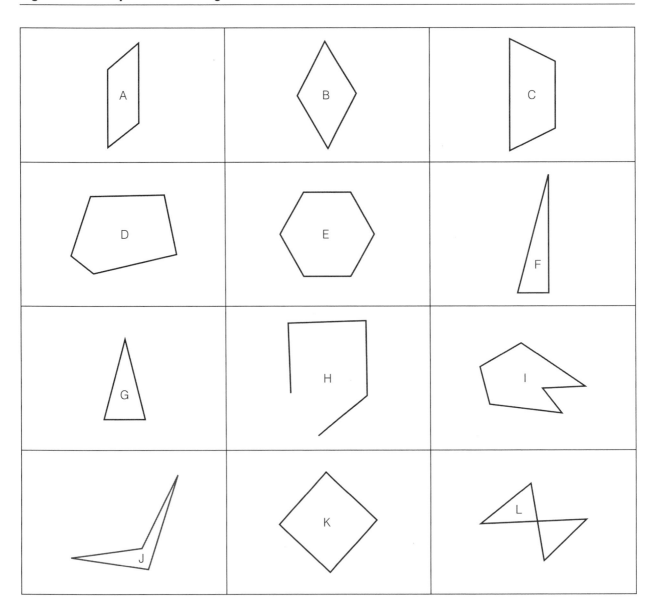

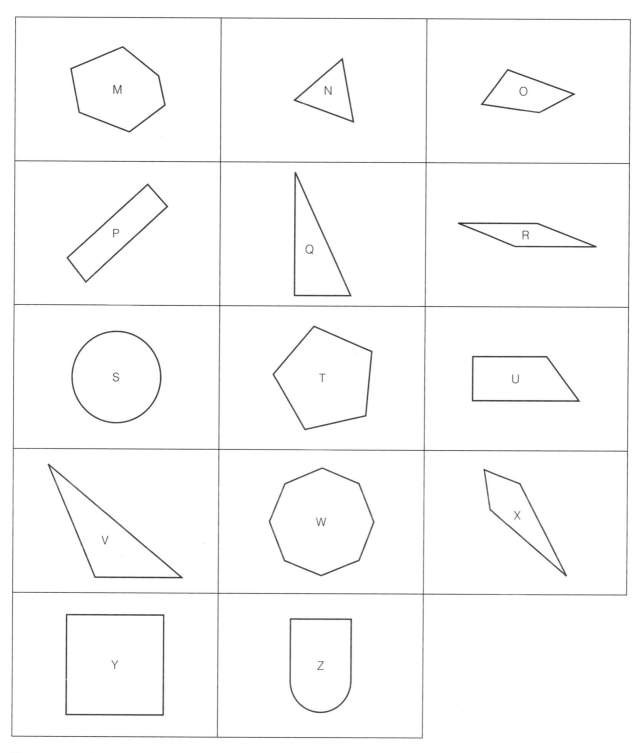

Figure 5.12: Shape cards.

*Visit **go.solution-tree.com/mathematics** for a free reproducible version of this figure.*

First, sort the shape cards into polygons and nonpolygons.

How did you define *polygon*? It is valuable for you to consider how you define various geometrical concepts, and how these cards align to your definitions. To refresh your understanding of the term *polygon*, it is a composition of two Greek words: *poly* and *gonia*. *Poly* means many, and *gonia* means angle or corner, so the literal meaning of the word is many angled. The number of angles also represents the number of sides in a polygon. Use this information to sort the shape cards. You might also practice *creating* examples of polygons and nonpolygons of your own, as this is an important activity for studying geometry. You can create additional shapes using blank cards to include in your sort. We've provided one blank card for you in figure 5.12 (page 128). If you are addressing this task within a collaborative team, you can compare the results of your sorting and discuss the validity of the shapes present in each set. This is a useful task for students as well. Observing the shapes students create and the decisions they make when sorting will provide valuable information regarding their thinking about geometry.

From this experience, try again to define *polygon*. Check your definition against this one: *A polygon is a closed two-dimensional shape made with straight line segments.* The definition you suggested might not be an exact match to this one, but any powerful mathematics definition for polygon will include that the shape is two-dimensional, that the sides must be straight (no loops, no curves), and that the shape must be closed (no openings, no gaps). After you have a good definition for polygon, this will help situate the remaining experiences with two-dimensional shapes in the set of shape cards. Examples of nonpolygons that might be a part of this experience are shapes with curved lines such as circles, half-circles, and shapes that are not closed. Which of the shape cards are nonpolygons? Cards H, S, and Z are nonpolygons. What about L? The shape on card L is actually a polygon, but it is not a *simple* polygon.

Consider the examples of simple and nonsimple polygons in table 5.1.

Table 5.1: Simple and Nonsimple Polygons

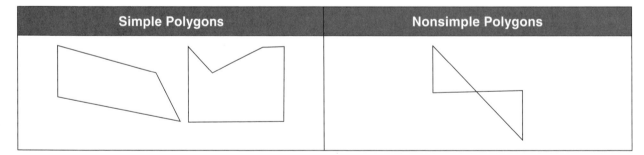

Simple Polygons	Nonsimple Polygons

Simple polygons are polygons that do not have any intersecting sides, while nonsimple polygons have intersecting sides. Simple polygons are most prevalent for grades 3–5, but it is important to know that polygons like the nonsimple polygon provided in table 5.1 are still polygons in order to avoid creating a potential misconception—or a rule that expires—for students about what shapes are polygons.

Step 3 in this task is to sort the simple polygons into triangles, quadrilaterals, and other polygons. What are the names of the "other" polygons in the set of shape cards? How might this list of polygon names, named based on the number of sides, help you (see table 5.2)?

Table 5.2: Names of Other Polygons

Number of Sides	Name of Polygon
5	Pentagon
6	Hexagon
7	Heptagon
8	Octagon
9	Nonagon
10	Decagon

In addition, other polygons might be named using geometry vocabulary such as presented in table 5.3. Use this information to further describe these other polygons.

Table 5.3: Categories of Polygons

Other Polygons	Definition
Regular	A polygon with all congruent sides and angles
Irregular	A polygon without all congruent sides or angles
Concave	A polygon with at least one interior angle greater than 180 degrees An alternative definition for a concave polygon is: If there exists two points inside the polygon connected by a line segment and a part of the line segment is outside the polygon, then the polygon is concave. For example,
Convex	A polygon with no interior angles greater than 180 degrees

Students in grade 3 should be able to name and define each of these polygons. They should use their observation, examination, and description skills to sort the polygons appropriately. You might also offer students opportunities to create, build, or draw examples of other polygons of their own.

Look at how you sorted the cards to create a set of triangles. You should only have shapes with exactly three sides in this set. Check your sorting of quadrilaterals. You should only have shapes with four sides in this set. The remaining simple polygons should be in the third set.

Now reconsider the set of triangles, and this time, name each triangle. Naming shapes is an important component of studying geometry. You may begin with informal names based on their attributes and build to more formal descriptions, but it is important to model the use of formal geometry shape names.

There are two ways to name a triangle: by its angles or by the length of its sides. See tables 5.4 and 5.5 for the naming of triangles. Again, you might practice creating examples of triangles on your own.

Table 5.4: Triangles Named by Sides

Triangle Name	Length of Sides	Shape Cards
Equilateral triangle	All sides have the same length.	N
Isosceles triangle	At least two sides have the same length.	G, N
Scalene triangle	No sides have the same length.	F, Q, V

You may notice that notations regarding the length of the sides or the size of the angles may not be present. For example, congruent sides and right angles are not indicated. As students move beyond elementary school, these designations will be necessary to demonstrate that the shapes are what they are named. Recall that considering relationships between shapes is an important component of two-dimensional geometry. Consider the six names of triangles provided in tables 5.4 and 5.5. Note that each triangle has angles and sides. With that notion in mind, which combination of triangles is possible? Use your knowledge of the six triangles to *classify* them by completing the chart in figure 5.13. The first two rows have been completed to help you get started.

Table 5.5: Triangles Named by Angles

Triangle Name	Size of Angles	Shape Cards
Right triangle	One angle is a right angle.	F, Q
Acute triangle	All angles are less than 90 degrees.	G, N
Obtuse triangle	One angle is greater than 90 degrees.	V

	Is always . . .	Is sometimes . . .	Is never . . .
An equilateral triangle	isosceles, acute		scalene, right, obtuse
An isosceles triangle		equilateral, right, acute, obtuse	scalene
A scalene triangle			
A right triangle			
An acute triangle			
An obtuse triangle			

Figure 5.13: Classification of triangles chart.

How did you use triangle definitions in the process of classifying the triangles? You might have had difficulty if you focused on nondefining attributes rather than exclusively on those attributes that define the different types of triangles. A completed Classification of Triangles Chart is included in appendix A (page 171).

Refer to your sorting of quadrilaterals. A quadrilateral is a polygon with four sides, so you should only have shapes with exactly four sides in the quadrilateral set. Common quadrilaterals present in K–2 geometry that become more formally defined and explored in grades 3–5 geometry are rectangles, squares, parallelograms, rhombuses (also called rhombi), and trapezoids. How do you know each is a quadrilateral? The first consideration is to check that the figure has four sides. Next, name each quadrilateral. Try to define these quadrilaterals before proceeding. Then, check your definitions with those provided in table 5.6 (page 134).

Be sure to note that you want to avoid defining a rectangle as a quadrilateral with two short sides and two long sides. These are attributes of some rectangles, but they are not *defining* attributes of rectangles and so they are not part of the definition for rectangle. That description limits the class of rectangles to exclude squares.

Table 5.6: Definitions of Common Quadrilaterals

Quadrilateral	Definition	Shape Cards
Parallelogram	A quadrilateral with opposite sides parallel	A, B, K, P, R, Y
Rectangle	A quadrilateral with four right angles	K, P, Y
Rhombus	A quadrilateral with all sides the same length	B, K, Y
Square	A quadrilateral with four right angles and all sides the same length	K, Y
Trapezoid	A quadrilateral with exactly one pair of parallel sides	C, U
Kite	A quadrilateral with exactly two pairs of distinct congruent, adjacent sides	X

Consider other possible relationships among these six types of quadrilaterals. What is the relationship between kites, parallelograms, rectangles, rhombuses, squares, and trapezoids? The relationship can be shown visually. Classify these quadrilaterals using the classifying diagram in figure 5.14 by placing the name of each of the six quadrilaterals on exactly one blank in the diagram.

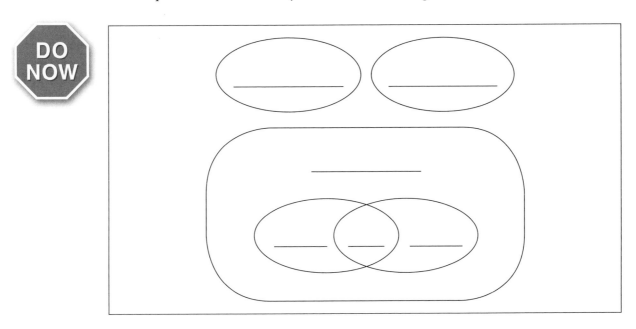

Figure 5.14: Diagram for classifying quadrilaterals.

How did you do? A key understanding in completing this diagram is knowing that rectangles, squares, and rhombuses are all parallelograms. Of these parallelograms, there is a common trait. How can you use this knowledge to complete the task in figure 5.11 (page 128) using attribute blocks if you were unable to complete it earlier? A completed Diagram for Classifying Quadrilaterals is provided in appendix B (page 173). Throughout the shape cards sorting task (see figure 5.11, page 128), you were engaged in Mathematical Practices that are similar to those used in the attribute train and block sorting tasks (see figure 5.4, page 123, and figure 5.7, page 126). The Mathematical Practice that stands out in this task is Mathematical Practice 6, "Attend to precision." When working with geometry concepts, it is important for teachers to attend to the appropriate use of geometry vocabulary, definitions, and tools to ensure that students do not obtain misconceptions during instruction.

The task in figure 5.15 (page 136) makes use of pattern blocks, just as they were used to explore fraction operations in chapter 4. Before proceeding, complete the pattern blocks task in figure 5.15.

The first part of this task is to name each block in the set of pattern blocks. This should be a review of two-dimensional shapes. The pattern block pieces are made of the following shapes: triangle, square, rhombus, hexagon, and trapezoid. Now, use a combination of two or more pattern blocks to build shapes you can name. Perhaps you used two equilateral triangles to build a rhombus, or you used two trapezoids to build a hexagon or a parallelogram.

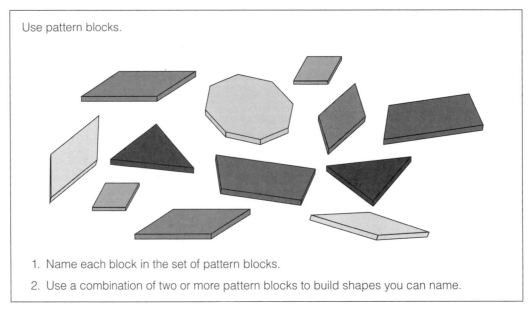

1. Name each block in the set of pattern blocks.

2. Use a combination of two or more pattern blocks to build shapes you can name.

Figure 5.15: Pattern blocks task.

If you did not compose those shapes, try to do so now. Composing (and decomposing) shapes is an important activity in geometry. Both two-dimensional and three-dimensional shapes can be composed and decomposed. Composing shapes is the act of taking two or more shapes to create another larger shape, and decomposing shapes is separating a shape into two or more smaller shapes. By composing and subsequently decomposing shapes, students apply their understanding of attributes and definitions of the individual shapes and newly composed shapes. Draw sketches of the shapes you composed using the pattern blocks. Consider other manipulatives that might be useful for exploring the composition of shapes in geometry. Tasks similar to this one reinforce students' abilities to reason with shapes and their attributes.

Recognizing Three-Dimensional Shapes

Starting with the next task (see figure 5.16), three-dimensional geometry is addressed. For this section, you will need to think about the following three-dimensional solids: spheres, cubes, right rectangular prisms, right circular cones, and right circular cylinders. You can acquire models of these solids by using some everyday objects. For instance, a ball is a model for a sphere, and a cereal box is a model for a right rectangular prism. A watercooler cup is a model for a right circular cone, and a can is a model for a right circular cylinder. Make a list of other everyday objects that can serve as models for three-dimensional shapes.

Use a set of two- and three-dimensional shapes.

1. Distinguish two-dimensional shapes from three-dimensional shapes.

2. Sort the three-dimensional shapes.

3. Describe defining attributes of the three-dimensional shapes.

4. Name the three-dimensional shapes.

Figure 5.16: Two- and three-dimensional shapes task.

Before beginning the sort with three-dimensional shapes, it will be helpful to consider the difference between two-dimensional shapes and three-dimensional shapes. In a practical sense, two-dimensional shapes are modeled as drawings or shapes on a plane, a two-dimensional surface. Because these shapes are two-dimensional (having only length and width), they have no thickness. This can be confusing because of the use of a three-dimensional model to represent a two-dimensional shape, such as a triangle cut out of construction paper (which really does have some thickness). In theory, one can't cut out or hold a triangle, because in concept, it only has two dimensions, but you need to create cutouts and shapes as a way to make the content accessible to learners. Three-dimensional shapes are modeled as solids in three dimensions as they have length, width, and height. Students need to understand the relationships that exist between two- and three-dimensional shapes. With a mixed pile of two- and three-dimensional shapes, students should be able to distinguish between these two classes of shapes.

Consider that a rectangular prism is composed of six rectangles and a cylinder is composed of two circles and a wrapped rectangle. Did you sort the three-dimensional shapes according to the polygons used to compose them? K–2 students might begin with an informal approach to sorting the three-dimensional shapes. For instance, they might sort the shapes into two groups, one group of three-dimensional shapes that can roll (spheres, cylinders, cones) and one group of three-dimensional shapes that cannot roll across a table (cubes, prisms). Again, instruction in grades 3–5 builds on that foundation. What sorting groups did you create? Perhaps you sorted by which shapes have flat sides and which do not or which shapes have only polygonal faces and which do not. Consider your observations and descriptions of each three-dimensional shape and make a list of the defining attributes of each shape. This is started for you in table 5.7.

Table 5.7: Attributes of Common Three-Dimensional Solids

Three-Dimensional Shapes	Example of a Defining Attribute
Sphere	No flat faces
Cube	Six faces
Right rectangular prism	Rectangular faces
Right circular cone	Only one base
Right circular cylinder	Two circular bases

As you work with these three-dimensional shapes, practice using their proper names and drawing each of them.

The Classroom

Now that you have explored your own thinking about plane and solid geometry concepts, turn your attention to explore what this will look like in the classroom. The included video links provide important insight into student thinking about geometry. The first video demonstrates the important foundational work that students need to accomplish in order to explore relationships within the set of quadrilaterals. In this video, grade 3 students are asked to make a square and a rectangle. We encourage you to watch the video in its entirety before proceeding.

www.solution-tree.com/Defining_and_Classifying
_Squares_and_Rectangles

Now that you have had the opportunity to watch students actively engage in developing understanding of squares and rectangles, what are your thoughts? There are other shapes that could be used as a context for the lesson; selecting shapes or pairs of shapes that students can explore is important for the task. Consider the focus for the lesson. How does the teacher facilitate discussion? What kinds of questions are posed? Note that the questions are meant to help students challenge their potential misunderstandings about shape. When students describe and compare the shapes, they are demonstrating what they are learning about the shapes.

Perhaps after viewing the entire video, you noticed that the focus of the lesson is not revealed in the teacher's introduction of the lesson or in the first instruction she gives. However, these two items provide an important foundation for the lesson. The introduction offers the students an opportunity to explore quadrilaterals, and the first instruction of using the available manipulative to make a square engages each student to recall how to use the manipulative and how to form the model for a square. During this event, the teacher quickly observes how students are interacting with the manipulative to create the model. When noticing that most students have completed the task, she asks the students to hold up what they've made.

What is really important at this point is that she does not indicate who is or who is not holding up a square. Instead, she invites the students to make the assessment by asking, "What do you see?" This gives students ownership in the lesson. You will note that the students respond in unison that all of the shapes held up are squares. It is at this point that the teacher indicates that she sees one shape being held up that is not a square. Again, she poses to the class the task of determining where the nonsquare is rather than simply pointing out the nonsquare and taking ownership away from the students. With the prompting to further observe the shapes being held up, a student responds that he thinks he sees the shape that is not a square. He explains his thinking, and the teacher gives a second student an opportunity to respond to the first student's conclusion. This exchange supports Mathematical Practice 3, "Construct viable arguments and critique the reasoning of others." In the safety of the learning environment, the student is willing to confront the inaccurate model for a square and to state his position clearly. However, the teacher's further questioning of the student who does not build the accurate model for a square leads to the student using the manipulative to make better sense of her understanding of a square. This teaching moment also represents the powerful impact that the right choice of manipulative can have on students' learning.

The next experience in this video is the teacher challenging the students to make a rectangle. Subsequently, the teacher asks the students to hold up their rectangles. She is operating on an assumption that students will most likely make the traditional rectangle with two long sides and two short sides. In preparation for this assumption, the teacher decides to introduce students to a different perspective of the rectangle by using the teacher move of "I saw someone . . ." By engaging students with a possible response from another student, the teacher can introduce a concept without causing alarm. Here the teacher says that she saw someone hold up a square in response to the request to make a rectangle. This is a critical point in the lesson because it is the marker for students developing an understanding of the relationship between squares and rectangles. The teacher then provides an opportunity for the students to engage in discourse about this new perspective. You can observe some students in the video making the declaration that "a square is a rectangle," but the strength of this statement is not evident from mere observation. Clearly, the teacher recognizes the need to further question students' understanding of the relationship between squares and rectangles.

The teacher asks students to share their thinking, and through the dialogue that follows, the students' understandings and misunderstandings are revealed. For instance, a student responds by saying, "A rectangle doesn't have all equal sides; it has two short sides and two long sides." This perspective is not surprising and is often the result of limited exposure to developing the appropriate definition of rectangle and limited exposure to models of rectangles that reflect this definition. This begs attention to Mathematical Practice 6, "Attend to precision," during instruction in mathematics. A quadrilateral with four sides (and four right angles)—two long sides and two short sides—is an example of a rectangle, but not the definition of rectangle. Again, the teacher inquires of the class who agrees with this statement. Upon seeing that the majority of the students does agree, the teacher confronts the students with the cognitive challenge that what the previous student said is indeed not correct. After allowing for additional discussion, the teacher asks, "Where are you now?"

One student in the class, who states that he is speaking for himself as well as his group, shares their results from comparing squares to rectangles—they both have four right angles and they both have opposite sides equal. With prompting by the teacher, the student is able to conclude that a square is a rectangle, but one with all equal sides. However, note that the discourse does not end with this declaration because the teacher needs more certainty that other students have also advanced their understanding of the relationship between squares and rectangles. The teacher engages the class by asking, "What did he say?" This is an excellent strategy for assessing students' clarification about what their peers have said and also provides students an opportunity to support or refute what they've heard another student say. In addition, the teacher uses all three layers of facilitation throughout the lesson—facilitating engagement of the whole class, small groups, and individual students.

Finally, the teacher challenges the students to make a square that is not a rectangle. The students determine that this cannot be done because a square is also a rectangle. At the conclusion of this lesson, you may wonder what other instructional moves the teacher could have made to encourage discourse and scaffold students to understand the relationship between a square and a rectangle. Note that this primary goal of the lesson was not presented in a straightforward fashion because simply telling students the relationship does not support their understanding of the relationship. Giving students an opportunity to explore the relationship is the best course of action.

Now take the time to watch the second video in its entirety.

www.solution-tree.com/Comparing_Plane_Shapes

Now that you have had the opportunity to view younger students compare attributes of two-dimensional shapes, what is your perspective about the progression of geometry? In this video, the teacher first narrows the discussion of shapes to two shapes: a circle and a rectangle. The goal of the lesson is to build students' skills of observation, description, and comparison of shapes. These skills serve as a foundation in geometry and carry across plane and solid geometry. They also give students context for Mathematical Practice 3, "Construct viable arguments and critique the reasoning of others."

Initially, the students' observations focus on the attribute of color. This is an acceptable anchor to include for younger learners. However, if you desire to avoid students focusing on the attribute of color as a difference between multiple shapes, simply present shapes of the same color to eliminate that difference. With further prompting, a student moves beyond color and describes the number of sides of the rectangle, and another student describes the circle as having only curves and no vertices. These descriptions include terminology that some young students might not have, but it is important to help students build formal mathematics terminology and to do so according to Mathematical Practice 6, "Attend to precision," because it is just as important to be precise with mathematical terminology as it is with mathematical computation. As the video continues, you will notice that another student has even more advanced geometry vocabulary when she states that the rectangle is "two-dimensional because it lays flat." Note that the strategy of thinking about a shape being two dimensional because it lays flat in a book is an informal way of characterizing two-dimensional shapes, not a way of defining two-dimensional shapes.

The teacher selects two more shapes for students to discuss: a triangle and a rectangle. In this section of the video, students again focus on the number of sides and the number of vertices. However, another student connects his understanding of the triangle to a real-life object (pizza); this strategy can be very helpful for students' developing understanding of shapes. To further the exploration of shapes, using the combination of *alike* and *different* helps students advance their mathematical language and their understanding of the shapes. The final comparison between a rectangle and circle provides an opportunity for students to distinguish shapes that have straight sides and shapes that do not have straight sides. It is important to note that the teacher's questions and the students' exploration of the shapes drive the learning experience. Furthermore, by using a limited number of shapes, the teacher is able to target students' focus better than if each student had many shapes to observe, describe, and compare.

TQE Process

At this point, it may be helpful to watch the first video again (page 138). Pay close attention to the tasks, questioning, and opportunities to collect evidence of student learning.

The TQE process can help you frame your observations. Teachers who have a deep understanding of the mathematics they teach:

- Select appropriate *tasks* to support identified learning goals
- Facilitate productive *questioning* during instruction to engage students in the Mathematical Practices
- Collect and use student *evidence* in the formative assessment process during instruction

This lesson's *task* focuses on classifying squares and rectangles, though as mentioned, this is not apparent at the beginning of the lesson. The goal of the lesson is originally presented as exploring quadrilaterals. The teacher designed this task with the expectation that many students will define rectangles as having two long sides and two short sides, excluding the possibility of a square being a rectangle. The sequence of the activities in this task highlights this common misconception; the learning outcome is for students to know that all squares are also rectangles. If the learning goal of this task had been presented at the beginning of the lesson, the dissonance of the lesson would be lost. Thus, it is important to consider how to present the learning goal in the design of the task when the plan is for students to discover a new relationship (or correct a commonly held misconception). Note also how the choice of manipulative (AngLegs) to model the shapes supports the teacher being able to see how the students are constructing the shapes, as the sides of the same length are the same color. This allows the teacher to quickly determine which students have constructed squares and which students have constructed rectangles that are not squares.

Notice how the *questioning* of the teacher guides the role of the student throughout the lesson. With the "What do you see?" and "What did he say?" type of questions, the students appear to be in charge of the lesson. However, the teacher is, in fact, guiding the lesson by asking the right questions and selecting the student responses that will move the class toward achieving the learning goal. The teacher uses questioning to create a climate in which students are leading the sense making and their strategies are guiding the work of the class. This climate is supported through questioning, appropriate use of student work, and the "I saw someone . . ." strategy. This strategy, when the teacher says she's seen another student take a certain action, is beneficial for students to think that other students advance the thinking that moves the class forward. It is important to consider and plan what examples or models will be helpful to present to students as a hypothetical situation to advance their learning. By asking other questions, such as "Where are you now?" and "What did he say?," the teacher is engaging students and encouraging discussion.

The teacher is able to collect *evidence* of student learning during the lesson. The choice of manipulative makes the recognition of who can accurately construct a square or a rectangle easy, and having the students display and analyze their squares leads to an example of Mathematical Practice 6, "Attend to precision." Clearly, the students have developed the norm of taking a risk to show their work in the class. This is important to note because the formative assessment process can support assessment of multiple students at one time, not just an occurrence between the teacher and a single student. The teacher also collects information on how students define rectangles, first by allowing them to construct them, and then, after seeing their constructions, by asking who agrees that a rectangle must have two short sides and two long sides. In seeing that all students agree with that definition, the teacher tells them that this is incorrect. With prompting by the teacher and some exploration, the class is able to conclude that a square is a rectangle, but one with all sides equal. The teacher continues the classroom discussion in order to collect more evidence that other students have advanced their understanding of the relationship between squares and rectangles.

An additional consideration is how to recognize and respond to student errors. In the next section, you will review geometry topics as they relate to common errors of students. This will provide another plan of action as you learn to address misconceptions by recognizing their source and thinking about ways to assist students.

The Response

Common difficulties in grades 3–5 involve the language of geometry. Students may confuse the vocabulary because there are simply so many new terms to learn in geometry, terms that will extend greatly beyond elementary school mathematics. It will help to use strategies such as a mathematics journal, a word wall, a classroom dictionary, and lots of discourse to support and reinforce the appropriate use of geometry vocabulary. Providing students opportunities to align geometry terms, descriptions, definitions (when appropriate), and images of shapes can be beneficial to helping students accommodate the many geometry concepts present in grades 3–5. You should deliberately use more than just the common ways of representing shapes, such as triangles with a horizontal line segment at the bottom of the drawing, as students need to accurately produce and identify a variety of representations.

Another frequent difficulty is with the definitions of geometrical terms that appear to be correct but in fact only help students develop misconceptions. For example, when rectangle is defined as a four-sided shape with two long sides and two short sides, this is really the description of one type of rectangle, and this description excludes the square as a rectangle, when in fact a square is a special case of a rectangle. Hence, an appropriate definition for rectangle is a four-sided shape (quadrilateral) with four right angles. The length of sides is not relevant to the definition of rectangle. However, if a rectangle has all sides of equal length, this type of rectangle is a square.

The next example deals with the language of *at least* and *exactly*. Each phrase brings a different perspective to a definition. While *at least* opens up a definition, *exactly* narrows the definition. For instance, consider the two possible definitions for isosceles triangle.

1.　An isosceles triangle is a triangle with at least two sides the same length.

2.　An isosceles triangle is a triangle with exactly two sides the same length.

The first definition opens up the possibility for equilateral triangles, triangles with all sides the same length, to also be isosceles triangles. However, the second definition would not include equilateral triangles. While both definitions are acceptable, the first, less restrictive definition is the one we have adopted in this book.

Consider these two accepted definitions for the trapezoid.

1.　A trapezoid is a quadrilateral with one pair of parallel sides.

2.　A trapezoid is a quadrilateral with exactly one pair of parallel sides.

The first definition opens up the possibility for parallelograms, rectangles, squares, and rhombuses to be trapezoids. However, the second definition would not accommodate quadrilaterals with more than one pair of parallel sides. In this case, the second, more restrictive definition is aligned with our views and is used in this book. What this means in general, though, is that it is important to be very clear about the supporting phrases used in mathematics definitions so that students do not develop misunderstandings in geometry.

Because language is at the forefront of difficulties in geometry, students *and* teachers must engage in Mathematical Practice 6, "Attend to precision," during geometry instruction. If teachers are precise with geometry language, then their students will be precise with language.

Reflections

1. What do you feel are the key points in this chapter?

2. What challenges might you face when implementing the key ideas from this chapter? How will you overcome them?

3. What are the important features for developing an understanding of geometry, and how will you ensure your instruction embeds the support needed for these features?

4. Select a recent lesson you have taught or observed focused on geometry. Relate this lesson to the TQE process.

5. What changes will you make to your planning and instruction based on what you read and considered from this chapter?

CHAPTER 6

Measurement

In grades 3–5, topics central to measurement include concepts related to perimeter, area, volume, elapsed time, angles, and conversion within systems. Contexts related to measurement offer opportunities for students to engage in problem solving.

The Challenge

The initial task in this chapter (figure 6.1) provides an opportunity for you to engage in problem solving related to measurement. This task involves the use of the geoboard and geoboard dot paper. If you do not have access to a geoboard, the activity can be completed using virtual geoboard manipulatives or the geoboard dot paper provided.

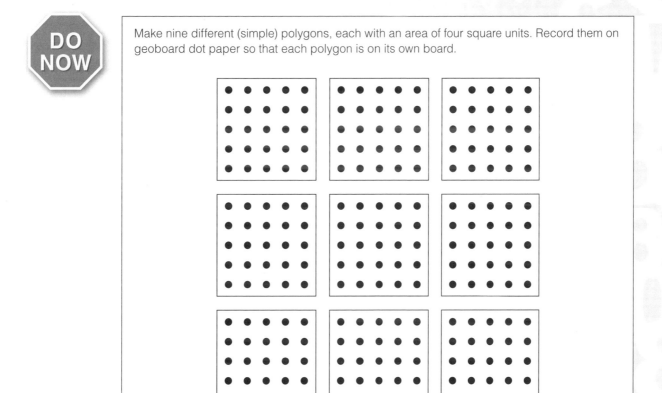

DO NOW

Make nine different (simple) polygons, each with an area of four square units. Record them on geoboard dot paper so that each polygon is on its own board.

Figure 6.1: Geoboard polygons task.

*Visit **go.solution-tree.com/mathematics** for a free reproducible version of this figure.*

In order to solve this task, you also need to define *different* in terms of the problem. In this problem, different means *not congruent*. Therefore, the polygons in figure 6.2 would *not* qualify as different because they are transformations of one another. In figure 6.2, you can see that the second figure was just a translation of the first, and the third figure was a rotation of the first figure. Polygons are the same if they are congruent, regardless of their location or orientation on the geoboard (see chapter 5 for more on polygons).

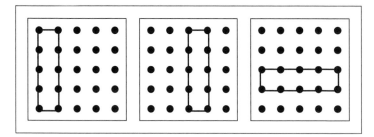

Figure 6.2: Polygons that are not different.

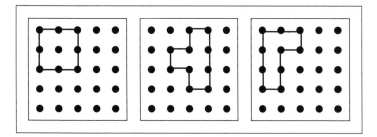

Figure 6.3: Three different polygons each with an area of four square units.

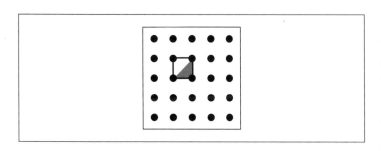

Figure 6.4: Defining a half-square unit.

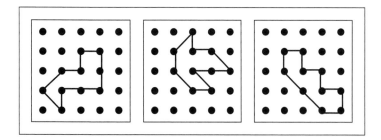

Figure 6.5: Four-square-unit polygons created using half-square units.

The other part of the task that must be clarified is how the area is determined. Area on a geoboard is typically measured using square units determined by the horizontal or vertical distance between two adjacent pegs. Therefore, the polygons in figure 6.2 each measure four square units in area and could represent one of the nine polygons used to complete the task in figure 6.1 (page 145). Three more possible polygons that you may have determined include those in figure 6.3.

Each of these polygons has an area that is clearly countable in that it can be determined by counting unit squares. Students in grade 3 are introduced to area by counting unit squares. However, in order to create nine polygons, each with an area of four square units, you must move beyond counting unit squares. One way to move beyond this is to count half-square units. The diagonal of a square divides the area of the square into two parts that are equal in measure. One of those parts can be counted as a half-square unit (see the shaded part of figure 6.4).

This allows you to create polygons like those in figure 6.5. Examine the polygons in figure 6.5 to confirm that the area is four square units in each case.

The area for each of the polygons in figure 6.5 can be determined by counting unit squares or half-square units. How is this different from the polygons in figure 6.6?

These polygons are not made up exclusively of squares and half-squares. These polygons are made up of halves of non-square rectangles. How is it helpful to think of the areas in this manner? The area of a triangle created by the diagonal of a rectangle is half the area of the rectangle. Examine the first polygon in figure 6.6. What rectangle could have been used to form that triangle? Figure 6.7 provides an overlay of the rectangles used to form the triangles in figure 6.6. Make sense of them and then try to use this technique to create additional four-square-unit polygons.

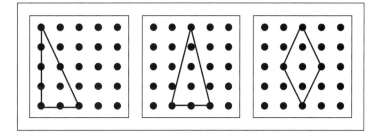

Figure 6.6: Four-square-unit polygons with parts beyond countable squares and half-squares.

By creating rectangles, the area becomes "countable" again, and the areas of the triangles formed by the rectangles are determined by taking half of the area of the rectangle. This sort of thinking helps students prepare for formulas for finding

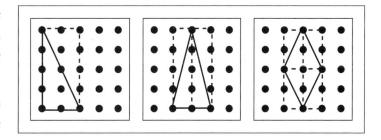

Figure 6.7: Four-square-unit polygons with rectangle overlays.

areas of polygons in later grades and provides an excellent context to support student engagement in Mathematical Practice 3, "Construct viable arguments and critique the reasoning of others" (see Bray, Dixon, and Martinez [2006], for a discussion of what this looks like with fourth-grade students).

The Progression

The domain of measurement contains several seemingly disjoint topics. Although it is difficult to see connections between measuring elapsed time and angle measurement, the links between length, perimeter, area, and volume are more transparent. Elapsed time and angle measure are connected in that they provide quantifications; they are different in that the attributes being quantified are quite distinct. Perimeter, area, and volume measure related attributes and provide an interesting avenue to explore as a progression. Following is a progression for building understanding of measurement.

- Tell time to the nearest minute.

- Solve word problems involving addition and subtraction of time intervals in minutes.

- Recognize perimeter and area as measureable attributes of plane figures.

- Estimate perimeter and area.

- Make sense of measuring area by counting unit squares and multiplying side lengths.

- Find areas of shapes composed of rectangles by finding areas of all nonoverlapping rectangles and adding those areas to find the area of the original figure.

- Distinguish and explore the relationship between area and perimeter.

- Recognize volume as a measureable attribute.

- Estimate volume.

- Measure volume by counting unit cubes.

- Determine volumes of right rectangular prisms by multiplying edge lengths or the area of the base by the height of the prism.

- Use decomposition to determine the volumes of solid figures composed of right rectangular prisms.

- Recognize angles as a measurable attribute.

- Draw angles, including acute, right, and obtuse angles.

- Measure angles.

Kindergarten Through Grade 2

The exploration of measurement begins in the primary grades with young learners identifying measureable attributes such as length (see chapter 6 in *Making Sense of Mathematics for Teaching Grades K–2* [Dixon et al., 2016] for an extensive discussion of measurement in the primary grades). Students first use direct comparison to relate sizes of objects and eventually use indirect comparisons leading to the use of units (nonstandard and standard) to quantify linear measures of objects. Students develop skills with the ruler in grade 2 and use it to measure lengths in whole units. Measuring time is also introduced in the primary grades, with students first telling time to the hour and half hour. Telling time extends to the nearest five minutes in grade 2.

Grade 3

In grade 3, time measurement is extended to telling and writing time to the nearest minute. In addition to telling time, measuring elapsed time is introduced. Students solve word problems describing addition and subtraction of time intervals using tools such as the open time line. These word problem types can be related to those for addition and subtraction of whole numbers (see chapter 1 for a discussion of addition and subtraction word problem structures). Grade 3 students also measure liquid volume and mass using grams, kilograms, and liters and solve word problems using these measures. However, a major focus regarding measurement in grade 3 involves area.

Students recognize area as a measureable attribute that reflects how much two-dimensional space is covered. Initially, students might use a variety of tools (geometric shapes, pieces of paper, bottle tops, and so on) to measure area. Without agreement of the tool used, however, students will be confronted with a variety of answers that do not support consensus. When given the same tool, such as square manipulatives, students can cover a given space and determine area by counting the square units. This leads to the use of a standard unit for area. This is connected to linear measurement and explored in earlier grades when students measure length. In grade 3, students measure area by counting rows of the same length, determining the number of unit squares needed to "tile" a rectangular region (see figure 6.8).

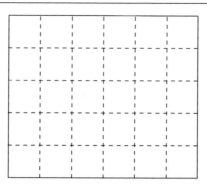

This rectangle is 6 units wide. There are 6 squares along the bottom row, and there are 5 rows of squares. The area is 30 square units.

Figure 6.8: Determining area by counting rows of tiles.

Eventually, students see that they can multiply side lengths to determine the area of a rectangle. Area is often confused with perimeter because perimeter is also explored in grade 3. Focus in this grade level is on distinguishing between perimeter and area but also exploring the relationship between perimeter and area. What becomes difficult here is that perimeter can also be determined by counting unit squares along the sides of a two-dimensional object. In figure 6.8, the perimeter of the rectangle could be determined by counting the six squares along the bottom, five squares along the side, six squares along the top, and five squares along the last side. This gives you a perimeter of 22 units, but because the squares were used to count the unit, students might think the measure is 22 *square* units and call it area.

Grade 4

In grade 4, students continue to solve problems involving areas of rectangular regions and perimeters of polygons. Focus is more directly on applying formulas to find these measures (area formulas for triangles and other quadrilaterals are addressed in grade 6). Students use different units within the same system to describe measures in terms of smaller units. For example, they use inches to describe something measured in feet by using the relationship that one foot is equivalent to twelve inches.

Angles are introduced as measureable attributes in grade 4. Students connect angle measurement to a circle with its center as the end points of the two rays that form the angle. Angles are measured in degrees, and each degree is $\frac{1}{360}$ of a turn around the circle (see figure 6.9). Students measure angles to the nearest degree with a protractor and draw angles to a specified degree measure.

Grade 5

Volume is introduced as a measureable attribute in grade 5 in much the same way area is introduced in grade 3. Students first determine volume by counting unit cubes (see figure 6.10, page 150), which are cubes with side lengths of one unit.

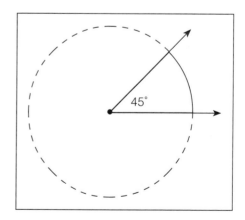

Figure 6.9: A 45° angle or $\frac{45}{360}$ of a turn around a circle.

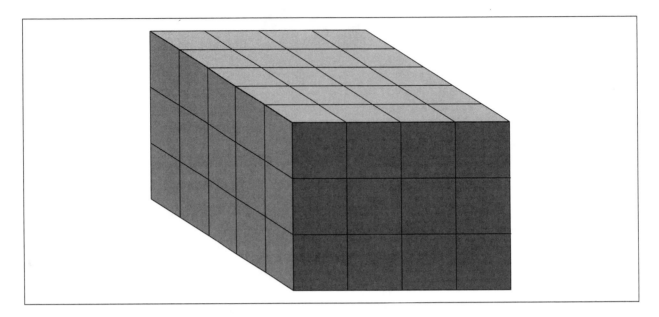

Figure 6.10: A rectangular prism with "countable" volume.

In grade 5, volume is limited to right rectangular prisms or solid figures composed of right rectangular prisms. Through engagement in Mathematical Practice 8, "Look for and express regularity in repeated reasoning," students develop the volume formulas for rectangular prisms of both length times width times height ($V = l \times w \times h$) and the area of the base times the height ($V = b \times h$).

The Mathematics

Students in grades 3–5 learn important aspects of measurement, including measuring elapsed time, connecting perimeter and area, exploring volume, deriving area formulas, and measuring angles. Perhaps the most important approach to helping students develop measurement concepts is for students to be actively engaged in measuring and discussing their experiences. What follows provides support for you to facilitate instruction that gives students these opportunities.

Measuring Elapsed Time

Measuring time intervals, or elapsed time, provides a nice connection to strategies for adding and sub-tracting whole numbers using an open number line (see chapter 1). However, rather than calculating with whole numbers on the number line, the number line represents time and can be thought of as an open time line. Students typically count up from the beginning time to the ending time in order to determine the elapsed time. This models the counting-up strategy discussed in chapter 1. Consider the elapsed time scenario provided in the task in figure 6.11. Solve it using an open time line.

Sasha is taking a flight from Orlando, Florida, to Manchester, New Hampshire. The plane is scheduled to take off at 7:15 a.m. and land at 11:45 a.m. How long should it take Sasha to fly from Orlando to Manchester?

Figure 6.11: Elapsed time for a flight task.

How did you solve the problem? Did you begin by sketching a time line and recording the time, 7:15, on the left of the line you drew? It is likely that you then began to make jumps of times that made sense to you. You might have jumped 45 minutes to get to the next hour, or you might have jumped by hours to 8:15, then 9:15, and so on. Using the open time line allows students to solve problems in ways that make sense to them and provides students with opportunities to make sense of one another's thinking as strategies are shared during instruction (Dixon, 2008). Consider the solution strategies provided in figure 6.12. Is there a solution strategy that closely matches how you solved the problem?

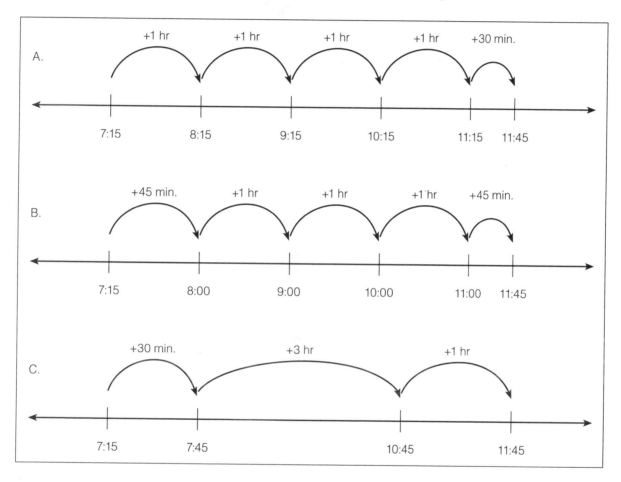

Figure 6.12: Solutions for Sasha's flight problem.

The choice of jumps influences the difficulty level of the final step in the solution process—that of combining the jumps to determine the total time elapsed. Solutions A and C result in a fairly straightforward last step of combining hours and then including the minutes. Solution B requires students to add the hours to get three hours but then to combine two sets of 45 minutes. Some students will make an hour by combining 45 minutes and 15 minutes, leaving 30 minutes left. Other students will make an hour with 30 minutes from each set of 45 minutes and then combine the two sets of remaining 15 minutes to get 30 minutes. Yet other students combine minutes to get 90 minutes and then convert that to one hour and 30 minutes. Each of these methods is valid, and students should choose what makes sense to them. That said, they should also make sense of each other's strategies. This provides a nice opportunity to support student engagement in Mathematical Practice 3, "Construct viable arguments and critique the reasoning of others."

Elapsed time problems become more challenging when different parts of the problem are unknown. In an elapsed time problem, the goal is often to determine the interval of time that elapses; however, the elapsed time can also be given with the goal to find the start or end time. In these instances, you can use word problem types related to those for addition and subtraction of whole numbers. For example, elapsed time problems include situations where the start time is unknown, the elapsed time is unknown, or the end time is unknown, which relate to join problems where the start is unknown, the change is unknown, or the result is unknown. Consider the problem and solution provided in figure 6.13. Did the student solve it correctly? How might you explain the student's thinking?

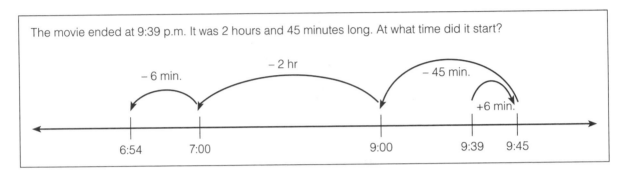

The movie ended at 9:39 p.m. It was 2 hours and 45 minutes long. At what time did it start?

Figure 6.13: A start unknown elapsed time problem.

This student used compensation to make the problem easier to solve. The student added six minutes onto 9:39 to get 9:45 so that it would be easier to subtract forty-five minutes and land on 9 p.m. Then the student subtracted two hours to land on 7:00. The student was not finished, because the student had to compensate for adding six minutes to the end time by subtracting six minutes from 7 p.m. to land on 6:54 p.m. as the start time for the movie. Exploring invented algorithms for adding and subtracting multidigit numbers (see chapter 1) supports this type of thinking with elapsed time.

Connecting Perimeter and Area

Early work with linear measurement provides the foundation for making sense of perimeter, area, and volume. When finding perimeter, misconceptions regarding linear measurement may still be present in students' thinking. For example, consider the student responses to the task in figure 6.14. Make sense of each student's reasoning before reading further.

Which student is correct? What were the bases of the other errors? Understanding that the perimeter is the distance around the outside of the square helps students determine perimeter accurately but also leads many students to make errors. In the bottom length of the square, five square units fit along that side, thus the length of the side is five. Therefore, the perimeter of the entire square is four times that length—or twenty units—meaning Austin is correct.

A common error in students' thinking is to count segment endpoints instead of spaces. Looking again at the bottom length of the square, and starting with the bottom left-hand corner, you can count six tick marks. Doing this for all four sides will result in twenty-four units, which is Colby's answer and is incorrect. Finally, where did Michele's solution come from? If you count the unit squares adjacent to the outside edge of the entire square, you will get sixteen, which would represent the area of the outside edge of the square.

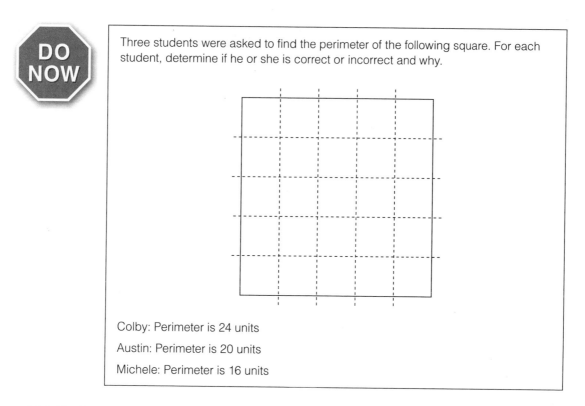

Figure 6.14: Finding the perimeter of a square.

Errors, such as those presented in Colby's and Michele's solutions, are often prevalent when students are asked to solve problems presented conceptually, as opposed to being given the side lengths and just asked to calculate the perimeter with numbers. Trying to determine the reasoning behind students' answers provides insight into how they may have been thinking about the problem, which will indicate which students need more experience with linear concepts—possibly with rulers—to help them make sense of length.

Determining perimeters of polygons is directly related to linear measurement, as the concept of perimeter is simply based on adding the measures of all the side lengths of a polygon. However, perimeter includes more than just calculating the length around a space. Being able to reason about perimeter is important so that students can compare perimeters with one another. Consider, for example, the task in figure 6.15. Solve the problem yourself before reading further.

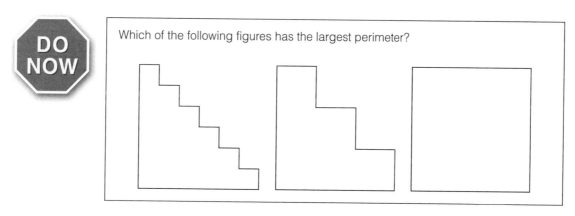

Figure 6.15: Comparing perimeter without calculating perimeter.

Looking at the three figures, it is common to think that the first figure has the largest perimeter because it has more corners than the other two figures. Students may look at the figures and think that the third figure has the largest perimeter because it has the largest area and think that a larger area equates to a larger perimeter. What is the solution to the problem? How did you solve it?

What else do the three figures have in common? First, all three figures have the same length and height. How is that going to help you solve the problem? Take a moment to compare the second and the third figure. If the figures are overlaid on top of one another, you can see that both perimeters line up until the "stair steps" begin (see figure 6.16).

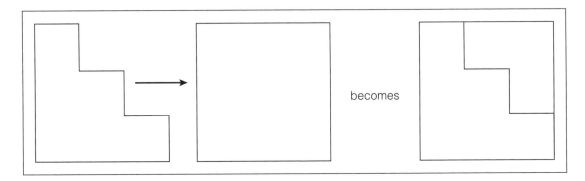

Figure 6.16: Overlaying figures 2 and 3.

How does the height of the stairs compare to the height of the square? If the height of the stairs is projected onto the height of the square, the heights are the same. The same happens with the lengths of the stairs compared to the top of the square. Thus, both figures have equal perimeters. What about the perimeter of the first figure? The first figure also has the same perimeter, because the height and length of each stair step can be projected onto the height and length of the other two figures. Though all three figures have different areas, the perimeters are the same.

Perimeter and area are often confused by students, and you may find them solving for perimeter when they are asked for the area or vice versa. Understanding the relationships between perimeter and area is important to help students make the distinction between each. To examine this yourself, solve the task in figure 6.17.

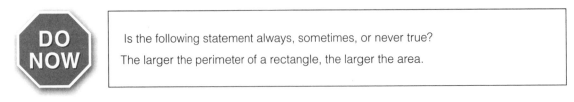

Figure 6.17: Relationship between perimeter and area.

How did you think about the statement? Did you draw rectangles and find examples to see if the statement is true?

Upon first glance, it appears as though the statement is always true. It makes sense that if the perimeter of a rectangle increases, the area will also increase. You can see with the two rectangles in figure 6.18, that this is the case.

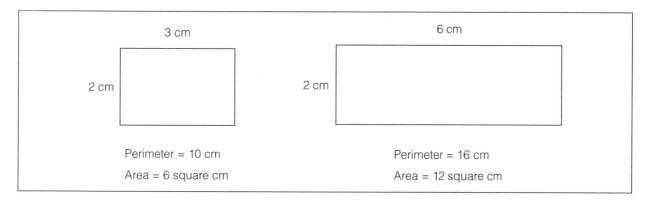

Figure 6.18: Larger perimeter and area with rectangles.

Can you find a case where the perimeter increases but the area does not? Examining the shapes in figure 6.19, you can see that as the perimeter increases, the area may either increase, decrease, or stay the same.

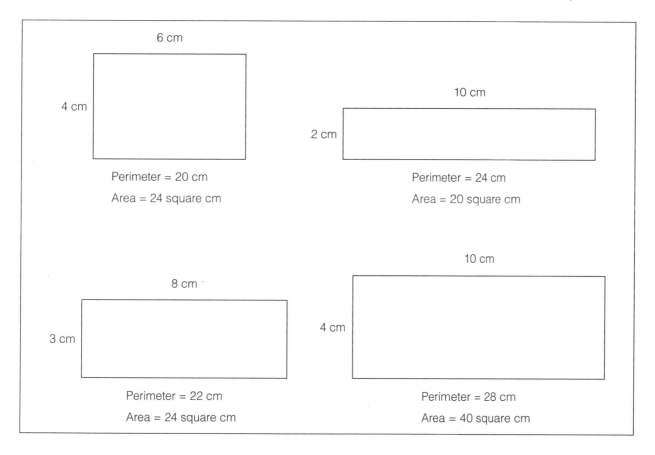

Figure 6.19: Examining perimeter and area.

From figure 6.19, it becomes evident that though you may have initially thought that the statement is always true, upon further examination you can see that this is not the case. Even though you may have found two rectangles where this is true, such as those in figure 6.18, two rectangles alone are not necessarily enough to make a generalization of this statement for *all* rectangles. Thus, finding more examples, such as those in figure 6.19, is needed to determine that the statement is only sometimes true.

Can you find an instance of two rectangles where the perimeters are the same but the areas are different? Try to find two figures yourself with the same perimeter. What do you notice about how their areas compare? Picking an example, such as the one shown in figure 6.20, you can see that though the perimeter is the same in both figures, the areas are not.

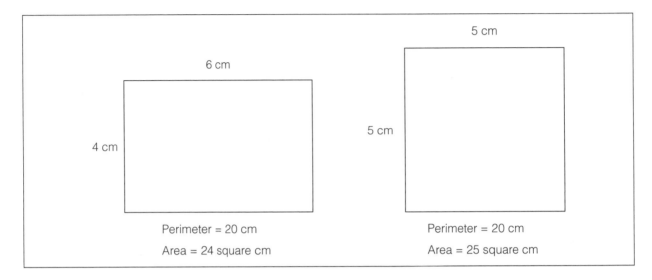

Figure 6.20: Two rectangles with the same perimeter but different areas.

Once students have experiences such as those just described with reasoning about perimeter and area, they can move toward finding the formulas for the perimeter and area of rectangles. This is something that students discover when they are given the opportunity to examine perimeters and areas of many rectangles. You might ask them to complete a table similar to the one provided in figure 6.21 and look for patterns.

When learners consider possibilities for patterns and develop the perimeter and area formulas from this process, they are engaging in Mathematical Practice 8, "Look for and express regularity in repeated reasoning."

Exploring Volume

Developing formulas to find the volume of rectangular prisms can be done with activities that allow for exploration of multiple strategies. For example, consider the task in figure 6.22.

How did you determine the volume? You may have found how many unit cubes were in a layer then multiplied by the number of layers. Or, you may have seen that the rectangular prism was a 5 × 4 × 4 rectangular prism and then multiplied the dimensions. Perhaps you found the area of the base of the prism by multiplying 4 × 4 or by mentally counting the cubes and then multiplied the area of the base times the height.

How would you expect students to approach this task for the first time? How would you expect students to make sense of volume? Knowing how students approach problems such as this will help you understand their thinking. Students should start their exploration of volume with the process of counting cubic units. They should record the dimensions for different rectangular prisms along with the volume and look for a relationship between the dimensions (see the discussion of the video in The Classroom section) similar to the activity in figure 6.21.

Rectangle	Length	Width	Perimeter	Possible Pattern for Perimeter	Area	Possible Pattern for Area
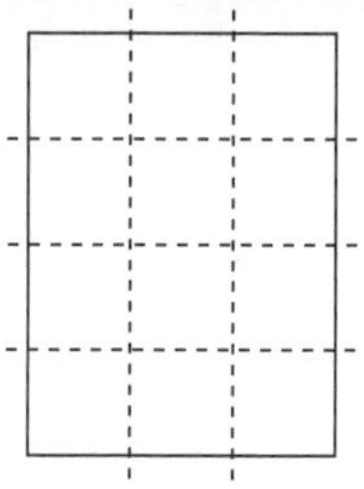						
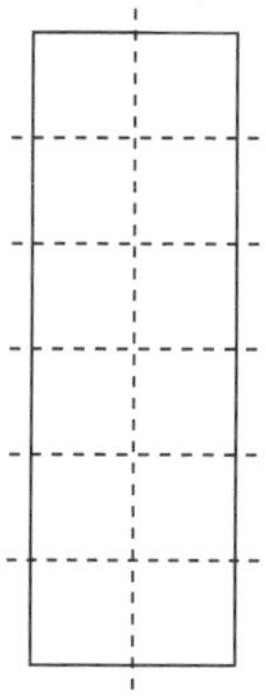						
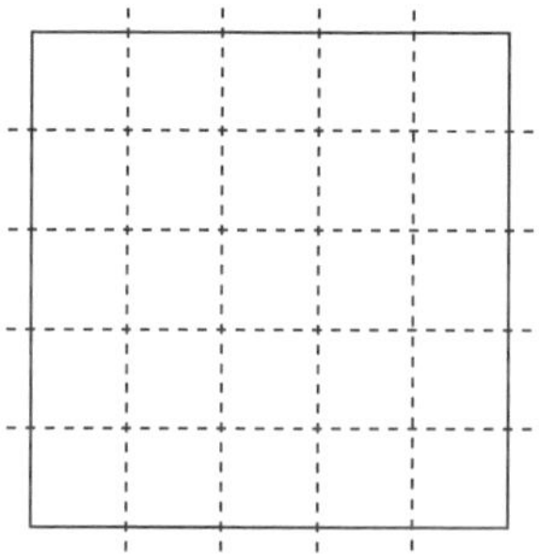						

Figure 6.21: Conjecturing about formulas for the perimeter and area of a rectangle.

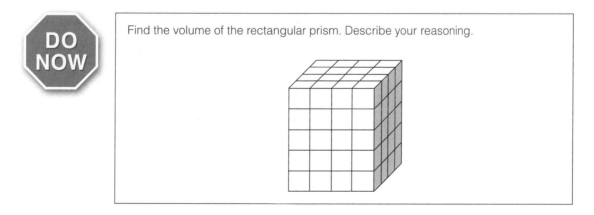

Find the volume of the rectangular prism. Describe your reasoning.

Figure 6.22: Finding volume.

Making sense of area formulas for polygons, specifically the rectangle, provides the foundation for students to derive the formula for the volume of right rectangular prisms. Consider the rectangular prism in figure 6.23. If you filled the prism with one layer of cubes, the layer would have the same number of cubes as the area of the base, in this case the *length × width* of the rectangle that forms the base, covered with cubic units.

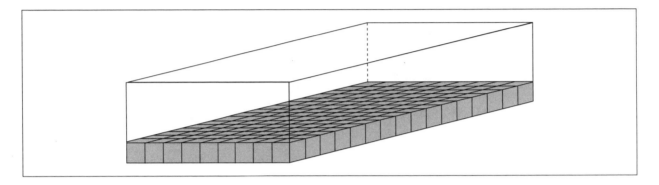

Figure 6.23: A rectangular prism with one layer filled.

If layers of cubic units were then added until the prism was filled, there would be layers to equal the height of the prism. In that way, the number of unit cubes that would fill the prism would be the product of the dimensions of the prism, often stated as $V = l \times w \times h$ or $V = B \times h$, where B is the area of the base and h is the height of the prism (note that area measures are identified with capital letters and linear measures use lowercase letters). Students should become familiar with both forms of the formula. However, using the formula $V = B \times h$ is preferred over $V = l \times w \times h$ because this formula will generalize to the formulas for volumes of all prisms and cylinders. For example, in middle school, when finding the volume of a cylinder, the base is a circle and the height is the height of the cylinder. Thus, the volume for a cylinder is the area of the base × height or $\pi r^2 h$. Students connect the formulas through a focus on coherence and by engaging in Mathematical Practice 7, "Look for and make use of structure."

Deriving Area Formulas

It is useful to think of the area formula for the rectangle as both length times width ($l \times w$) as well as base times height ($b \times h$). The formula $l \times w$ might more closely relate to how students develop the formula for the area of a rectangle by looking at the relationship between the lengths and widths of rectangles and their areas. However, $b \times h$ provides a foundation for connecting the formula for the area of a rectangle to area formulas for parallelograms, triangles, and even trapezoids and circles in later grades. Once students understand that the formula for the area of the rectangle can also be represented as $b \times h$, these other formulas can be derived.

Consider the parallelogram. In grade 6, students decompose parallelograms and then compose them into rectangles (see figure 6.24). This process helps students see that a parallelogram can be decomposed and composed to form a rectangle, and so the formula for the area of a rectangle, $b \times h$, can be applied to the formula for the area of a parallelogram. One key understanding developed alongside the area of a parallelogram is the requirement that the height of a figure is perpendicular to the base.

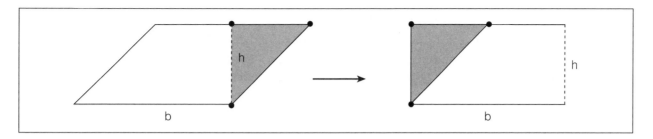

Figure 6.24: A parallelogram transformed to create a rectangle with the same area.

Notice that when the parallelogram is decomposed and composed as a rectangle, the base of the parallelogram is maintained, as is the height. The dimensions are the base and height of the composed rectangle. This reinforces that if the two quadrilaterals have the same base and height then they have the same area and, hence, the same area formula.

The formula for the area of a parallelogram is applied to find the area formula for the triangle. All types of triangles (right, obtuse, and acute) can be formed by finding half of a parallelogram determined by the diagonal of the parallelogram (see figure 6.25). This exploration leads to the derivation of the formula for the area of the triangle as $A = \frac{1}{2}(b \times h)$. This exploration is supported by tasks similar to the one provided in figure 6.1 (page 145).

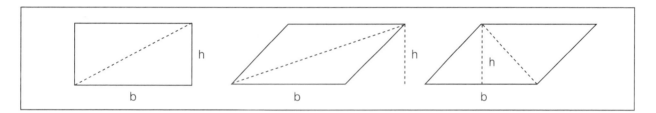

Figure 6.25: Right, obtuse, and acute triangles formed from diagonals of parallelograms.

A more challenging exploration is to derive the formula for the area of a trapezoid from the formula for the area of a parallelogram. Consider the task in figure 6.26. How might you apply the formula for the area of a parallelogram to find the formula for the area of the trapezoid? Be sure to explore this task prior to continuing.

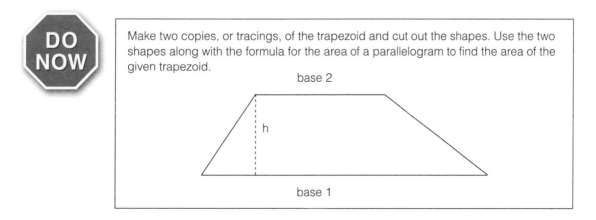

DO NOW Make two copies, or tracings, of the trapezoid and cut out the shapes. Use the two shapes along with the formula for the area of a parallelogram to find the area of the given trapezoid.

base 2

h

base 1

Figure 6.26: Trapezoid area task using congruent trapezoids.

How can you connect the two trapezoid shapes you have cut out to a parallelogram? The first step in solving the problem in figure 6.26 (page 159) is to arrange the two copies of the trapezoid so that they form a parallelogram, as shown in figure 6.27. Notice that the height of the parallelogram is the same as the height of the original trapezoid. But what is the new base?

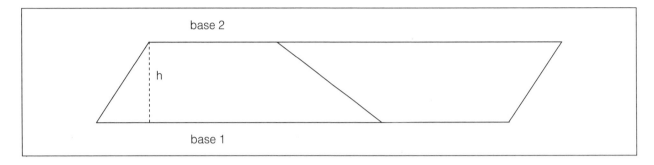

Figure 6.27: Parallelogram composed of two copies of the original trapezoid.

Notice that the base of the parallelogram consists of base 1 *and* base 2 of the original trapezoid. Therefore, the base of the parallelogram can be thought of as base 1 + base 2. The area of the parallelogram would be the sum of base 1 and base 2 times the height or $(b_1 + b_2) \times h$. However, the area of the original trapezoid is half of the parallelogram, so the formula for the area of the trapezoid is $\frac{1}{2}(b_1 + b_2) \times h$. See chapter 5 in *Making Sense of Mathematics for Teaching Grades 6–8* (Nolan et al., 2016) for a more in-depth discussion of deriving the area formula for the trapezoid.

The area of a circle, however, is less straightforward, but can still be connected to a parallelogram. What would happen if you took the circle and cut it into small sectors, like cutting up a pie or pizza? What happens as you make these slices smaller and smaller? As the circle is decomposed into smaller and smaller sectors, or slices, and the slices are rearranged as shown in figure 6.28, the shape begins to resemble a parallelogram.

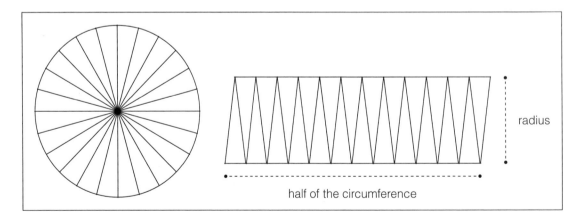

Figure 6.28: Area of a circle.

Eventually, the base of the parallelogram will approach a straight line as the slices become infinitesimally small. How can this be used to find the formula for the area of the circle? Why can the base of the parallelogram be described as half the circumference of the circle? If you examine the original circle, half of the sectors are oriented in one direction and the other half are oriented in the opposite direction. This leaves half of the circumference of the circle as the base of the parallelogram (as shown in figure 6.28). Because the circumference of the circle is π times the diameter, the base of the parallelogram would be one-half this value or πr (since the radius is half the diameter). The height of the parallelogram is the radius of the circle, or r. When the area of the parallelogram is found, the area of the circle then becomes πr^2. When area formulas are derived in this manner, the coherence among the formulas and their connections to the formulas for the areas of rectangles and parallelograms as $b \times h$ become evident; additionally there is less to memorize because the formulas are understood.

Measuring Angles

Developing a conceptual understanding of angle measurement also provides an opportunity to highlight the coherence of mathematics. In grade 4, students make sense of angle measures by considering the arc made where the endpoints of the rays that form the angle intersect at the center of a circle. The angle is measured in degrees, and there are 360 degrees in a circle. The arc created by the intersecting rays of the angle determines the measure, in degrees, of the angle (see figure 6.9, page 149, for an illustration of a 45° angle). Students measure angles such as this with a protractor but also see that because eight of these angles could fit on the circle, one of them is ⅛ of a circle and 360 divided by 8 is 45. This sort of exploration provides a foundation for proportional reasoning, which is stressed in grade 6. Thinking of angles as rotations of rays will link to rigid motion transformations, specifically to rotations that are addressed in grade 8.

The Classroom

Now that you have made sense of measurement, think about what instruction looks like when the focus is on developing conceptual understanding with topics related to measurement. The included video links provide opportunities to observe students in action with selected tasks. The first video offers a window into a fifth-grade class where students explore making boxes with a volume of thirty-six cubic units and ultimately generalize the formula for finding the volume of rectangular prisms.

As you watch, take note of how the formula for the volume of rectangular prisms is developed. How does the teacher use questioning to provide opportunities for the students to make sense of the task? How does the teacher help students look for and make use of patterns? Watch before proceeding.

www.solution-tree.com/Finding
_Volume_of_Rectangular_Prisms

Now that you have watched the video, what did you notice? Who generates the data for the table? Who looks for the patterns? If you were the teacher, what would you consider as an extension to this lesson if you feel that the students have made sense of the formula for the volume of rectangular prisms? This responds to the fourth critical question of the PLC culture, "What will you do if the students know it?" (DuFour et al., 2010).

At this point, it might make sense to provide students with a different volume and ask them to describe potential dimensions of the rectangular prism with that volume. You could provide a volume and two of the dimensions and have students deduce the value of the missing dimension. You could also have students write explanations for how they could derive the formula for the volume of rectangular prisms as the area of the base times the height. What is important is that you provide students opportunities to extend their thinking when they demonstrate they have already met the learning goal. You can then use this evidence to adjust instruction so that students have the most meaningful mathematics learning experience possible.

The second video extends understanding of area to the middle grades, where students use formulas for areas of polygons to find areas of shapes composed of different polygons. The task involves students determining the area of a tiled surface surrounding a swimming pool. Before proceeding, solve the task yourself in figure 6.29 and then watch the second video.

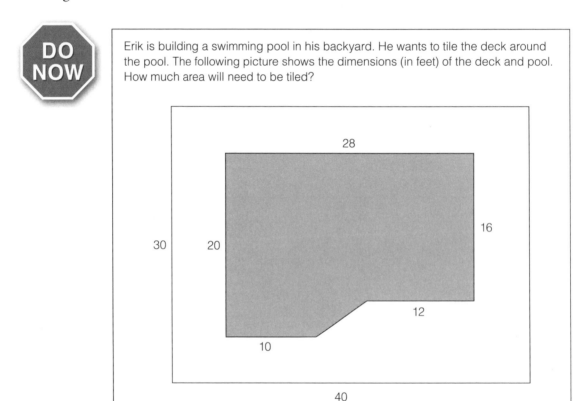

Figure 6.29: Erik's pool deck tiling problem.

www.solution-tree.com/Finding_Area_in_Context

Who makes sense of the problem? How does the teacher help students make sense of one another's thinking? How do the explorations that take place in the intermediate grades help prepare students for this middle school task?

Notice that the teacher asks a student to unpack the problem and then provides the entire class the opportunity to make sense of the problem before continuing to solve it. All too often, teachers take over the problem solving and turn tasks into simple procedures before students have the opportunity to persevere in solving them without assistance. In this lesson, the teacher provides the time for students to come up with strategies and then has students compare their strategies to one another rather than providing a strategy of her own.

The teacher poses appropriate questions and has students share their answers. The first student who shares her answer for the area of the tiled region says the answer is 700 feet. Rather than correcting this student, the teacher asks students to provide the correct answer of 700 feet *squared* and then has the original student make sense of her error. Her error is similar to one that occurs in the intermediate grades when students confuse perimeter and area. This student used a linear unit of feet rather than a square unit of feet squared. The teacher helps the student clarify this common error before moving on to compare solution strategies. Once the correct answer is shared, the emphasis of discussion is on comparing solution strategies. This helps students engage in Mathematical Practice 7, "Look for and make use of structure," to support the idea that area can be decomposed in many ways.

TQE Process

At this point, it may be helpful to watch the first video again (page 161). Pay close attention to the tasks, questioning, and opportunities to collect evidence of student learning.

The TQE process can help you frame your observations. Teachers who have a deep understanding of the mathematics they teach:

- Select appropriate *tasks* to support identified learning goals

- Facilitate productive *questioning* during instruction to engage students in Mathematical Practices

- Collect and use student *evidence* in the formative assessment process during instruction

The *task* chosen for this lesson begins with students using cubes to create different rectangular prisms. Before ever discussing a formula or procedure for finding the volume of a rectangular prism, the task calls for students to *build* rectangular prisms with a given volume. This allows for students to explore different possibilities for the dimensions of a box that is composed of thirty-six cubes. Collecting the information and posting it on the board give students a common frame to make sense of the data. The design of the task facilitates looking for patterns in rectangular prisms with the same volume so that students might more readily see that multiplying the dimensions provides the same volume in each instance. The teacher also ensures that students are provided the formula in different ways, describing the volume formula with both $l \times w \times h$ as well as $B \times h$, to capture different ways the students might see the pattern. The goal is for students to engage in Mathematical Practice 8, "Look for and express regularity in repeated reasoning." It is important to note that Mathematical Practice 8 can sometimes be confused with Mathematical Practice 7, "Look for and make use of structure"; in this lesson, the students are engaged in Mathematical Practice 8 rather than Mathematical Practice 7 because they are looking for commonalities *across* examples rather than within them.

The teacher uses *questioning* to reinforce the goals of the lesson. When she collects information to complete the chart with dimensions and cubes, her questions reinforce the pattern that is the focus of the task—the number of cubes is always the same. She also circulates around the room, questioning students in small groups to provide opportunities for students to verbalize the patterns they observe. This action also reinforces engagement with Mathematical Practice 8, "Look for and express regularity in repeated reasoning."

The students provide *evidence* of their learning as they participate in the task. When students are working at the beginning of the lesson, the teacher watches what the students are doing and listens to their conversations. This allows her to understand what the students already know about volume. This form of preassessment provides the teacher with information about the vocabulary students are comfortable with and what they already know about shapes and volume. As she circulates, she is collecting evidence of the students' engagement with the task and their level of understanding in order to adjust questions and guide the learning process. This evidence is important to ensure that the lesson is providing the support and enrichment for students needed to reach—and extend—the learning goal of the lesson.

The Response

Typical areas of difficulty related to measurement occur when applying formulas without understanding; this is further complicated when students fail to properly distinguish the relationships within and between two- and three-dimensional shapes. For example, as noted, students often confuse the concepts of perimeter and area. When students approach measurement as a collection of formulas, they are likely to confuse these concepts because the measures are treated simply as calculations without meaning. Even students who seem to understand the concepts of perimeter, area, and volume often mislabel the measures. They are likely to forget to include the unit, square unit, or cubic unit with the measure. In these cases, students need support to engage in Mathematical Practice 6, "Attend to precision."

Misconceptions that might be conceptual—or possibly just due to carelessness—involve using the wrong dimensions for calculating area. For example, it is common for students to use the side length rather than the height for calculating areas of triangles and nonrectangular parallelograms. Many of these errors can be resolved by supporting students to attend to precision, reinforcing how to develop area formulas, and making certain that students can accurately identify the attributes of shapes, such as the height of a triangle.

Students should use reasoning and estimation to ensure that their answers make sense. This is especially important when performing conversions within measurement systems. For example, students should be able to indicate that the same object measured in feet should require more units to describe the measure in inches and fewer units to describe the measure in yards. When students check to see if their answers are reasonable, measurement errors—like dividing rather than multiplying when changing the unit from meters to centimeters—can be avoided.

Measurement includes the concept of time, and it is very common for students to experience difficulties in learning how to tell time and to calculate elapsed time. After students make sense of the open time line for determining elapsed time, they typically experience success with these sorts of problems; however, there is often confusion when the unknown is not the elapsed time but rather the start or end time. Students often represent the problem accurately on the open time line but then report the given elapsed time as the solution rather than the missing start or end time. This can be resolved by having students make a chart like the one in figure 6.30 to help organize their reasoning. By organizing their work, students are able to determine what is given in the problem and use the missing value as the solution they seek.

Start Time:	
Elapsed Time:	
End Time:	

Figure 6.30: An elapsed time table for determining what is unknown.

Because measurement concepts are varied, expect students to be challenged by the amount of vocabulary they will have to acquire. Each measurement concept carries its own unique set of vocabulary terms. It will be important for students to be organized in developing their understanding of the various measurement vocabulary and engaged in discourse that will support their understanding.

Reflections

1. What do you feel are the key points in this chapter?

2. What challenges might you face when implementing the key ideas from this chapter? How will you overcome them?

3. What are the important features for developing an understanding of measurement, and how will you ensure your instruction embeds the support needed for these features?

4. Select a recent lesson you have taught or observed focused on measurement. Relate this lesson to the TQE process.

5. What changes will you make to your planning and instruction based on what you read and considered from this chapter?

Next Steps

An important role of mathematics teachers is to help students understand mathematics as a focused, coherent, and rigorous area of study, regardless of the specific content standards used. To teach mathematics with such depth, you must have a strong understanding of the mathematics yourself as well as a myriad of teaching strategies and tools with which to engage students. Hopefully, by providing the necessary knowledge, tools, and opportunities for you to become a *learner* of mathematics once more, this book has empowered you to fill this role.

Now what? How do you take what you learned from *doing* mathematics and make good use of it as the *teacher* of mathematics?

Our position is that you first need to apply what you learned to your lesson planning. Are you planning for instruction that focuses on teaching concepts before procedures? How is your planning aligned to developing learning progressions? How will you ensure that your lessons do not end up as a collection of activities? What follows are strategies that will help you use what you experienced as learners and apply it to what you do as teachers.

Focus on Content

At the heart of meaningful mathematics experiences is mathematics content. A focus on content addresses the *what* of mathematics instruction. What is the mathematical idea or concept you want students to develop and learn as a result of the lesson you facilitate? With your collaborative team, discuss the content that will best serve your students as you progress through the school year. Everything that happens in a mathematics lesson—every task, every activity, every question, every element of the formative assessment process—provides an opportunity to strengthen students' understanding of mathematics content. Thus, it is important for you and your team to engage in collaborative planning about the mathematics content of a unit before the unit begins. Having made sense of mathematics for teaching provides you with a focus on content that will help you and your students have more meaningful and productive experiences with mathematics.

Select Good Tasks

As you've seen throughout this book, your focus on content is revealed in the tasks you select for students to engage in during instruction, so be sure to address this element of instruction during planning. Good tasks are those that support students in learning meaningful mathematics (concepts and, when appropriate, procedures). Other byproducts of good tasks include students engaging in meaningful discourse, developing critical thinking, having multiple ways of representing their thinking (definitions, equations, drawings, and so on), and building fluency (choosing strategies that are most efficient for a given task) in mathematics.

Good tasks also support students in acquiring proficiency with the Mathematical Practices, thereby supporting students' development in mathematics that will last beyond their current grade of study. As you teach, you have the opportunity to engage in the formative assessment process through the use of good tasks. By selecting good tasks, you set the stage for your students to develop strong conceptual understanding of mathematics. We modeled this for you through the tasks provided in this book.

Align Instruction With the Progression of Mathematics

Knowing how mathematics progresses within and across grades is a valuable asset for planning mathematics lessons. As students develop mathematically, you want their classroom experiences to be aligned with how the mathematics should progress. These understandings are important in both planning and implementing instruction processes. In this book, we've facilitated the alignment of instruction with the progression of mathematics within and across grades.

Build Your Mathematics Content Knowledge

Throughout this book, we have addressed mathematics content that is meaningful for your grade band. We have also addressed the content from the perspective that teachers need to facilitate meaningful mathematics instruction. In each chapter, we encouraged you to engage with the mathematics for the purpose of building your mathematics content knowledge by doing mathematics. Our aim was to provide you the support you needed for your understanding of mathematics so that you could subsequently engage your students in similar ways.

Observe Other Teachers of Mathematics

Making Sense of Mathematics for Teaching Grades 3–5 has provided you the opportunity to observe mathematics teaching in action. Through videos and examples, you were able to see students engaged in meaningful mathematics based on rich tasks. We hope this provided an opportunity for you to nurture discourse within your collaborative teams about teaching and learning mathematics. For each video, our aim was to guide you to examine the teacher moves and student exchanges that support the students' learning of mathematics. We are confident that each video provides nuggets of insight and confirmation that will help you clarify your thinking about and improve your teaching of mathematics. We encourage you to continue this practice by observing your fellow teachers when possible and inviting them to observe you.

Respond Appropriately to Students' Struggles With Mathematics

Students' progress in mathematics is often met with some level of struggle with understanding mathematics concepts and applying procedures. Some students even struggle with the language (the words, symbols, and so on) of mathematics. Some misunderstandings are unintentionally perpetuated when mathematics is not deeply understood by teachers (such as, subtracting always makes smaller, or multiplication always makes larger). By preparing for common misunderstandings and errors, you will be better able to help students successfully engage with mathematics and overcome barriers to understanding.

Using the formative assessment process to determine what students know and do not know provides opportunities for you and your collaborative team to reflect together to improve instruction.

Now What?

How has *Making Sense of Mathematics for Teaching Grades 3–5* helped prepare you for your next steps? How will you use the TQE process to inform your practice?

- How will you select appropriate *tasks* to support identified learning goals?

- How will you facilitate productive *questioning* during instruction to engage students in the Mathematical Practices?

- How will you collect and use student *evidence* in the formative assessment process during instruction?

In responding to these questions within your collaborative team, your focus should also include the four critical, guiding questions of PLCs (DuFour et al., 2010).

1. What do we want students to learn and be able to do?

2. How will we know if they know it?

3. How will we respond if they don't know it?

4. How will we respond if they do know it?

Now that you have reached the conclusion of this book, we also ask you to respond to these three questions in the spirit of continuing the reflective process.

1. What do you know now that you did not know before interacting with this book?

2. What do you still need to learn now that you have completed this book?

3. How will you obtain the knowledge you still need?

Appendix A: Completed Classification of Triangles Chart

	Is always . . .	Is sometimes . . .	Is never . . .
An equilateral triangle	isosceles, acute		scalene, right, obtuse
An isosceles triangle		equilateral, right, acute, obtuse	scalene
A scalene triangle		right, acute, obtuse	equilateral, isosceles
A right triangle		isosceles, scalene	equilateral, acute, obtuse
An acute triangle		equilateral, isosceles, scalene	right, obtuse
An obtuse triangle		scalene, isosceles	equilateral, right, acute

Appendix B:
Completed Diagram for
Classifying Quadrilaterals

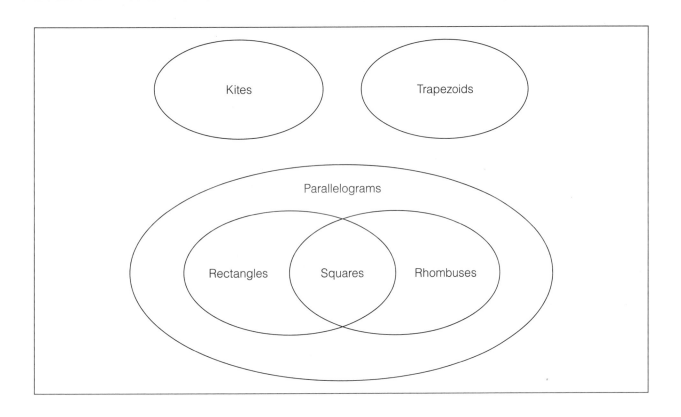

References

Ball, D. L., Thames, M. H., & Phelps, G. (2008). Content knowledge for teaching: What makes it special? *Journal of Teacher Education, 59*(5), 389–407.

Bray, W. S., Dixon, J. K., & Martinez, M. (2006). Fostering communication about measuring area in a transitional language class. *Teaching Children Mathematics, 13*(3), 132–138.

Carpenter, T. P., Fennema, E., Franke, M. L., Levi, L., & Empson, S. B. (2015). *Children's mathematics: Cognitively guided instruction* (2nd ed.). Portsmouth, NH: Heinemann.

Clements, T. B. (2011). *The role of cognitive and metacognitive reading comprehension strategies in the reading and interpretation of mathematical word problem texts: Reading clinicians' perceptions of domain relevance and elementary students' cognitive strategy use.* Unpublished doctoral dissertation, University of Central Florida, Orlando.

Dixon, J. K. (2008). Tracking time: Representing elapsed time on an open timeline. *Teaching Children Mathematics, 15*(1), 18–24.

Dixon, J. K., Adams, T. L., & Nolan, E. C. (2015). *Beyond the Common Core: A handbook for mathematics in a PLC at Work, grades K–5.* T. D. Kanold (Ed.). Bloomington, IN: Solution Tree Press.

Dixon, J. K., Andreasen, J. B., Avila, C. L., Bawatneh, Z., Deichert, D., Howse, T., et al. (2014). Redefining the whole: Common errors in elementary preservice teachers' self-authored word problems for fraction subtraction. *Investigations in Mathematics Learning, 7*(1), 1–22.

Dixon, J. K., Andreasen, J. B., Roy, G. J., Wheeldon, D. A., & Tobias, J. M. (2011). Developing prospective teachers' productive disposition toward fraction operations. In D. J. Brahier & W. R. Speer (Eds.), *Motivation and disposition: Pathways to learning mathematics* (73rd NCTM Yearbook, pp. 279–289). Reston, VA: National Council of Teachers of Mathematics.

Dixon, J. K., Nolan, E. C., Adams, T. L., Brooks, L. A., & Howse, T. D. (2016). *Making sense of mathematics for teaching grades K–2.* Bloomington, IN: Solution Tree Press.

Dixon, J. K., & Tobias, J. M. (2013). The "whole" story: Understanding fraction computation. *Mathematics Teaching in the Middle School, 19*(3), 156–163.

DuFour, R., DuFour, R., Eaker, R., & Many, T. (2010). *Learning by doing: A handbook for Professional Learning Communities at Work* (2nd ed.). Bloomington, IN: Solution Tree Press.

Fisher, D., & Frey, N. (2003). Writing instruction for struggling adolescent readers: A gradual release model. *Journal of Adolescent and Adult Literacy, 46*(5), 396–405.

Karp, K. S., Bush, S. B., & Dougherty, B. J. (2014). 13 rules that expire. *Teaching Children Mathematics, 21*(1), 18–25.

Kilpatrick, J., Swafford, J., & Findell, B. (Eds.). (2001). *Adding it up: Helping children learn mathematics.* Washington, DC: National Academies Press.

Kisa, M. T., & Stein, M. K. (2015). Learning to see teaching in new ways: A foundation for maintaining cognitive demand. *American Educational Research Journal, 52*(1), 105–136.

Lamon, S. J. (2005). *Teaching fractions and ratios for understanding: Essential content knowledge and instructional strategies for teachers* (2nd ed.). Mahwah, NJ: Erlbaum.

Larson, M. R., Fennell, F. S., Adams, T. L., Dixon, J. K., Kobett, B. M., & Wray, J. A. (2012). *Common Core mathematics in a PLC at Work, grades 3–5*. T. D. Kanold (Ed.). Bloomington, IN: Solution Tree Press.

National Council of Supervisors of Mathematics. (2014). *It's TIME: Themes and imperatives for mathematics education*. Bloomington, IN: Solution Tree Press.

National Council of Teachers of Mathematics. (2014). *Principles to actions: Ensuring mathematical success for all*. Reston, VA: Author.

National Governors Association Center for Best Practices & Council of Chief State School Officers. (2010). *Common Core State Standards for mathematics*. Washington, DC: Authors. Accessed at www.corestandards.org /assets/CCSSI_Math%20Standards.pdf on January 31, 2015.

Nolan, E. C., Dixon, J. K., Roy, G. J., & Andreasen, J. B. (2016). *Making sense of mathematics for teaching grades 6–8*. Bloomington, IN: Solution Tree Press.

Stein, M. K., & Smith, M. S. (1998). Mathematical tasks as a framework for reflection: From research to practice. *Mathematics Teaching in the Middle School, 3*(4), 268–275.

Tobias, J. M. (2013). Prospective elementary teachers' development of fraction language for defining the whole. *Journal of Mathematics Teacher Education, 16*(2), 85–103.

Index

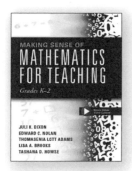

Making Sense of Mathematics for Teaching Grades K–2
Juli K. Dixon, Edward C. Nolan, Thomasenia Lott Adams, Lisa A. Brooks, and Tashana D. Howse

Develop a deep understanding of mathematics. With this user-friendly resource, grades K–2 teachers will explore strategies and techniques to effectively learn and teach significant mathematics concepts and provide all students with the precise, accurate information they need to achieve academic success.
BKF695

Making Sense of Mathematics for Teaching Grades 6–8
Edward C. Nolan, Juli K. Dixon, George J. Roy, and Janet B. Andreasen

Develop a deep understanding of mathematics. With this user-friendly resource, grades 6–8 teachers will explore strategies and techniques to effectively learn and teach significant mathematics concepts and provide all students with the precise, accurate information they need to achieve academic success.
BKF697

Making Sense of Mathematics for Teaching High School
Edward C. Nolan, Juli K. Dixon, Farshid Safi, and Erhan Selcuk Haciomeroglu

Develop a deep understanding of mathematics. With this user-friendly resource, high school teachers will explore strategies and techniques to effectively learn and teach significant mathematics concepts and provide all students with the precise, accurate information they need to achieve academic success.
BKF698

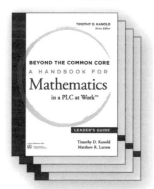

Beyond the Common Core series
Edited by Timothy D. Kanold

Designed to go well beyond the content of your state's standards, this series offers K–12 mathematics instructors and other educators in PLCs an action-oriented guide for focusing curriculum and assessments to positively impact student achievement.
BKF627, BKF628, BKF626, BKF634

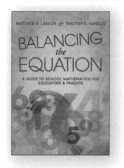

Balancing the Equation
By Matthew R. Larson and Timothy D. Kanold

This book focuses on educators and parents who seek to improve students' understanding and success in mathematics. The authors tackle misconceptions about mathematics education and draw on peer-reviewed research about the instructional elements that can significantly improve student learning.
BKF723

DIG DEEP INTO CONTENT
DIXON · NOLAN · ADAMS
MATHEMATICS

Bring Dixon Nolan Adams Mathematics experts to your school

Janet B. Andreasen
Guy Barmoha
Lisa Brooks
Kristopher Childs
Craig Cullen
Brian Dean

Lakesia L. Dupree
Jennifer Eli
Erhan Selcuk Haciomeroglu
Tashana Howse
Stephanie Luke
Amanda Miller

Samantha Neff
George J. Roy
Farshid Safi
Jennifer Tobias
Taylar Wenzel

Juli K.
Dixon

Edward C.
Nolan

Thomasenia
Lott Adams

Our Services

1. Big-Picture Shifts in Content and Instruction

Introduce content-based strategies to transform teaching and advance learning.

2. Content Institutes

Build the capacity of teachers on important concepts and learning progressions for grades K–2, 3–5, 6–8, and 9–12 based upon the *Making Sense of Mathematics for Teaching* series.

3. Implementation Workshops

Support teachers to apply new strategies gained from Service 2 into instruction using the ten high-leverage team actions from the *Beyond the Common Core* series.

4. On-Site Support

Discover how to unpack learning progressions within and across teacher teams; focus teacher observations and evaluations on moving mathematics instruction forward; and support implementation of a focused, coherent, and rigorous curriculum.

Evidence of Effectiveness

Pasco County School District | Land O' Lakes, FL

Demographics
- 4,937 Teachers
- 68,904 Students
- 52% Free and reduced lunch

Discovery Education Benchmark Assessments

Grade	EOY 2014 % DE	EOY 2015 % DE
2	49%	66%
3	59%	72%
4	63%	70%
5	62%	75%

> **The River Ridge High School Geometry PLC went from ninth out of fourteen high schools in terms of Geometry EOC proficiency in 2013–2014 to first out of fourteen high schools in Pasco County, Florida, for the 2014–2015 school year."**
>
> —Katia Clouse, Geometry PLC leader, River Ridge High School, New Port Richey, Florida

Contact your local representative
888.409.1682